Byzantium and Its Army

284-1081

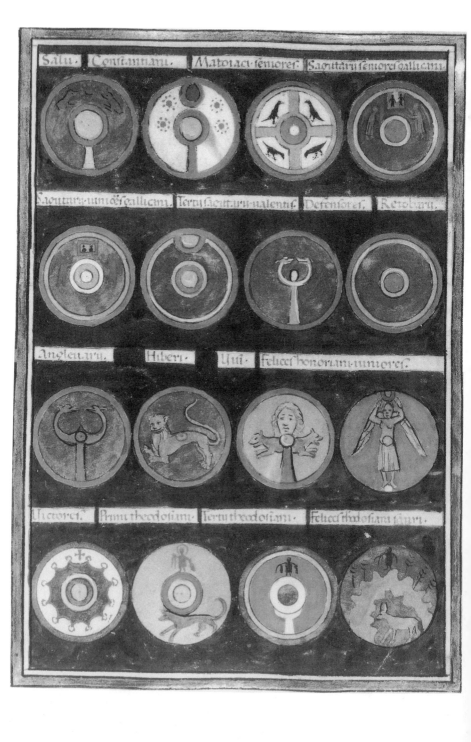

WARREN TREADGOLD

Byzantium and Its Army
284–1081

STANFORD UNIVERSITY PRESS

Stanford University Press
Stanford, California
©1995 by the Board of Trustees of the
Leland Stanford Junior University

Printed in the United States of America

CIP data are at the end of the book

The illustration on the dust jacket is the Renais-
sance frontispiece from the *Notitia Dignitatum*. It is
reproduced by permission of the Bodleian Library,
Oxford.

The illustrations on the title-page spread are designs for shields from the *Notitia Dignitatum*. They
are reproduced by permission of the Bodleian
Library, Oxford.

TO IRINA ANDREESCU-TREADGOLD,
MY WIFE AND FAITHFUL COMRADE IN ARMS,
ON OUR TENTH ANNIVERSARY

Preface

This book was written by accident. While working on a general history of Byzantium, I kept encountering unanswered questions about the Byzantine army, and a surprising amount of evidence for the answers. The subject is so central to Byzantine history that I was unwilling to give it cursory treatment, but reexamining it in any depth in the general book would have exaggerated the army's importance and interrupted the rest of the story. So, as I researched and wrote, I gathered material that I at first expected to put into an article or articles, but finally decided should be a book of its own, though a short one.

It has been kept short by omitting the period after 1081 and focusing on the main evidence for understanding the army's role in Byzantine history—chiefly the army's size, organization, and pay. Most of the history of Byzantine warfare is so closely related to other events that I saved my remarks on it for the general history. Even so, plenty of room remains for future studies of the army, soldiers, officers, strategy, and more specialized topics.[1] I only hope that such work will take account of the questions discussed here, correct me when I am wrong, and in any case try to make progress instead of defending the Principle of Unripe Time so well diagnosed in Byzantine studies by Michael Hendy.[2] Explaining why nothing can be done is always safe and easy; but writing nothing at all is safer and easier, and equally useful.

1. The excellent new book of Mark Bartusis, *The Late Byzantine Army: Arms and Society, 1204–1453* (Philadelphia, 1992), reached me just after I sent my present work to the press. Definitive for its period, Bartusis's book should serve as a model for future historians of the earlier Byzantine army. Yet the army was so different after 1204 from what it had been before 1081 that nothing in Bartusis's book required me to alter what I had written here.

2. Hendy, *Studies*, 3 and 12.

Byzantine military history has suffered considerably from a tendency to overvalue modern scholarship at the expense of original sources. Here I cite in my notes only books and articles that I found useful for this subject, and I include in my bibliography only works that I cite. Most previous research on the Byzantine army proved to be of only marginal use here because, whatever its merits, it passed over the evidence for the army's size, organization, and pay that forms the core of this book. My bibliography also omits most translations and reprints, which readers can find easily enough for themselves in library catalogues. All translations given in the text or notes are my own.

Since the army's development continued unbroken from Roman times to the eleventh century, Byzantine military history has also suffered from the recent tendency to exaggerate the differences between Rome and Byzantium.[3] Of course the empire changed between the time of Augustus and the various dates when we begin to call it the Byzantine Empire (I use 284; some use 324, 395, 476, 565, 610, or 717), and up to the final fall of Constantinople. But those changes can best be understood by understanding what had come before them. To avoid making an arbitrary distinction between Byzantium and Rome, the forms I use here for Greek names and terms are Latinized (or sometimes Anglicized) ones, not the forms based on Classical Greek that many Byzantinists now favor.[4]

For funding, I am pleased to thank several institutions that were aware only of supporting my general history but incidentally supported this book as well: the National Endowment for the Humanities, the Earhart Foundation, the Wilbur Foundation, the Florida International University Foundation, and All Souls College, Oxford. I can assure them that the other book is coming, I hope within a year, and that this book has contributed considerably to it.[5] I would also like to thank Nicholas Purcell for help in obtaining the illustrations, my cartographer, Helen Sherman, and above all my editor, Paul Psoinos, for his usual exemplary work, which saved me from a number of errors.

For whom is this book meant? For anyone interested in either Byzantium or its army. I have avoided jargon and advanced mathematics, which the modest extent and limited complexity of the evidence hardly require. Sophisticated theoretical models are dangerous at this early stage of basic

3. On this debate, see Treadgold, "Break in Byzantium."

4. None of the established systems of transliterating Greek is perfect, and each has its advantages. But some scholars can be disturbingly passionate about the matter of transliteration, as if they were trying to use Classical Greek forms to force acceptance of a sharp break between Rome and Byzantium on those who disagree with them.

5. My *History of the Byzantine State and Society* was completed in November 1993 and should soon be published, also by Stanford University Press.

research, when any complicated argument that leads to an improbable conclusion is likely to be wrong. Yet most of my discussion of the army's size, organization, and pay is based on evidence that is good by the standards of ancient and medieval history. Although the evidence for state budgets is somewhat less so, and the estimates for population that I have borrowed are quite rough, I am still convinced that they are close enough to reality to be helpful. As for those who think that history is totally subjective, they have no grounds to object if the rest of us prefer our way of thinking to theirs.

W. T.
Berlin
September 1992

Contents

Tables and Maps

Byzantium and Its Army
284–1081

Introduction

The Byzantine Empire was almost always ready to fight, and often fought for its life. During much of its history its provinces were military districts called themes, garrisoned by soldiers and governed by generals. Some two-thirds of its emperors led troops before or after their accession, and acclamation by the army, not coronation or inheritance, was what made a man emperor. The army overthrew twenty-odd rulers, and tried to oust many more. It was large and expensive; but on the whole it served its purpose. It held on to nearly all the empire's land in the fourth and fifth centuries, conquered half as much again in the sixth, held half the original territory through the fierce invasions of the next two centuries, and by the eleventh century doubled the empire's eighth-century size. Despite losing a surprising number of battles, the army succeeded in preserving both itself and Byzantium.

Byzantine historians, while making many generalizations like these, have never written a general book on the army before. One of them has noted that "the study of Byzantine military organization and history would seem to be in its infancy," and so it is.[1] Though everyone admits that the army changed a great deal over the years, no one seems quite sure how and when it changed. For every period, doubts remain about how big the army was, how many men were in its various units, how much of it was cavalry, how high its pay and total payroll were, and when, why, and how it received land grants in the themes.

Historians of Rome have made much more progress. To begin with, most of them would accept the axiom, "In any general study of the Roman army in its different phases it is essential to have some notion of its

---

1. Dennis, *Maurice's Strategikon*, xxiii.

size and how much troops were paid."[2] They have reckoned the Roman army at about 290,000 men under Augustus and about 375,000 men under Septimius Severus, with some variations in between.[3] Most Roman historians agree that every legion had about 5,500 men, only some 120 of them cavalry, while the auxiliary troops had units of 500 and 1,000 men, and the Praetorian Guard 4,500 men under Augustus and 5,000 after Domitian.[4]

Roman historians know that basic pay under Augustus was 225 denarii a year, and they are now fairly sure that after three increases it was 600 denarii under Severus.[5] They are coming near to agreeing on the amount of the Roman military budget, one estimating 445 million sesterces (111.25 million denarii) under Augustus and another 472 million sesterces (118 million denarii) in the second century.[6] Though such figures are still being refined within restricted margins for error, they have already proved valuable for focusing and clarifying discussions of the Roman army and economy.

The reason historians of Byzantium lag behind cannot be a lack of information, because their evidence is, if anything, better than that for the Roman army. In fact, since the Byzantine Empire is just a modern name for the eastern part of the Roman Empire in its later phase, Roman historians have used a good deal of early Byzantine evidence for the army. Byzantine sources include some important kinds of evidence missing for the earlier Roman period, including detailed military manuals and rank lists, two comprehensive payroll figures, and several totals for the number of soldiers, one of which is itemized by major units.

Yet what one reads about the Byzantine army in general works is usually vague. While Roman military reforms are always attributed to specific emperors, Byzantine military changes are commonly spoken of as processes of gradual evolution, as if soldiers simply decided for themselves whether they were soldiers or not, what and how they should be paid, where to gather in units, and how those units should be organized. The different corps of the themes seem to take shape gradually over a period of years ending only when they are first mentioned in the sources. Later, when new themes and the units known as the tagmata are found, their

2. Duncan-Jones, "Pay and Numbers," 541.
3. For the army under Augustus, see Hopkins, "Taxes and Trade," 125; for the army under Severus, see MacMullen, "Roman Emperors' Army Costs," 571–72. These estimates are based on multiplying the number of units by their official strength.
4. Watson, *Roman Soldier*, 13, 15, 17, and 62 (with 175 n.137).
5. Ibid., 91; cf. MacMullen, "Roman Emperors' Army Costs," 580, and most recently Speidel, "Roman Army Pay Scales."
6. Hopkins, "Taxes and Trade," 124–25; Starr, *Roman Empire*, 86–88. MacMullen, "Roman Emperors' Army Costs," 580, excluding the navy, arrives at figures of 105 million denarii for the second century and 78.75 million denarii earlier.

soldiers seem to appear from nowhere. Finding the soldiers or the money to pay them was apparently not a problem for the Byzantines, or at least seems not to be an interesting problem for us.

More detailed studies of the army can fill many pages without providing a much clearer picture. Efforts to corroborate and interpret the extensive documentation on the army's numbers, organization, and pay have been rejected as unduly speculative. At the same time, generalizations about the army's social and economic role have been made on the basis of a few selected bits of evidence, or without any evidence, or even in defiance of explicit evidence, which the modern generalizations are used to dismiss. Nurtured by such neglect of the sources, the study of the Byzantine army has not only failed to grow beyond its infancy but sometimes appears to be regressing.

For example, in a careful and useful study of the Byzantine reaction to the Arab invasions published in 1976, Ralph-Johannes Lilie accepted and used the detailed figures given by Arab geographers for the size of the army, and concluded that the themes and their military land grants were introduced together in the period between 650 and 680.[7] But in an article published in 1984 Lilie concluded from an ambiguous passage in the eighth-century lawbook known as the *Ecloga* that no military lands existed then, so that the themes must have developed gradually over two centuries.[8] By 1987, realizing that the Byzantine government could not have supported an army nearly as large as the geographers describe without relying on land grants, he declared that no figures in the sources could be used because they were unverifiable, as if his interpretation of the *Ecloga* could be verified.[9]

Using an approach that seems diametrically opposed to Lilie's but turns out to have much the same result, Friedhelm Winkelmann has argued that the Arab geographers' figures must be treated with such respect that they cannot be corrected to make sense of them. Winkelmann argued that four discrepancies in the dozens of numbers the geographers cite, rather than being mistakes made in transmitting a single original source, as everyone had previously assumed, represented real changes in the Byzantine army.[10] This interpretation necessarily leads to the conclusion, which he made no attempt to draw or defend, that the army lost 14,000 men in inexplicable places at a time when the empire was expanding strongly.[11] In a subsequent book on Byzantine ranks, Winkelmann pursued his method of col-

7. Lilie, *Byzantinische Reaktion*, 287–338.
8. Lilie, "Zweihundertjährige Reform."
9. Lilie, "Byzantinische Staatsfinanzen." For my response, see Treadgold, "On the Value," with Lilie's rejoinder, "Stellungnahme."
10. Winkelmann, "Probleme."
11. See Treadgold, "Remarks."

lecting texts while rejecting all "Byzantine or modern schematizing" and any attempts to find "a clear arrangement or logic in the system."[12] But the assumption that the Byzantines used a system of ranks with no internal logic is not only speculative but implausible, and requires rejecting much Byzantine evidence. The method resembles writing a grammar of a language without trying to learn it.

At the other extreme, Speros Vryonis has tried to substantiate his claim that Byzantium had "a money economy in the 7–9th centuries" by an estimate of the payroll of the themes in Asia Minor. He compares a payroll of the Armeniac Theme in 811 with a list of salaries of thematic commanders under Leo VI (r. 886–912), and calculates the total payroll by assuming that the payrolls of the themes were more or less proportional to the salaries of their commanders. But during the intervening hundred years the Armeniac Theme is known to have been divided into seven parts. If Vryonis's assumption means anything, the payroll of the Armeniac Theme in 811 should have been proportional not to the later salary of the commander of the Armeniacs but to the sum of the later salaries of the commanders of the Armeniacs, Charsianum, Paphlagonia, Chaldia, Colonia, Sebastea, and Leontocome, all of which were in the Armeniac Theme in 811. If so, the correct total for the payroll of the themes of Asia Minor in 811 would be not 690,300 nomismata, as Vryonis estimates, but just 219,600 nomismata, less than a third as much. Vryonis then tries to corroborate his calculations by treating a payroll captured on the Strymon River in 809 as if it were the payroll of the Theme of Strymon, which appeared almost a century later. Finally, Vryonis uses these conclusions to generalize about the prosperity of Asia Minor two additional centuries later, in the late eleventh century.[13] The whole discussion, which repeatedly ignores important and well-documented changes in the army between the seventh and eleventh centuries, is not even speculative, but simply erroneous.

Walter Kaegi has recently managed to combine both arbitrary skepticism and arbitrary speculation. He first rejects as "exaggerated" the total of 150,000 men for the army in 559 given by Agathias, though Agathias was a contemporary and a friend of several officials who should have had access to the correct figure. Then Kaegi, citing no evidence, makes vari-

12. Winkelmann, *Byzantinische Rang- und Ämterstruktur*, 69.

13. See Vryonis, *Decline*, 2–6, citing his "Attic Hoard," 298–99 (my quotation is from p. 299). In the list on pp. 4–5 of Vryonis's book, the salaries for the commanders of the seven themes that made up the Armeniacs in 811 total 130 pounds of gold, and those of all the commanders in Asia Minor 305 pounds (omitting Thrace, Macedonia, Samos, and the Aegean as not in Asia Minor, and Mesopotamia and Lycandus as not yet within the empire in 811). If the Armeniac payroll of 1,300 pounds in 811 represented the same proportion, the total would be 3,050 pounds of gold ($\times$ 72 = 219,600 nomismata).

ous estimates of his own for parts of the army in 630. These estimates confuse the empire's field army, to which Agathias must be referring, with the frontier troops, who by Agathias's time were no longer classed as soldiers. For example, Kaegi estimates 25,000 soldiers in Egypt, where no field army was stationed, and treats the frontier troops in Isauria as if they were part of the field Army of the East, from which they were quite separate. Though Kaegi's estimates add up to 102,000 to 122,000 men, he arrives at a total between 98,000 and 130,000. But even his lowest figure would be compatible with Agathias, since Kaegi himself states that in 630 the army "was almost certainly smaller than that of Justinian's reign," perhaps "by as much as one-third." Thus a plausible report from a reliable source is rejected on the basis of unsupported modern guesses that actually tend to agree with it.[14]

John Haldon, who accepts Agathias's total, rejects the Arab geographers' figure of 24,000 men for the tagmata in the ninth century. Though this number can be corroborated from official Byzantine documents, Haldon finds it too large to fit his Marxist interpretation of the tagmata as an elite of "praetorians" designed to defend imperial ideology. He writes (with the italics in the original):[15]

[I]t is methodologically inadequate simply to analyze the texts which give such figures for their internal and comparative consistency and to assume that whatever figures thus result *must* be "accurate." We must also ask whether or not—given what we know of the nature, capacity, and dynamic of the social formation in question . . . —the results of the analysis are *feasible*. Do they fit in with what is otherwise known—or better, assumed [*sic*]—about the society in question? If figures are arrived at which do not accord with such assumptions, then what the "evidence" *appears* to "tell" us must be re-assessed, the evidence itself must possibly be set aside (even if temporarily) as impossible to interpret in a contextually adequate manner.

Despite its refreshing frankness, this defense of ideology against evidence is unlikely to convince anyone with assumptions different from Haldon's.

Though these authorities all imply that little more can be made of the evidence for the size and pay of the army than they do, their conclusions are almost entirely incompatible with each other. Lilie argues that Byzantine rank lists are so unreliable that nothing can be deduced from them about the army's size or pay. Winkelmann argues that the rank lists

14. Kaegi, *Byzantium*, 39 – 41.
15. Haldon, *Byzantine Praetorians*, 92, with 338 – 53 for his conception of the tagmata. For his views on Agathias, see Haldon, *Byzantium*, 251 – 53, where his own estimate is actually a bit higher than Agathias's figure. Cf. Winkelmann's acceptance of the Arabs' figure for the size of the tagmata (though only for the year 899) in Winkelmann, "Probleme," 29.

are so reliable that minor inconsistencies in them are evidence not of errors in the lists but of an illogical system from which nothing can be deduced. While ignoring the details, Vryonis is willing to make almost any deductions from statistics in the sources as long as they suggest that the army payroll was high. Kaegi is unwilling to make any deductions from statistics in the sources, even when his own guesses agree with them. Haldon will allow only deductions that agree with assumptions he has made before consulting the statistics. While Lilie, Kaegi, and Haldon have made some significant contributions to Byzantine military history, their attitudes make any satisfactory overall study of the subject impossible. We can hardly expect to advance much farther as long as we avoid considering the bulk of the evidence.

Yet the main reason that no one has yet tried to study all the evidence on the army is probably not that the evidence is unreliable, so difficult to use that nothing can be said about it, so easy to use that anything can be said about it, inferior to guesswork, or ideologically unpalatable. The real problem is that the army is such an integral part of Byzantine history that a proper study of it requires looking at sources stretching over hundreds of years, in the process disturbing many generalizations that have been formulated without doing such work. At the beginning, with so little previous research to build upon, one is also likely to make mistakes.

I have made my share of them in my earlier work on the Byzantine army in the eighth and ninth centuries, mostly through ignorance of earlier and later evidence. For instance, in computing the military payroll I assumed that the officers called decarchs ("commanders of ten") commanded ten men besides themselves, though diagrams in a military manual dating from about 600 show decarchs leading ten men including themselves.[16] This and two smaller mistakes led me to overestimate the size of the army by over 12,000 men. At the same time I assumed that almost 15,000 oarsmen of the themes were paid separately from the soldiers, because I failed to notice that official documents of the tenth century showed oarsmen and soldiers being paid together.[17] Since these mistakes tended to cancel each other out, they gave a total only slightly higher than the recorded amount of the ninth-century military payroll; but since they left out of that payroll sums that I then included elsewhere, I overestimated both the army's size and its payroll by more than a tenth. The present book, which corrects those errors, probably includes other mistakes that I could have avoided if I knew everything.

16. Cf. Maurice, *Strategicon*, III.1 – 4, with Treadgold, *Byzantine State Finances*, 97, 104 – 8, and 118.
17. Cf. Treadgold, ibid., 34 – 35, with Treadgold, "Army," 104 – 6.

That one can go wrong using the sources, however, does not demonstrate that something is wrong with the sources. The only means of showing that the evidence is unusable would be to make a thorough and careful effort to use it, and by doing so arrive at conclusions that could be shown to be self-contradictory, incoherent, impossible, or at least highly unlikely. If, on the other hand, most of the evidence can be shown to be self-consistent and intelligible, only two possibilities remain. Either most of the evidence is reliable and the conclusions it indicates are essentially correct, or it results from a gigantic practical joke concocted by dozens of Byzantines and Arabs over many centuries working in concert to deceive others about what the army was like.

For the present purpose the subject can be limited somewhat. Here I confine myself to basic questions and to the period between 284, the accession of Diocletian, and 1081, the accession of Alexius I Comnenus. Diocletian, besides being for various reasons the first emperor who can be considered "Byzantine," began far-reaching changes in the army that shaped it for some time thereafter. Though Alexius I made major changes as well, the main reason for stopping with him is that by 1081 the old army of the themes and tagmata had practically disintegrated, so that the later army was of a kind unlike what had gone before. Since the themes and tagmata are known to have included components that dated from the fourth century, 1081 represented the end of a course of development, if not the end of the Byzantine army. I shall begin with an outline of Byzantine military history up to that date.

CHAPTER ONE

The Roman Army's
Second Millennium

The first Roman legion, then the same as the whole Roman army, went back to the time of the kings of Rome, allegedly to the eighth century B.C. This army is said to have been divided into two legions in the early fifth century B.C. Under the Republic legions multiplied, served along with auxiliary troops contributed by Roman allies, and became permanent and professional units instead of temporary citizen levies. Republican generals used this army to conquer most of the Mediterranean basin, Julius Caesar used it to conquer the Republic, and his successors as emperors used it to defend Roman territory, to make some new conquests, and to keep themselves in power. The Roman army thus had a thousand years of tradition behind it by 284, the accession of Diocletian.[1]

Yet Diocletian took over an army that for three-quarters of a century had failed to keep Germans and Persians out of the empire but succeeded in killing all but three of his twenty-seven predecessors. The fundamental problem was that four different sectors of the frontier constantly needed defending: the East, threatened by the Persian Empire, and the Lower Danube, Upper Danube, and Rhine rivers, all threatened by German tribes. Large armies under responsible commanders had to be stationed at all four trouble spots. Since the emperor could only be in one sector at a time, the generals in each of the other three had to be left an army

1. Most of this chapter is summarized from the narrative chapters of my forthcoming *History of the Byzantine State and Society.* The main events also appear in context, with fuller references, in such standard works as Stein's *Histoire de Bas-Empire* and Ostrogorsky's *History of the Byzantine State*, though my interpretations sometimes differ from theirs. Where I differ with them on matters of fact, I include footnotes here to explain.

that was large enough to repel the enemy, which unfortunately was also large enough to support a rebellion. When a general's troops proclaimed him emperor, he would march away from the frontier, letting in the barbarians.

THE DEFENSIVE ARMY OF DIOCLETIAN

Diocletian worked hard to make the army less prone to rebel and better at defeating the enemy. To make the army stronger, he increased its size. Though the amount of the increase is controversial and will be discussed later, Diocletian certainly enforced a strict system of conscription.[2] He required soldiers' sons to enlist, and demanded that taxpayers either produce recruits or pay for bounties to attract them. To make the army more contented and efficient, Diocletian regularized its pay. This consisted largely of food, arms, and uniforms supplied in kind that are difficult to evaluate and again will be discussed later.[3]

Perhaps most important, to give each weak point in the frontier a capable commander who would not proclaim himself emperor, by 293 Diocletian chose three trusted generals and proclaimed them emperors himself. He became senior emperor in the East, and after some shifting of responsibilities took over the eastern frontier while his junior emperor Galerius guarded the Lower Danube. In the West another senior emperor—though not quite as senior as Diocletian—held the Upper Danube with a junior emperor to hold the Rhine. Today this system of two senior and two junior emperors is often called the tetrarchy, though Diocletian considered the main division to be twofold, between East and West.

Each of the four emperors commanded the soldiers in his sector, most of whom were stationed along the frontiers. Diocletian grouped them into a chain of regional commands under dukes (*duces*), who were independent of the provincial governors and sometimes defended two or three small provinces. The dukes commanded forces of infantry legions and other cavalry and infantry units, and the dukes along the river frontiers had fleets. The emperors, who also kept small mobile reserves wherever they were, mustered the dukes' troops when they were needed for campaigns. These measures, Diocletian hoped, would provide basic security at home and abroad.

For some years the system worked remarkably well. Diocletian and his colleagues defeated the Persians, the Germans, and whatever rebels appeared, and secured the frontiers and internal order for the first time anyone could remember. In 299 Diocletian even annexed some border terri-

2. See below, pp. 44–59.
3. See below, pp. 148–56.

tory from Persia; though his intention was evidently to punish Persian aggression rather than to expand, this was the empire's first foreign conquest in a hundred years. In 305 Diocletian abdicated voluntarily, allowing his subordinate Galerius to become senior emperor of the East and to choose a junior colleague, Maximin. In this way the tetrarchy was supposed to renew itself indefinitely.

Yet without Diocletian's restraining influence, civil war broke out in the West within a year of his abdication. In 307 Galerius led an army into Italy to restore order, but he had to withdraw when many of his men deserted to the rebel western emperor Maxentius. Several years of fighting and intrigue left both East and West split between hostile emperors. In 312 Constantine I, the emperor on the Rhine, eliminated Maxentius, the emperor based at Rome and in charge of the Upper Danube. The next year Galerius's successor Licinius, the emperor for the Lower Danube, finished off Maximin, the emperor for the Persian frontier. Constantine took the Lower Danube sector from Licinius in 317, and completed his conquest of the empire by defeating his rival in 324. He founded Constantinople near the site of his final victory in a naval battle.

Having disbanded the old Praetorian Guard of the Roman emperors, Constantine created a new cavalry corps known as the Scholae as his own guardsmen and agents. During his conquests Constantine had assembled a sizable field army, probably drawn in large part from the mobile reserves of his rivals. He kept it distinct from the frontier troops, making it a standing force of infantry and cavalry that was to accompany the emperor wherever he went. But Constantine kept separate administrations for the four parts of the empire. These he entrusted to his three surviving sons and a nephew, who inherited them at his death in 337.

Constantine's son Constantius II held the eastern frontier, and divided the Lower Danube with his brother Constans I after the troops lynched its intended ruler, Constantine's nephew. The three brothers took over the frontier forces in their domains and divided the field army, which they put under masters of soldiers (*magistri militum*). At first each emperor had one master of soldiers for cavalry and one for infantry; but emperors soon began to appoint separate masters of soldiers for the field forces deployed in the provinces and for those kept "in the Emperor's Presence," the praesental army (*praesentales*). Besides his praesental army, Constantius maintained a field army of the East to watch the Persian frontier, and after the assassination of his brother Constans in 350 Constantius kept another field army in Illyricum on the Lower Danube.

The army defended the East rather well until the emperor Julian arrived from the West after his cousin Constantius's death and invaded the Persian Empire in 363. Julian's advance to the Persian capital of Ctesiphon accomplished nothing; Julian died of a wound, and the expedition ran out of supplies. The guardsman whom the army chose as Julian's successor brought his men out safely by agreeing to some cessions of border territory to the Persians. This failure was more Julian's fault than that of the army, which emerged with limited losses.

The next year, when the throne fell vacant again, the army chose another bodyguard, Valentinian I. He decided to become emperor of the West, and named his brother Valens emperor of the East. After the brothers divided the field forces, Valens deployed his share in three armies under masters of soldiers: one praesental, one for the East, and a third for Thrace, on his part of the Lower Danube frontier. The rest of the Lower Danube was Valentinian's, under a Master of Soldiers for Illyricum.

While the field armies gained in importance, the frontier forces became second-class troops. A law of 372 provided that recruits who were not strong or tall enough for the field armies should be enlisted as frontier soldiers.[4] These troops were usually adequate to deal with bandits and rioters, but they were less good at fighting foreign enemies. This came to be a problem, because the Huns had appeared to the northeast, frightening the Goths, the Germans settled across the Lower Danube, into seeking refuge in imperial territory.

In 378 the temporarily united Goths inflicted a crushing defeat on the eastern field armies near Adrianople in Thrace, killing Valens and many of his men. This chaotic battle, caused by various Byzantine mistakes, seems not to have resulted from any basic weakness in the army beforehand, but it certainly caused weakness afterward. To save the situation, the western emperor Gratian, Valentinian's son, chose the capable general Theodosius as eastern emperor. Besides Valens' territories, Theodosius I received most of Illyricum, not only because the Goths threatened it but because its army, having suffered no losses at Adrianople, was the empire's only effective force in the region.

To replace the losses at Adrianople, Theodosius feverishly recruited new soldiers, including many Germans, some of them deserters from the Goths, and other barbarians. Ending the practice of appointing separate commanders for infantry and cavalry, he united the field armies of Illyricum, Thrace, the East, and the Emperor's Presence, each under a single master of soldiers. With reinforcements from Gratian, Theodosius managed to keep the Goths more or less confined to northern Thrace. Their offshoots, the Visigoths and Ostrogoths, eventually agreed to make peace with the empire. The Ostrogoths settled in Gratian's part of Illyricum and the Visigoths in Thrace, officially as Byzantine allies but with almost complete independence.

4. *Theodosian Code*, VII.22.8.

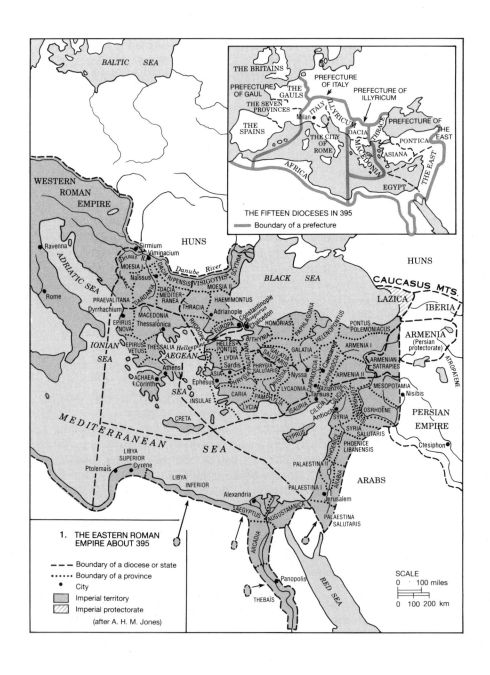

BALTIC SEA

THE BRITAINS

PREFECTURE OF ITALY

PREFECTURE OF GAUL

THE GAULS

PREFECTURE OF ILLYRICUM

THE SEVEN PROVINCES

ITALY

ILLYRICUM

THRACE

PREFECTURE OF THE EAST

THE SPAINS

Milan

DACIA

PONTICA

THE CITY OF ROME

MACEDONIA

ASIANA

AFRICA

EGYPT

THE EAST

THE FIFTEEN DIOCESES IN 395
━━━ Boundary of a prefecture

WESTERN ROMAN EMPIRE

ADRIATIC SEA

Ravenna

Sirmium
Viminacium

HUNS

HUNS

BLACK SEA

CAUCASUS MTS.

Drinus R.

MOESIA I

DACIA

Danube River

SCYTHIA

LAZICA

IBERIA

Rome

Naissus

RIPENSIS

VISIGOTHS

MOESIA II

PRAEVALITANA

DACIA MEDITER-RANEA

DARDANIA

THRACIA

HAEMIMONTUS

Dyrrhachium

MACEDONIA

EPIRUS NOVA

Thessalonica

Adrianople

RHODOPE

EUROPA

Constantinople
Bosporus
Chalcedon

HONORIAS

PAPHLAGONIA

PONTUS POLEMONIACUS

ARMENIA (Persian protectorate)

IONIAN SEA

EPIRUS VETUS

THESSALIA

Hellespont

HELLES-PONTUS

BITHYNIA

PHRYGIA PACATIANA

GALATIA SALUTARIS

GALATIA

HELENOPONTUS

ARMENIA I

ARMENIAN SATRAPIES

AEGEAN

LYDIA

Sardis

PHRYGIA SALUTARIS

CAPPADOCIA I

Caesarea

CAPPADOCIA II

ATROPATENE

ACHAEA
Corinth

Athens

ASIA

Ephesus

SEA

PHRYGIA

PISIDIA

LYCAONIA

Nyssa
Nazianzus

Tarsus

ARMENIA II

MESOPOTAMIA

Nisibis

CARIA

PAMPHYLIA

CILICIA I

EUPHRATENSIS

OSRHOËNE

PERSIAN EMPIRE

INSULAE

LYCIA

ISAURIA

CILICIA II

Antioch

SYRIA

CRETA

CYPRUS

SYRIA SALUTARIS

PHOENICE

PHOENICE LIBANENSIS

Ctesiphon

MEDITERRANEAN SEA

LIBYA SUPERIOR

Cyrene

PALAESTINA II

ARABS

Ptolemaïs

LIBYA INFERIOR

Alexandria

PALAESTINA I

Jerusalem

PALAESTINA SALUTARIS

AEGYPTUS

AUGUSTAMNICA

1. THE EASTERN ROMAN EMPIRE ABOUT 395

ARCADIA

Panopolis

THEBAÏS

RED SEA

SCALE

0   100 miles

0   100 200 km

--- Boundary of a diocese or state
•••••• Boundary of a province
• City
▨ Imperial territory
▨ Imperial protectorate
(after A. H. M. Jones)

Yet Theodosius gained time to continue rebuilding the army. Even without the Army of Illyricum, which he returned to Gratian, he was able to defeat Ostrogoth raiders in 386 and Gratian's murderer Maximus in 389. Though Theodosius then established Gratian's brother Valentinian II in the West, he kept the Army of Illyricum for himself. He also transferred some western field troops to the East in 388, and with them expanded the praesental army into two praesental armies of similar organization.[5] In 394 Theodosius won another war, this time with western rebels who had murdered Valentinian II. The next year Theodosius died, dividing a somewhat strengthened empire between his two sons, Arcadius in the East and Honorius in the West.

Theodosius had taken most of the eastern field army with him to the West; on his death, it was to be returned to the East. While the advisers of his two young sons quarreled with each other, the eastern field army did return, to murder Arcadius's adviser Rufinus. Arcadius's new adviser Eutropius then reassembled the field armies of Illyricum, Thrace, the East, and the two praesental armies. The organization of the eastern forces at this time is largely known from the *Notitia Dignitatum,* a comprehensive list of the empire's principal officers and officials. The portion for the eastern empire dates to about 395; the portion for the West is rather later.[6] The eastern *Notitia* catalogues the legions and other units belonging to the East's five field armies and fifteen ducates of border troops.

Though the organization of the eastern army scarcely changed throughout the fifth century, this was a far from easy time for either the army or the Byzantines. The Visigoths ravaged Illyricum for several years, until they left for the western empire. In 400 Gaïnas, a Visigoth Master of Soldiers in the Emperor's Presence, briefly took over Arcadius's government in Constantinople, before being driven out and killed. The Huns repeatedly raided Thrace and Illyricum, forcing the Byzantines to pay them tribute and to fortify Constantinople with an almost impregnable wall. The Byzantines had temporarily to evacuate much of the Danube frontier, where the Huns raided at will until they turned to attacking the western empire in 450.

While the eastern emperors happened to be weak rulers, Germans and other barbarians remained strong in the armies, and Aspar, an Alan Master of Soldiers in the Emperor's Presence, was virtual ruler of the East by 457. To balance the influence of Aspar and his Germans, the eastern emperor Leo I recruited many Isaurians, warlike mountaineers from southeast Anatolia. The Isaurian leader Zeno first became head of the imperial

5. On this transfer of troops from West to East and the organization of the two armies in the Emperor's Presence, see Hoffmann, *Spätrömische Bewegungsheer,* I, 469–507.

6. Hoffman, ibid., 516–19, dates the portion of the *Notitia* for the East between 392 and 394, while Mann, "What Was the *Notitia Dignitatum* for?" 1–9, more plausibly puts it in 395 or soon afterward.

guard, which included the newly created corps of Excubitors. Then Leo named Zeno Master of Soldiers for Thrace, and made him presumptive heir to the throne by a marriage to the emperor's daughter.

In 468 Leo launched the one great eastern offensive of the century, a joint expedition with the West to reconquer North Africa from the Vandals. Its success would probably have saved the West. But the campaign was a catastrophic failure, which doomed the West and left the East seriously weakened. Apparently with some reason, many blamed the defeat on treachery by barbarian officers in both the western and the eastern armies, and by Aspar in particular. Three years later Leo managed to murder Aspar and to replace him with Zeno.

But Aspar's murder enraged the many Ostrogoths in the army. They joined the Ostrogoths still settled in Illyricum in ravaging Thrace, and had to be bought off. When Zeno succeeded to the throne in 474 he inherited a serious Ostrogoth problem. He only solved it, after years of fighting, by sending the Ostrogoths to Italy in 488, supposedly to punish the Germans who had recently overthrown the last western emperor. Perhaps to limit the number of barbarians in the army, and in any case to control them, Zeno legislated that all recruitment should be monitored by the central government.[7]

Despite all these internal and external troubles, between Diocletian's accession in 284 and Zeno's death in 491 the eastern part of the empire gained slightly more territory than it lost. Diocletian had conquered a little land from Persia that Julian had forfeited along with a bit more; but Theodosius had annexed a larger area in Armenia by a peaceful agreement with Persia. The Byzantines temporarily withdrew from some of the Danube frontier region several times, but they always reoccupied the whole of it later. While the tetrarchy had given rise to civil wars among its members and their heirs, no one from outside the system ever broke into it more than momentarily in the East; after Constantine no eastern rebel of any sort did so. In the East, though not in the West, the changes Diocletian made in the army achieved more or less what he had intended.

THE PROFESSIONAL ARMY OF ANASTASIUS

After putting down a revolt by the Isaurians, Zeno's successor Anastasius I finally brought the fifth-century military crises to an end. His success seems to be connected with a change he made in the soldiers' pay. About 498, as part of more extensive financial reforms, Anastasius replaced issues of rations, uniforms, and arms with cash allowances that let the men

---

7. *Justinian Code*, XII.35.17. The date of 472 suggested by the editor is impossible, because Zeno only became emperor in 474.

purchase whatever they needed. These new allowances were evidently generous—so generous that the army attracted large numbers of native volunteers. The forced conscription prevalent during the fourth century was abandoned, and the barbarian mercenaries who had been so numerous during the fifth century became much less important.[8] No new barbarian generals tried to take over the empire, and the army became a much more effective instrument.

The first test of the reformed army came in 502 with an invasion of Armenia by the Persian king. Anastasius mustered an army of almost unprecedented size on the eastern frontier. Though at first the commanders failed to coordinate the campaign properly, the Byzantines soon forced the Persians to sue for peace. In 506 Anastasius anchored the Persian frontier by strongly fortifying the border town of Dara. Later, after putting down a serious military rebellion, Anastasius left the army so strong that Justinian I, who became emperor in 527, could realistically hope to reconquer the lost western provinces.

First Justinian had to dispose of a war with Persia. To do so, he created a new field Army of Armenia that supplemented the Army of the East in the north. Though Justinian transferred some experienced troops to the Army of Armenia, he recruited a number of new soldiers that equaled the new unit's full strength.[9] Finding these recruits seems to have presented no difficulty. Faced by two field armies instead of one, the Persians suffered several defeats and in 532 agreed to a peace with no time limit, the so-called Perpetual Peace. Under its terms Justinian paid a substantial sum to the Persian king, but he offset it by suspending the pay of the garrison troops on the eastern frontier.[10]

The same year Justinian sent a great expedition, largely composed of soldiers from the Army of the East, to conquer the Kingdom of the Vandals in Africa. The commander was the brilliant Master of Soldiers for the East, Belisarius. He and his army defeated the Vandals in two pitched battles and completed their assignment within a year. Belisarius sent back to Constantinople the Vandal king, the Vandals' treasury, and the surviving Vandals, who were enrolled in the Army of the East. With still more new recruits, and probably some troops from the East that the Vandals replaced, Justinian created a new mobile Army of Africa and five new ducates of African border troops.

Scarcely pausing for breath, in 535 the emperor sent Belisarius to conquer Italy from the Ostrogoths. The next year Justinian seems to have

8. These facts, both the generosity of the allowances and the availability of volunteers, are noted by Jones, *Later Roman Empire*, 668–74, though he fails to make the apparent connection of cause and effect. See below, pp. 153–54.

9. See *Justinian Code*, I.29.5.

10. Procopius, *Secret History*, 24.12–13.

united the fleets under a new Quaestor of the Army. This quaestor had jurisdiction over both the Lower Danube and the eastern Mediterranean, enabling him to transfer ships where they were needed.[11] The same year Belisarius took southern Italy and Rome. His initial force was so small that he was able to advance to the Ostrogoths' capital at Ravenna only after receiving successive reinforcements. Nonetheless, with the help of a little trickery, Belisarius conquered Ravenna and all Italy south of the Po before he was recalled in 540 to fight the Persians. He left behind a new Army of Italy, and brought with him to Constantinople the Ostrogoths' king and treasury.

The Persian king Khusrau I, noticing that Justinian had sent much of the Army of the East to the West, broke the Perpetual Peace after eight years. The king invaded Syria, swept aside the unpaid frontier troops, and sacked Antioch, the Syrian metropolis. Many of the frontier troops simply abandoned their posts. Only when the mobile Army of Armenia arrived did the Byzantines put up a creditable defense. After Belisarius returned from Italy with many of his troops, he was able to raid Persian Mesopotamia while Khusrau was away. Though the eastern frontier troops were in disarray, their pay resumed as the peace lapsed, and the field armies seemed to be as good as ever.

At this point, beginning in 541, the empire suffered a devastating epidemic of bubonic plague, a disease never before seen in the Mediterranean world. The outbreak lasted four years, and spread throughout the empire. Justinian himself caught it, and almost died. When he recovered, he dismissed Belisarius for plotting to seize the throne if it became vacant. Certainly the plague caused enormous loss of life among both soldiers and taxpayers, and terrible financial problems for Justinian. Among other expedients, he delayed the army's pay.

The effects of the plague and overdue pay soon showed in the army's performance. The Ostrogoths made a strong recovery and retook most of Italy, where Byzantine troops began deserting to them. Much of Byzantine Africa fell to the local Moors, some Byzantine troops deserted to them, and the remaining soldiers mutinied. Fortunately for the empire, the Persians had also caught the plague, and agreed to a truce at an affordable price in 545. Justinian evidently took this opportunity to cancel the regular pay of all his border troops, apparently including the fleets. Though the African army ended its mutiny, late pay caused even the praesental armies to riot and the garrison of Rome to surrender to the Ostrogoths.

11. Since Justinian's *Novel* 51 of 536, which created the Quaestor of the Army, survives only in part, the command remains somewhat obscure; cf. Stein, *Histoire du Bas-Empire*, II, 474–75.

By 552 the treasury had recovered enough to let Justinian send a sizable army to Italy and, in a last gasp of conquest, troops to back a rebellion against the Visigothic king of Spain. Within a year Justinian's commander for Italy, Narses, defeated the Ostrogoths twice, killed their last two kings, and cleared them from most of Italy, while Byzantine forces started taking southern Spain. In 554 Justinian counted Italy as conquered, as it nearly was. But in 558 the plague returned, and military pay again fell into arrear. Consequently Justinian never managed to take more than the southern fifth of Spain from the Visigoths. Narses seems not to have finished off the last remnants of the Ostrogoths until 561, when Justinian also made peace with Persia.

At his death in 565, despite both epidemics of plague, Justinian left the empire enlarged by Africa, Italy, and southern Spain, each of which had a new field army. The original eastern empire still had its four field armies and the new Army of Armenia, and the frontier forces survived, if only as unpaid irregulars. Justinian had given his armies enormous tasks and often inadequate support, but on the whole they had fought well. He had always found recruits to raise new armies, and to replace the losses in the old ones caused by battles and the plague.

Yet Justinian's new conquests were hard to hold. Within four years of his death, Byzantine Spain was attacked by the neighboring Visigoths, Africa by the Moors, and Italy by the Lombards. All three were serious invasions, but the Lombards had most success, taking the north and most of the interior of the Italian peninsula by 572. Justinian's successor Justin II sent no help to the West, but provoked a war in the East by aiding an Armenian rebellion against Persia. The Persians retaliated with an invasion that took Dara, the main Byzantine stronghold on the frontier. At the news Justin became insane.

Justin's empress turned for help to his Count of the Excubitors Tiberius, who became the real ruler. To deal with the emergency on the Persian frontier, Tiberius negotiated truces with the Persians and the Avars, a coalition of tribes related to the Huns that had arrived in force on the Danube frontier. Tiberius transferred soldiers from the armies of Illyricum and Thrace to the Persian frontier, and recruited a new corps of Byzantines and barbarians called the Federates that he attached to the Army of the East. By 578 these Federates were ready to fight, and with their help the army defeated the Persians and advanced into Persian territory.

But the enlarged army on the Persian frontier threatened to mutiny when it could not be paid on time, and the Avars and their vassals the Slavs took advantage of the absence of so many troops to cross the Danube. As the Slavs raided all the way to Greece and the Lombards advanced in Italy, the Byzantines had the better of their war with the Persians, but were

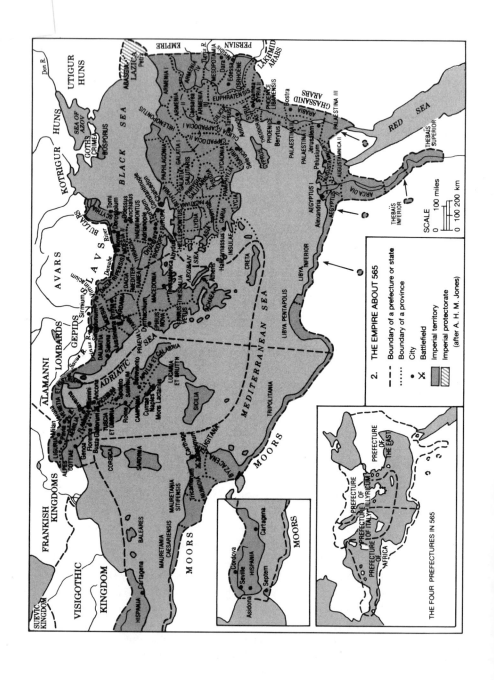

THE EMPIRE ABOUT 565

— — — Boundary of a prefecture or state
· · · · · · Boundary of a province
● City
✕ Battlefield
▨ Imperial territory
▨ Imperial protectorate

(after A. H. M. Jones)

SCALE
0   100 miles
0 100 200 km

THE FOUR PREFECTURES IN 565

PREFECTURE OF THE EAST
PREFECTURE OF ILLYRICUM
PREFECTURE OF ITALY
PREFECTURE OF AFRICA

unable to bring it to an end. Meanwhile Justin was succeeded by Tiberius, who in turn was succeeded by Maurice, Tiberius's commander against the Persians.

Maurice inherited a badly depleted treasury and three major wars. The Avar and Slav advance became so alarming that he had to send some troops back to the Balkans; but he left Italy and Africa to defend themselves against the Lombards and Moors under military governors called exarchs. Money ran low, and in 588 Maurice ordered his troops to accept issues of arms instead of their arms allowances. But at this the eastern armies mutinied; they only returned to allegiance when they were paid as usual the next year.

Yet the war was also taking a toll on the Persians. In 590 rebels overthrew the Persian king, and his son Khusrau II fled to the empire and appealed for help. Maurice sent an army that restored Khusrau, who returned Dara and ceded most of Armenia to Byzantium. Having won one of his wars, Maurice transferred troops from the East to the Balkans, though money remained short. In 593 Maurice ordered his men to live off the land north of the Danube to save on campaign rations, but the order was abandoned when they threatened to mutiny. The next year Maurice ordered allowances for both arms and uniforms to be replaced by issues in kind. Although he tried to avoid a mutiny by promising that soldiers who died in battle would be replaced by their sons, the soldiers demanded and received both this concession and their full pay.

Despite these tensions between the army and the government, the soldiers did good service, defeating the Avars and Slavs again and again until by 599 the Balkans were practically cleared of invaders and the Danube frontier reestablished. Troops could now have been spared for Italy, but the government seems to have had no money to send them there. In 602 Maurice tried again to save on rations by ordering the soldiers to winter north of the Danube. This time they not only mutinied but marched on Constantinople, where they killed the parsimonious emperor and replaced him with the junior officer Phocas.

Khusrau II, vowing to avenge his benefactor Maurice, first supported a pretender alleged to be Maurice's son. Then, when the pretender died, Khusrau started to take Byzantine Armenia and Mesopotamia for himself. A rebellion against Phocas started in Africa and spread to Egypt, allowing the Persians to conquer Armenia and Mesopotamia and to invade Syria and Anatolia. The empire seemed to be on the verge of disintegration; Phocas, lacking legitimacy, was unable to restore order. In 610 a rebel fleet from Africa killed the usurper and replaced him with Heraclius, son of the Exarch of Africa.

Heraclius took over much the worst military crisis that the eastern empire had seen since Diocletian. The armies were exhausted and demoralized by civil war and their defeats by the Persians. While the troops fought hard for Syria, sometimes under Heraclius himself, the Persians overran it along with Cilicia and Palestine. The Avars and Slavs poured across the Danube, shattering the Army of Illyricum and crippling the Army of Thrace. This time the invaders conquered almost the whole Balkan peninsula except for some coastlands. By 616, after the Visigoths had taken most of the rest of Byzantine Spain, the empire held little more than Anatolia, Africa, and Egypt, with scraps of Thrace, Greece, and Italy.

The loss of so much land made meeting the army payroll almost impossible. The unpaid Italian army rebelled. In 616 Heraclius cut military pay in half, probably by substituting arms and uniforms for cash allowances as Maurice had tried to do in 594. The emergency was so obviously dire that this time the soldiers accepted the measure, which reduced their incomes but left them able to live. Heraclius sent the Army of Italy its pay and put down its revolt. But the Persians went on to raid Anatolia up to the Asian suburbs of Constantinople and then to invade Egypt, which they conquered by 620.

For the first time, the eastern empire was truly fighting for survival. Again desperate for money, Heraclius arranged a huge loan from the Church, including most of the Church's gold and silver plate. The emperor mustered in Anatolia what was left of the praesental armies and the armies of Thrace, Armenia, and the East, and prepared to attack the Persians. Making a truce with the Avars, Heraclius defeated and expelled the Persians from Anatolia in 622. Although he had to interrupt his attack when the Avars broke their truce, by 624 he led an army into Persian Armenia and Atropatene, where he put Khusrau II and his army to flight. The next year three Persian armies converged on Persian Armenia to attack the emperor, but he defeated them all.

In 626 the Persians joined the Avars in besieging Constantinople, but their efforts were poorly coordinated and the siege failed. Byzantine fortunes continued to improve. The Slavs rebelled against the Avars, and Heraclius defeated the Persians again in Armenia. Then he struck through Atropatene into Mesopotamia, and defeated the Persians not far from their capital at Ctesiphon. In 628 Khusrau II was overthrown by his son, who agreed to restore the frontier as it had been before the war.

Heraclius thus regained Egypt and Syria and Byzantine Mesopotamia and Armenia, and returned the eastern armies to their stations. Though it was a splendid victory, the Slavs were still in the Balkans and the empire had been weakened and impoverished. In 633 the Arabs, newly converted to Islam, began to raid Palestine. The next year they defeated the Duke of Palestine, and then the commander of the Army of the East. When Heraclius mustered a large army against them, they crushed it in 636 at the battle of the Yarmūk River. They then took most of Syria and Mesopotamia and invaded Egypt, where in 640 they defeated reinforcements from the praesental armies and the Army of Thrace.[12] Heraclius died the next year after seeing his triumph over the Persians turn into abject defeat against the Arabs.

The Byzantine army had fought doggedly and capably through crisis after crisis. But it still faced long years of warfare against a fresh and enthusiastic enemy. Since the army could barely carry on as it was, reducing its size or cost further seemed out of the question. Yet even at half its former pay it appears to have put a crushing burden on the treasury, which any further losses of taxpaying territory would aggravate. Though Heraclius's son Constantine III managed to meet his army payroll in 641, this was considered quite an accomplishment. He soon died, and the Byzantines in Egypt surrendered. After some domestic unrest, Heraclius's grandson Constans II became emperor just before he turned twelve.

THE THEMES OF CONSTANS II

Constans grew up quickly. He inherited little more than Anatolia, Armenia, Africa, and part of Italy, all of them threatened by the enemy. Though he tried to retake Egypt, the expensive expedition he sent there failed. Then the Arabs built a fleet and began raiding by sea. Africa rebelled in 646, but two years later Arab raiders killed its exarch; his successor made his submission to the emperor and began sending the annual surplus of his revenues to Constantinople. Italy rebelled, but its exarch died of the plague and his rebellion ended. While the Arabs took Armenia, fortunately for Constans they were occupied first with completing their conquest of Persia and then with a major civil war. In 659 the Arab governor of Syria agreed to pay tribute in return for a truce. So far Constans had survived on luck and the revenues of Africa, neither of which seemed likely to continue for long.

In 662, leaving his son Constantine IV to rule for him in Constantinople, Constans set sail on an expedition to the West. He never returned. After spending six years bolstering the defenses of Italy and Africa, he was assassinated in a military revolt on Sicily. The Arabs, with their civil war over, began raiding Anatolia, where much of the army rebelled. Apparently the empire's days were numbered, since it had already lost more than half its territory in thirty years and now had even fewer resources to meet a much stronger and richer enemy. Surprisingly, however,

12. The Egyptian chronicler John of Nikiu, 178 and 191, refers to the Byzantine commanders in Egypt as "generals of the local levies"; but since he says that these "local levies" came from Constantinople, they were probably the praesental armies, mistranslated at some point in the tangled tradition of John of Nikiu's work.

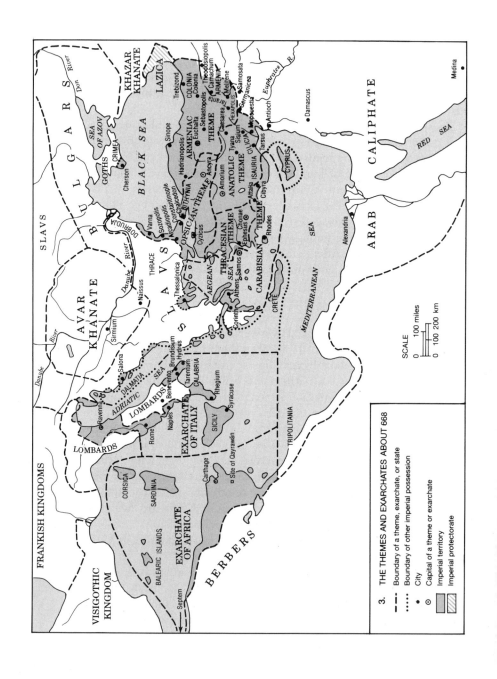

FRANKISH KINGDOMS

VISIGOTHIC KINGDOM

SLAVS

BULGARS

AVAR KHANATE

KHAZAR KHANATE

LAZICA

BLACK SEA

Don River

SEA OF AZOV

CRIMEA

GOTHS

Cherson

Sinope

Trebizond

COLONIA
Colonia

THEODOSIOPOLIS
Theodosiopolis

Camachum

ARMENIA

Satala

Samosata

Melitene

ARMENIAC THEME

Sebastopolis

Euchaita

Hadrianopolis

Caesarea

Tarranica

Mopsuestia

HEXAPOLIS

Antioch

Damascus

Euphrates R.

Medina

ARAB CALIPHATE

RED SEA

Varna

Sozopolis

Constantinople

Chalcedon

Cyzicus

BITHYNIA

Ancyra

OPSICIAN THEME

Amorium

ANATOLIC THEME

Tyana

Sisium

ISAURIA

CILICIA

Tarsus

Attalia

Cibyra

CYPRUS

SLAVS

THRACE

Naissus

Danube River

Sirmium

Thessalonica

AEGEAN SEA

Chonae

Ephesus

THRACESIAN THEME

Athens

Samos

Corinth

Rhodes

CARABISIAN THEME

CRETE

MEDITERRANEAN SEA

Alexandria

Salona

DALMATIA

ADRIATIC SEA

Ravenna

LOMBARDS

Rome

Naples

Benevento

Hydrus

Brundisium

Tarentum

CALABRIA

Rheghium

Syracuse

SICILY

EXARCHATE OF ITALY

CORSICA

SARDINIA

BALEARIC ISLANDS

Carthage

Site of Qayrawān

EXARCHATE OF AFRICA

Septem

BERBERS

TRIPOLITANIA

SCALE

0   100 miles

0 100 200 km

3.   THE THEMES AND EXARCHATES ABOUT 668

— · — Boundary of a theme, exarchate, or state

· · · · · Boundary of other imperial possession

•   City

⊙   Capital of a theme or exarchate

▨   Imperial territory

▨   Imperial protectorate

the Byzantines began to put up much stiffer resistance. And for the first time the scanty sources begin to refer to the Byzantine armies as themes (*themata*), under the command of generals called strategi (*stratēgoi*).

These themes were simply the mobile armies of the previous period, now stationed in specific districts also called themes. Since Greek had become the empire's dominant language, the armies had Hellenized names. The Army of Armenia became the Armeniac Theme in eastern Anatolia. The Army of the East became the Anatolic Theme—meaning "Eastern" rather than "Anatolian"—though it had retreated to central Anatolia after what had been the East was mostly lost. The Army of Thrace became the Thracesian Theme, in western Anatolia where Heraclius had withdrawn it.[13] The two praesental armies, recently known as the Obsequium or "Retinue," became the Opsician Theme in northwest Anatolia and southern Thrace. The Opsician was the most senior theme, and its commander had the special title of count. Of less obvious origin is the Carabisian Theme, a corps of marines named after a Greek word for ship (*karabis*) and based in Greece, the Aegean islands, and the southern shore of Anatolia.[14]

At least in later years, the soldiers of the themes supported themselves from land grants within their districts. Modern historians long believed that the military lands and the themes were introduced together by Heraclius, and enabled him to defeat the Persians.[15] But this theory has come under sustained attack, and for good reasons. First, apart from one vague and problematic reference, no source mentions the themes during Heraclius's reign. Second, if the themes helped Heraclius defeat the Persians, it is hard to see why they should have failed him so badly against the Arabs a few years later. Third, the themes as we know them were permanently stationed in Asia Minor, poorly placed for an invasion of Persia. What their positions rather suggest is a retreat before the Arabs.

The next theory to gain currency was that the themes and military lands were introduced gradually. The themes are well attested in the latter part of the seventh century; but the military lands are only mentioned by name in legal texts of the tenth century, though the sources seem to assume that some military lands existed by the late eighth century. The most extreme gradualist theory holds that the themes originally did not include any military lands at all, but that military lands slowly evolved over two hundred years as soldiers settled down and bought property.[16] But critics of the gradualist theory have pointed out that after the mid-seventh century

13. See Lilie, "'Thrakien' und 'Thrakesion,'" who refutes the older theory that the Thracesian Theme was of later origin.

14. That Greece was a part of the original Carabisian Theme is plausibly maintained by Charanis, "Observations," 6–11. On this theme's origin, see below, pp. 72–73.

15. See Ostrogorsky, *History*, 95–100, with the earlier works he cites.

16. See Lilie, "Zweihundertjährige Reform," with his references.

the empire could hardly afford to pay its troops enough to live, let alone enough to buy land.

The state's only remaining means of supporting its soldiers seems to have been to give them the land. We shall see that the land the soldiers received is most likely to have come from the imperial estates, which formed a large part of the empire in the sixth century but thereafter practically disappeared.[17] Apparently the military lands were introduced under Constans II. According to a recent reconstruction, a group of lead seals that become common at just this time reveals a system by which state warehouses sold the troops their arms after they had been settled on military lands.[18] Though the gradualists have objected that the soldiers would have lacked the cash to buy arms, this objection can be met by supposing that the warehouses accepted payment in kind.[19]

If the military lands began this early, and the themes began no earlier, the military lands were probably introduced along with the themes. The one source to date the creation of the themes attributes it to "the men after Heraclius," an apparent reference to Constans II and his advisers.[20] The sources first mention themes by name after 662, when Constans left for the West with men from the Opsician Theme while the Armeniac Theme stayed in the East.[21] References to themes are frequent thereafter. The first seal of a warehouse that seems to have supplied the themes probably dates from 659. Afterward such seals are common. Finally, coins minted after 658 are much rarer at Anatolian archeological sites than earlier coins, suggesting that the state was spending much less money there.[22]

All this evidence points to the three years from 659 to 662 as the time when the themes and military lands were introduced in the East. These were precisely the dates of the truce Constans made with the Arabs, which provided just enough respite from warfare for soldiers to be redeployed in themes and settled on military lands. This was also about the time when the government would have run out of money to pay the army.

It was also the time when the Byzantines' enormous losses of territory abruptly stopped. The advantage of the themes was that they gave soldiers a personal stake in holding their lands. When the soldiers died, their heirs would take over their lands with the same incentive. Although Constans'

17. See below, pp. 171–73 and 178.

18. Hendy, *Studies*, 626–62.

19. See below, pp. 184–86.

20. The reference is in Constantine VII, *De Thematibus*, p. 60. Though Constantine lived in the tenth century and often wrote antiquarian nonsense, as an emperor he had access to state archives, and his antiquarianism has no bearing on this subject.

21. See Theophanes, 348, and Gouillard, "Aux origines," 295. Though these sources refer to 668, both themes must have been organized by 662, because Constans could hardly have organized eastern themes while he was in the West.

22. See Hendy, *Studies*, 626 and 641; and below, pp. 181–84 and 169–70.

main reason for creating the themes was probably financial, their military value proved to be just as important.

Did Constans introduce the system of military lands in the West, where he spent the years from 663 to 668? This seems the obvious explanation of what he was doing there. Italy and Africa had serious defensive and financial problems. While both continued to be called exarchates, their organization seems to have been compatible with the theme system, because parts of both later became the themes of Sicily and Sardinia. Lead seals show that state warehouses of the sort that apparently complemented military lands were operating in Africa by 674 and in Sicily by 697, when Sicily seems still to have been part of the Exarchate of Italy.[23]

Soldiers and officers in northern Italy had substantial landholdings in the later seventh and eighth centuries, and at least some of these seem likely to have been grants from imperial estates, especially those clustered around the old western imperial capital of Ravenna.[24] In 664, when the self-appointed Exarch of Africa refused to send additional money to Constans' government, the exarch's own soldiers rather surprisingly overthrew him.[25] After eighteen years of virtual independence, the only apparent reason the African soldiers had for loyalty to Constans was an offer of military lands.

Though the soldiers would have been glad enough to receive land grants, creating the themes did give a dangerous amount of independence to their commanders. As early as 668 the Strategus of the Armeniac Theme rebelled, and the Count of the Opsician Theme had Constans murdered. Though both rebellions ended in submission to Constantine IV, they encouraged the Arabs to attack Anatolia and Africa.

In 670 Arab troops established forward bases at Qayrawān in Africa and Cyzicus in the Opsician Theme. They occupied Cyzicus continuously from 674 to 677, raiding around the Sea of Marmara up to the suburbs of Constantinople. Finally Constantine IV drove off their fleet with an incendiary compound we call Greek Fire, and as their army retreated it was defeated by a force drawn from the themes. The Arabs made peace, with nothing to show for their campaign.

The Byzantines acquired another dangerous neighbor in 681, when the

23. For a seal of a warehouse of Africa dated to 673/74, see Morrisson and Seibt, "Sceaux," 234–36; for a seal of a warehouse of Sicily dated to 696/97, see Zacos et al., *Byzantine Lead Seals*, I.1, 274–75, no. 197.

24. The abundant evidence is noted by Brown, *Gentlemen*, 101–8, who rightly points out that soldiers could acquire land by means other than government grants but seems too eager to exclude the possibility of such grants.

25. See al-Nuwayrī, tr. in de Slane, *Ibn Khaldun*, I, 324, where the emperor Heraclius is Constans II (whose real name was Heraclius Constantine), and the occasion must have been Constans' financial demands of 664 (*Liber Pontificalis*, I, 344), soon before the Arab invasion of Africa in 45 A.H. (665/66).

Turkish tribe of the Bulgars crossed the Danube and subjugated the Slavs of northern Thrace. Though Constantine tried to expel them, they defeated his army and captured the Byzantine outposts on the Black Sea coast. The emperor made peace, but to guard against the Bulgars he made the European part of the Opsician Theme into an independent Theme of Thrace.

Under a treaty with the Arabs made in 687, Constantine's son and successor Justinian II accepted some Christian refugees from Syria known as Mardaïtes. Justinian made them permanent oarsmen for the marines of the Carabisian Theme, settling them in southern Anatolia and the Aegean islands. He also separated Greece from the Carabisians to make it a new Theme of Hellas, which apparently received its own Mardaïtes in 689.[26] Thus the thematic fleet became a considerably more professional force. Justinian tried to make a similar addition to the army by capturing Slavs in Thrace and enrolling them in the Opsician Theme; but captives proved less reliable than willing refugees, and in their first battle most of the Slavs deserted to the Arabs.

Justinian seems to have blamed the Slavs' desertion on the Strategus of the Anatolics Leontius, whom he jailed. On being released in 695, Leontius took his revenge, overthrowing and exiling Justinian. This was only the second time since Constantine I that a legitimate eastern emperor had been deposed, and the disastrous exception was Phocas. Leontius's sole claim on power was the support of the army, but he could not take the army's loyalty for granted.

In 697 the Arabs seized the African exarch's headquarters at Carthage. Leontius speedily embarked an expeditionary force on the Carabisian fleet that retook Carthage and the region around it. But the next year the Arabs drove out the expedition, which returned to Crete. Rather than take the blame for losing Africa, the Carabisian officers proclaimed emperor their second-ranking admiral Apsimar. He took the imperial name Tiberius, sailed to Constantinople, and deposed Leontius.

Tiberius gave up on the African mainland, though he apparently tried to contain the Arabs by turning the African islands into a Theme of Sardinia and separating a new Theme of Sicily from Italy.[27] In the East the Arabs exploited Byzantine instability by conquering the parts of the Ar-

26. See Treadgold, "Army," 115–18.
27. Both themes appear for the first time in an Arab list identified by Oikonomidès, "Liste arabe," 121–30; but I am not persuaded by Oikonomidès's argument that the list should be dated before 695 because Hellas is missing (so are the Thracesians, the Carabisians, and the Exarchate of Ravenna, to fit the erroneous idea that the empire had only six "patricians" in its provinces). In fact, the mention of Sardinia as an independent theme implies a date after the fall of Carthage in 698. Sicily is first attested as a theme ca. 700, and was probably created ca. 699, also as a response to the fall of Carthage; cf. Brown, *Gentlemen*, 48 and n.20.

meniac Theme east of the Euphrates, and eastern Cilicia in the Anatolics. Usurpations had done such obvious harm to the empire that in 705 Justinian II was able to return from exile with an army of Bulgars and depose and execute Tiberius.

But the cycle of political failure and military rebellion continued. After the Arabs raided far into the Anatolic Theme, Justinian was overthrown again in 711 by a naval expedition he had sent to stop a revolt in the Crimea. When the Arabs took western Cilicia and the Hexapolis in the southeastern Armeniacs, the current usurper was overthrown in 713 by the Count of the Opsician, though the count was blinded before he could be crowned. As the Arabs prepared a land and sea campaign to take Constantinople, the Opsician Theme deposed the new emperor Anastasius II in 715. In 717 the Strategus of the Anatolics Leo seized Constantinople, shortly before the Arabs put it under siege by land and sea.

Leo III had to deal with a determined effort by the Arabs to conquer the empire by taking its capital. The siege lasted over a year. The Byzantine navy attacked the Arab fleet early, and burned some of it with Greek Fire. Though the Arabs were weakened by this attack, a harsh winter, desertions by Christians in the Arab fleet, and disease, they only withdrew the next summer after a Byzantine army ambushed reinforcements sent by the caliph. This victory gave Leo enough prestige to put down a revolt backed by the Count of the Opsician. In 727 Leo put down a rebellion by the Carabisian Theme, which seems to have led him to move its headquarters from Samos to southern Anatolia, farther away from the capital.[28] The Carabisians then became known as the Cibyrrhaeot Theme, after the port of Cibyra on the Anatolian coast.

During the Arab siege of Constantinople, the Theme of Sicily had temporarily rebelled and Byzantine control over Italy was loosened; this was probably the time when the empire lost effective control over Sardinia. But after the siege Leo halted the Arab advance on the eastern frontier, and in a few places rolled it back. In the future the Arabs often raided Anatolia, but they conquered no more of it for any length of time. Already their conquests on the eastern frontier had advanced very slowly since the themes were created, and all their gains since then had come during the empire's internal troubles between 695 and 717. Yet while the themes greatly slowed the Arab conquest, they had also raised most of the rebellions that had plagued Byzantium since their creation. As the savior of the empire from the Arab siege, Leo himself managed to die in bed in his palace, as only one of his eight predecessors had done since the foundation of the themes. Yet he had found no permanent solution to the problem of military rebellions.

28. For Samos as the theme's original headquarters, see Charanis, "Observations," 9–10, citing Constantine VII, *De Thematibus*, 81.

THE TAGMATA OF CONSTANTINE V

Leo's death in 741 set off a revolt against his son Constantine V by Artavasdus, Count of the Opsician Theme. Artavasdus seized Constantinople within a month, and held it for over two years. But the Anatolic and Thracesian themes backed Constantine, who defeated Artavasdus, besieged him in the capital, and finally starved him out and blinded him in 743.[29] This civil war of two years and a half marked the fifth time the Opsician Theme had rebelled since its creation. It was plainly too large to be so close to the capital, even after the Theme of Thrace had been separated from it.

To limit the power of the Opsician Theme, Constantine set up several units called the tagmata or regiments, which he made distinct from all the themes. Three senior tagmata, the Scholae, Excubitors, and Watch, had the names of old companies of guards, but Constantine turned them into crack cavalry regiments. Three junior tagmata, the Numera, Walls, and Optimates, had also existed earlier in a different form; they now became infantry regiments, with the Numera and Walls serving as garrison troops for Constantinople and the Optimates manning the baggage train of the senior tagmata on campaigns.

The commanders of the tagmata were known as domestics, except for the Drungary of the Watch and the Count of the Walls. By the tenth century, and probably from the beginning, the soldiers of the cavalry tagmata were stationed partly in Thrace, including new land that Constantine took from the Slavs, and partly in northwestern Anatolia. The stations of the tagmata in Anatolia were divided between the remainder of the Opsician theme and a new small district of the Optimates.

In this period of poor sources, the date of Constantine's creation of the tagmata is not recorded. The Opsician Theme backed another revolt in 766, when it was probably punished again by having its eastern half made into a new Bucellarian Theme, first mentioned in 767.[30] The tagmata themselves are already attested at the date of this revolt, and before 766 the only apparent reason for breaking up the Opsician was the rebellion of Artavasdus that ended in 743.[31] By 745 Constantine was invading the

29. See Treadgold, "Missing Year."
30. Theophanes, 438 and 440.
31. To be precise, the Domestic of the Excubitors is attested when he joined the revolt of 766 (Theophanes, 438). Since the Domestic of the Scholae had a more senior rank, he must also have existed then, though he is first attested in 767 (Theophanes, 440). There seems to be no reason to suppose a later date for the creation of the Watch, Numera, Walls, and Optimates as tagmata, since all of them took their names and the titles of many of their officers from earlier units; tagmata that were certainly formed later had entirely new names and were manned by new recruits. Besides, the function of the Scholae and Excubitors as

caliphate, probably accompanied by the tagmata, and sending back settlers to Thrace, probably into land the tagmatic troops had just cleared of Slavs.[32] This campaign marked the first successful Byzantine invasion of Arab territory in a generation.

The tagmata, which Constantine seems to have created mainly to limit the power of the Opsician Theme to revolt, proved to be a useful instrument both for extending Byzantine control in Thrace and for offensive campaigns against the Arabs and Bulgars. Although the empire's final bout of the plague interrupted operations for several years beginning in 746, in later campaigns Constantine destroyed the Arab border strongholds of Melitene and Theodosiopolis, capturing still more settlers for Thrace, and conquered the border fort of Camachum.[33] Then he conquered more of Thrace, and campaigned against the Bulgars with considerable success until his death in 775. Though in 751 the Lombards seized the empire's last possessions in central Italy, these had been weakly held for a long time.

The empress Irene, who ruled for Constantine's underage grandson Constantine VI after 780, continued extending the empire's holdings in Thrace. About 789 she divided the Theme of Thrace, making the western part into a Theme of Macedonia. Her successor Nicephorus I, probably a former Strategus of the Armeniacs, made further annexations. He reoccupied not just more of Thrace but most of Greece, which had long been held by the Slavs. In Greece he created new themes of the Peloponnesus, Cephalonia, and Thessalonica in 809, resettling them with Byzantines, including Mardaïte oarsmen from the Theme of Hellas. These former oarsmen, known as the Mardaïtes of the West, were stationed in the themes of Peloponnesus and Cephalonia and served as marines.[34] Nicephorus also recruited a fourth cavalry tagma, the Hicanati, which was partly composed of the sons of officers in other units.

In 811 Nicephorus made a major campaign against the Bulgars and defeated them soundly; but he then fell into an ambush in a mountain valley and was killed along with many of his men. This largely accidental defeat allowed the Bulgars to conquer the part of Thrace annexed by Irene and Nicephorus. The territories in Thrace that fell to the Bulgars were poorly defended, probably because they had never received an adequate garrison, unlike Nicephorus's new themes in Greece, which the Bulgars did not

---

a mobile force appears to imply the existence of the Optimates to supply a baggage train, the Watch to guard the emperor, and the Numera and Walls to guard Constantinople. The theory of Haldon, *Byzantine Praetorians*, 236–41, that Irene created the Watch in 786/87 is based on a misreading of the sources; cf. Treadgold, *Byzantine Revival*, 81–82 with n. 95.

32. Theophanes, 422.
33. See Lilie, *Byzantinische Reaktion*, 164–65.
34. See Treadgold, "Army," 116–19.

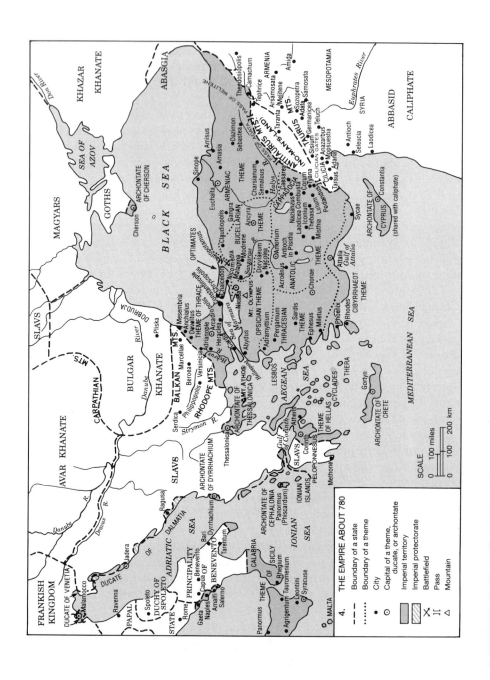

4. THE EMPIRE ABOUT 780

Boundary of a state
Boundary of a theme
City
Capital of a theme, ducate, or archontate
Imperial territory
Imperial protectorate
Battlefield
Pass
Mountain

SCALE
0   100 miles
0   100   200 km

FRANKISH KINGDOM

KHAZAR KHANATE

DON River

ABASGIA

ARMENIA
Amida

MESOPOTAMIA

Euphrates River

SYRIA

ABBASID CALIPHATE

MAGYARS

SEA OF AZOV

GOTHS

ARCHONTATE OF CHERSON

Cherson

BLACK SEA

Sinope
Amisus
Amasia
Euchaita
Claudiopolis

Theodosiopolis
Camachum
Teprice
Arsamosata
Melitene
PASS OF MELITENE
NO-MAN'S-LAND
Sozopetra
Adata
Samosata
Sisium
Germanicea
Teluch
CILICIAN GATES
Anazarbus
Mopsuestia
Tarsus
Adana

Dazimon
Sebastea
Semalnus

ANTITAURUS MTS.
TAURUS MTS.

ARMENIAC THEME
Gangra
Charsianum
Caesarea
CAPPADOCIA

Antioch
Seleucia
Laodicea

ARCHONTATE OF CYPRUS
(shared with caliphate)
Constantia

SLAVS

CARPATHIAN MTS.

BULGAR KHANATE

Pliska

DOBRUDJA

Danube

AVAR KHANATE

R.

Danube
Drawus R.

Ragusa

Jadera
DUCATE OF VENETIA
Malamocco
Ravenna
PAPAL STATE
Rome
Gaeta
Naples
Amalfi
DUCHY OF SPOLETO
Spoleto
PRINCIPALITY OF BENEVENTO
Benevento
Capua
Salerno
Tarentum
Bari
DALMATIA
ADRIATIC SEA
GULF OF
Panormus
THEME OF SICILY
Rhegium
Leontini
Syracuse
Agrigentum
Tauromenium
MALTA

ARCHONTATE OF DYRRHACHIUM
Dyrrhachium
ARCHONTATE OF CEPHALONIA
Panormus (Phiscardum)
IONIAN ISLANDS
IONIAN SEA
CALABRIA

SLAVS
Athens
SLAVS
Corinth
Gulf of Corinth
THEME OF HELLAS
PELOPONNESUS THEME
Methone

Serdica
Philippopolis
Versinicia
Beroea
Marcellae
BALKAN MTS.
Mesembria
Anchialus
Develtus
Adrianople
THEME OF THRACE
Arcadiopolis
Heraclea
RHODOPE MTS.
Strymon R.
Hebrus R.
ARCHONTATE OF THESSALONICA
MT. ATHOS
Thessalonica

LESBOS

AEGEAN SEA

CYCLADES
THERA
ARCHONTATE OF CRETE
Gortyn

MEDITERRANEAN SEA

OPTIMATES
Mesopotamia
Chrysopolis
Chalcedon
Nicomedia
Malagina
Nicaea
BUCELLARIAN THEME
Dorylaeum
Nacolea
OPSICIAN THEME
Mt. OLYMPUS THEME
Sea of Marmara
Abydus
Adramyttium
Pergamum
THRACESIAN THEME
Sardis
Ephesus
Miletus
Phoenix
Rhodes

Ancyra
Modrene
Sangarius
Amorium
Acroinus
ANATOLIC THEME
Chonae

Sycae

Antioch in Pisidia
Iconium
Laodicea Combusta
Nazianzus
Nyssa
Thebasa
Lulum
Podandus
Misthia
CYBYRRHAEOT THEME
Attalia
Gulf of Attalia

Halys
Tyana
CILICIA

attack. The Bulgars then began to raid the rest of Thrace, though without trying to conquer it.

When the new emperor Michael I failed to stop them, he had to abdicate in favor of his Strategus of the Anatolics, who became Leo V. Leo finally defeated the Bulgars in an ambush of his own, and obtained a peace that restored the Thracian frontier as it had been before Irene. About 819 Leo, probably provoked by sea raiding by the emergent Russians, made two coastal parts of the Armeniac Theme into the new military districts of Paphlagonia and Chaldia.[35] But Leo was assassinated in 820 by conspirators, and his Domestic of the Excubitors became emperor as Michael II.

Leo's murder began a civil war between Michael II and Thomas the Slav, a senior officer of the Anatolic Theme. Most of the army except the Armeniac and Opsician themes backed Thomas, who besieged Michael in Constantinople by land and sea. Michael managed to defeat and execute Thomas in 823, but only put down the last of the rebels in Anatolia the next year. This civil war especially weakened the naval themes of the Cibyrrhaeots, Peloponnesus, and Cephalonia, which had backed Thomas. Two years later a rebellion broke out in Sicily, and the rebels soon appealed for help to the Arabs of Africa. While Michael's fleet was trying to recover Sicily in 828, a band of Arab adventurers seized Crete. Since Crete had never been part of the system of themes, it had no proper garrison, which it had seemed not to need, and was easy prey for the Arabs. When Michael died in 829 most of the Theme of Sicily held out, but Crete had become a nest of Arab pirates.

By and large the themes had continued to provide an adequate defense. During the century after they were created, the empire had held most of its land except for the gradual slipping away of Africa and Italy. Neither of these was formally a theme, both took several decades to be lost, and the main factor in their loss was probably the empire's internal instability between 695 and 717. This had also allowed the Arabs to take Cilicia and western Armenia. The civil war between 820 and 824 in turn contributed to the Arab conquests on Sicily and Crete, the latter of which was not a theme.

After Constantine V created the tagmata, military revolts had become somewhat less frequent, and the empire had even been able to recover some territory. Constantine himself, Irene, and Nicephorus had all retaken parts of Thrace, though the reconquests of the latter two rulers were lost before long. The empire's other significant gains were Nicephorus's new themes in Greece, though these had been won through mostly peaceful occupation at the expense of unwarlike Slavs. While the themes

35. See Treadgold, "Three Byzantine Provinces."

and tagmata could defend the empire well enough, they could not yet expand it aggressively, and they still rebelled distressingly often.

THE FLEXIBLE ARMY OF THEOPHILUS

The succession of Michael II's son Theophilus took place without a revolt. Soon Theophilus was campaigning against the Arabs, but with more enthusiasm than success. In 834 he gave asylum to a group of religious rebels from the caliphate known as Khurramites, who converted to Christianity and joined the Byzantine army. More Khurramites arrived in 837, when Theophilus raided the caliphate in force. But the next year the caliph retaliated with a great raid on Asia Minor. As the Khurramites rebelled, the caliph defeated the Byzantines and sacked Ancyra and Amorium, headquarters of the Bucellarian and Anatolic themes.

By 839 Theophilus roused himself to lead an army against the Khurramites, who promptly submitted. They agreed to let their company be divided into fifteen parts, which were incorporated into fifteen different themes and other districts. The fifteen units that received Khurramites included two new themes, Dyrrhachium in today's Albania and the Climata in the Crimea, and three new districts called cleisurae, or mountain passes, meant to guard the Arab frontier. The Cleisura of Charsianum was created in the border region of the Armeniacs, and the cleisurae of Cappadocia and Seleucia in the border region of the Anatolics. While resettling the Khurramites at the beginning of 840, Theophilus also seems to have made extensive military reforms, reorganizing the army's command structure and raising its pay.[36]

Theophilus's reforms brought an almost immediate improvement in the themes' performance. In 840 and 841 the cleisurae of Cappadocia and Charsianum handily defeated Arab raiders, who had been accustomed to plunder the border areas with impunity. Theophilus evidently made the Cleisura of Cappadocia a theme in recognition of its valor. After Theophilus's death in 842 Arab raids usually took a route to the northeast of the cleisurae, where Theophilus had for some reason left a section of the Upper Euphrates with no special command to defend it.[37]

Under Theophilus's son Michael III, the Byzantines tried to retake Crete in 843, but the island was easily defensible and the expedition failed. To replace a stillborn Theme of Crete, a new Theme of the Aegean Sea was separated from the Cibyrrhaeot Theme.[38] About this time the Byz-

---

36. See below, pp. 104 and 119–35.
37. See Treadgold, *Byzantine Revival*, 312–25 and 347–57.
38. On this and other changes in the army between 843 and 899, see Treadgold, "Army," 86–88.

antines acquired a new enemy on land when the Paulicians, a heretical religious sect, founded a rebel principality around the city of Tephrice on the border of the Armeniac Theme. Allying themselves with the Arabs of nearby Melitene, the Paulicians also raided across the poorly defended frontier along the Upper Euphrates. Though about 861 a new Theme of Colonia was separated from the Armeniacs to fill the gap, it remained a weak point because it received no additional troops, unlike the cleisurae that Theophilus had reinforced with Khurramites. Yet the Byzantines continued to fight well against the Arabs and Paulicians, until in 863 they inflicted severe defeats on both which marked the end of serious Arab raiding in Anatolia.

Basil I, who founded the durable Macedonian dynasty by murdering the irresponsible Michael III, devoted himself to curbing Arab piracy and the still dangerous Paulicians. Basil greatly strengthened the Imperial Fleet based in Constantinople by giving it its own professional marines. These seem to have been introduced around 870, after which the navy regularly defeated Arab pirates. The navy also added the heel of Italy to the Theme of Cephalonia and briefly took all of Cyprus, which the empire had long shared with the caliphate.[39] The Arabs captured Syracuse in Sicily only because Basil was then using the Imperial Fleet to move marble for a church he was building in the capital, not to reinforce the Syracusans. Basil's wars with the Paulicians were successful; in 879 his army crushed them and retook their stronghold of Tephrice.

Basil's heir Leo VI fought an indecisive and inglorious war with the Bulgars that led him to create two new frontier districts, Nicopolis from Cephalonia and Strymon from Macedonia. From 900, however, Leo began to advance the eastern frontier for the first time since the seventh century. He created new themes of Mesopotamia and Sebastea and new cleisurae of Lycandus and Leontocome ("Leoville"), his name for Tephrice. These commands combined newly conquered land with land from earlier themes, which were in turn partly compensated with territory from their neighbors. The new territory was garrisoned with largely Armenian recruits. Leo's military reforms included changes in the command structure and an increase in thematic cavalry.[40]

By sea Leo was less successful. An Arab naval expedition surprised and sacked Thessalonica. The last of Sicily fell to the Arabs, leaving nothing of that theme but the toe of Italy, which became known as the Theme of

39. Basil later had to restore the power-sharing arrangement with the Arabs on Cyprus, and apparently compensated for his lost theme on the island by creating a new Theme of Samos from the Theme of the Aegean Sea. Basil also protected the Byzantine possessions on the Adriatic coast by setting up a Theme of Dalmatia, though unlike other themes it had only a token garrison.

40. See below, pp. 105–6.

Calabria. Leo turned the heel of Italy, previously a part of the Theme of Cephalonia, into a Theme of Longobardia.[41] In 911 Leo tried to retake Crete, but his expedition, like previous attacks on the island, was a costly failure. After this the empire made no significant conquests for almost a quarter century, mostly because of internal troubles and a war with Bulgaria.

Once peace was made with the Bulgars, the empire went on the offensive against the Arabs. In 934 Byzantine forces captured the Arabs' chief border stronghold of Melitene. Soon thereafter the large tribe of the Banū Ḥabīb fled to the empire, converted to Christianity, and were enlisted to garrison five small new themes that stretched north from Melitene along the frontier. The Byzantines now began to make regular raids on Arab territory in Syria, Mesopotamia, and Armenia. In 949 the Byzantines again tried to recapture Crete, but failed.[42] Though the same year they took Theodosiopolis, the Arabs' main base in Armenia, the emir of Aleppo Sayf al-Dawlah managed to keep them from making more conquests for another ten years.

During the century or so after Theophilus's military reform of 840, the army's performance was reassuring but not spectacular. Military rebellions virtually ended, and for almost the first time in Byzantine history practically all of the empire's territory became secure from raids. If only limited conquests had been made on the eastern frontier, part of the reason was that the mountainous terrain made conquests there slow and difficult. Probably a more important reason was simply that the Byzantines had long been accustomed to being on the defensive, so that the ambitions of the empire's emperors and generals had become rather modest. As soon as more ambitious emperors and generals appeared and tried to do more, the army proved capable of astonishing exploits.

About 959, under the dashing young emperor Romanus II, the tagmata were divided into eastern and western commands, headed by a Domestic of the East and a Domestic of the West. This signaled the beginning of some major campaigns of conquest. In 961 the Domestic of the East Nicephorus Phocas finally succeeded in retaking Crete and making it a theme. Next Nicephorus ravaged Arab Cilicia and sacked the center of Arab resistance at Aleppo. He only interrupted his campaign when the emperor Romanus died. The widowed empress invited Phocas to marry her and become co-emperor along with her six-year-old son, Basil II.

As Nicephorus II, Phocas led his army back to Cilicia, this time to con-

---

41. Longobardia is first attested in a salary list of Leo VI (Constantine VII, *De Ceremoniis*, 696–97) datable to 910; see Treadgold, "Army," 93–98.

42. Afterward they created a new Theme of the Cyclades, which is attested in the *Escorial Tacticon* of 971/75, did not exist in 949, and is unlikely to have been created after 961 since it was probably meant to be a defense against the Cretan Arabs.

quer it. First he took Cyprus, in 964.[43] He completed the conquest of Cilicia in 965, dividing it into a half-dozen new themes.[44] Most of their garrisons were probably Armenian. In 967 the prince of Taron in Armenia willed his principality to Nicephorus, who joined it to the empire by annexing parts of western Armenia that had long been more or less subject to the empire. These became more than a dozen new themes, garrisoned by native Armenian troops. To avoid fragmenting Byzantine power too much among these little districts, Nicephorus put them under the general command of the Strategus of Chaldia, who received the grander title of duke.[45]

Nicephorus had still more ambitious plans, and expanded his heavy-armed cavalry to prepare for more conquests in Syria. But he had little interest in fighting elsewhere. He invited the Russians to attack Bulgaria for him; when the German emperor attacked the Italian themes, Nicephorus entrusted the war to a new general commander with the title of Catepan of Italy. In 968 the emperor made a major campaign in northern Mesopotamia and Syria. He apparently took Edessa and made it a theme, then captured the forts around Antioch and blockaded the ancient Syrian capital itself, leaving a force to continue the siege. Antioch surrendered and became a theme in 969.

That same year, despite all his triumphs, Nicephorus II was murdered by his neglected empress and his envious Domestic of the East, John Tzimisces. A brilliant general in his own right, Tzimisces became the emperor John I, ruling for the still underage Basil II. John took over a military crisis in the north, where the Russians had conquered the Bulgars and were threatening Byzantine territory. But in the south Byzantine forces had the Emirate of Aleppo at their mercy. In 970 the Aleppines made a treaty accepting Byzantine overlordship and formally ceding the region of Antioch to the empire.

Then John seems to have reorganized the army on the eastern frontier. He grouped the thirty-odd small frontier themes and two new themes around Antioch under three dukes with authority over the local strategi. Leaving the Duke of Chaldia only with authority over the far north, he put the central sector under a Duke of Mesopotamia and the southern

---

43. Scylitzes, 270, dates the expulsion of the Arabs from Cyprus to the second year of Nicephorus (after August 16, 964), and it seems to have preceded the embassy of Nicephorus to Aleppo in the fall of 964 (Yaḥyā of Antioch, 794–95). Lemerle, "Vie ancienne," 93 n. 96, notes that the usual date of 965 seems slightly too late.

44. These themes were Tarsus, Mopsuestia, Anazarbus, Germanicea, Adata, and Hexacomia; see Oikonomidès, *Listes*, 355, 356, 359, 360.

45. The themes were Taron, Chantiarte, Chortzine, Cama, Chauzizium, Melte, Artze, Ocomium(?), Chuët, Muzarium, Caludia, Erkne, Zermium, Chasanara, and Limnia. On these and the new Ducate of Chaldia, see Oikonomidès, *Listes*, 354, 359–63, and (on Ocomium) 268 n. 26.

sector under a Duke of Antioch. Apparently John extended the dukes' commands to seven more small themes that he separated from the older themes nearest the frontier.[46] John also founded a new Tagma of the Immortals, taking its name from a Persian corps mentioned by Herodotus.

The following year John led his Immortals and other troops against the Russians occupying Bulgaria. The emperor trounced the Russians twice, besieged them in the Bulgarian fort of Dristra, and forced them to withdraw to Russia. John annexed eastern Bulgaria and divided it into six themes under new dukes of Adrianople and Thessalonica. These dukes also seem to have had responsibility for six more themes that he separated from the old frontier themes on the pattern of the eastern frontier.[47] A little later John seems to have extended Byzantine control farther up the Danube, where he created two more themes.[48] The new garrisons seem to have consisted partly of natives, partly of settlers brought from the East.

Having reestablished the Danube frontier for the first time since the early seventh century, John turned to campaigning in the East. After raiding Arab Mesopotamia, in 975 the emperor invaded southern Syria down to northern Palestine, which belonged to the Fatimid Caliphate of Egypt. On his return he set up new themes on the coast between Tripoli, which the Fatimids still held, and the Byzantine base of Antioch.[49] John said that

46. Though Kühn, *Byzantinische Armee*, 126 and 167–68, attributes this reorganization to Nicephorus II, it probably belongs to John I, because it parallels a similar reorganization on the Balkan frontier that must be his, and it depended upon the elevation of Antioch to a ducate. Nicephorus put Antioch not under a duke but under a strategus at the end of his reign; see Cheynet and Vannier, *Études prosopographiques*, 19 n. 16. The new themes around Antioch were Palatza and Artach, and the themes detached from others were probably Soteropolis (from Chaldia), Romanopolis (from Mesopotamia), Coptus (from Sebastea), Taranta (from Lycandus), Cymbalaeus (from Charsianum), Podandus (from Cappadocia), and Irenopolis (from Seleucia). On all these commands, cf. Oikonomidès, *Listes*, 354–63, though at 362 I would identify Irenopolis with that city in Isauria, not an Irenopolis in eastern Cilicia.

47. The new themes were Beroea in Greece, Drugubitia, Beroea in Thrace, Dristra, and the Mesopotamia of the West. The themes detached from others were Jericho (from Dyrrhachium), Larissa (from Thessalonica), New Strymon (from Strymon), Paralia or "The Seacoasts" (from Macedonia), the Euxine (from Thrace), and the Bosporus (from Cherson). On all of these districts, see Oikonomidès, *Listes*, 354–58, 361–63, and 266 and n. 24 (where the completion Par[alia] is confirmed by Scylitzes, 368, who locates that command near Abydus). Note that unlike Oikonomidès I locate the Theme of Larissa in Thessaly, assuming that Anatolian Larissa remained part of the Theme of Sebastea. Besides a strategus, the Mesopotamia of the West had a catepan, apparently to command a fleet on the Danube.

48. These were Ras and Morava; see Nesbitt and Oikonomidès, *Catalogue*, I, 100–101 and 195–96. The date of these themes' creation must be conjectured; if it was in 973, the *Escorial Tacticon* should be dated before then, though the *Tacticon* cannot be earlier than 971.

49. On the new themes, see Yaḥyā of Antioch, 369, who is somewhat vague but names Balaneae and Gabala; Oikonomidès, *Listes*, 261 n. 19, notes that seals confirm the existence of Gabala and add Laodicea; Antaradus, later attested as a theme, should probably be added as well.

he intended to take the coast of Palestine and Jerusalem itself, and such conquests would hardly have been more remarkable than those he had already made. But the next year he unexpectedly died.

Thus Basil II became senior emperor at the age of eighteen. John's Domestic of the East and relative Bardas Sclerus promptly rebelled and gained the support of almost the whole army of Asia Minor. Basil called on Bardas Phocas, Nicephorus II's nephew, who won over many of Sclerus's troops and drove Sclerus into exile after four years of civil war. Meanwhile the power of the Bulgars had begun to revive, and in 986 they defeated Basil in battle. Sclerus took this as a signal to return from exile and resume his rebellion, and instead of putting down the rebellion Phocas joined it, took it over from Sclerus, and seized all of Anatolia. Basil appealed for help from the Russians, who supplied him with a band of mercenaries. These crushed the rebels in a three-year civil war, and became a permanent unit of the army known as the Varangian Guard.

By 990 Basil II was finally master of the empire. He first attacked the king of Iberia, who as punishment for backing Phocas had to bequeath his kingdom to the empire. Then Basil began a war with the Bulgars, who during the rebellions had retaken much of eastern Bulgaria. The emperor had to interrupt his campaigns to repulse attacks by the Fatimids on the eastern frontier, probably creating three new themes in the process, and to claim his inheritance in Iberia, which he made a ducate in 1000.[50] But the Byzantines gradually retook all of eastern Bulgaria and more, establishing three new themes and a Ducate of Paradunavum ("Beside the Danube") to coordinate the region's defense.[51] Basil raided western Bulgaria until 1004, when he apparently thought he had punished the Bulgars enough.

After doing little campaigning for about ten years, in 1014 Basil captured much of the Bulgar army in a mountain pass. When the Bulgars captured some of his men, the emperor retaliated by blinding all his prisoners. This allowed Basil to raid the heart of western Bulgaria. By 1018 the Bulgars had become so discouraged that most of them surrendered. Basil established a Ducate of Bulgaria in the central part of the conquered

50. The new eastern themes were probably Sizara (cf. Yaḥyā of Antioch, 457−58), Teluch, and the Euphrates Cities. The latter two are first attested about 1030 (Scylitzes, 381 and 387), but they are unlikely to have been created after 1000, when the empire was at peace with the Fatimids, and the ease of the Fatimid raid on Germanicea in 998 seems to indicate that they did not exist at that date. The gap they filled would have been left by the loss of Edessa during the civil wars.

51. The new themes were Philippopolis, Pliska, and Great Preslav. The Theme of Little Preslav apparently replaced the Mesopotamia of the West, and the Ducate of Paradunavum was the new name of the Theme of Dristra. See Nesbitt and Oikonomidès, *Catalogue*, I, for the seals attesting these commands as well as Mesembria, which may also have become a theme at this time since no other date seems appropriate.

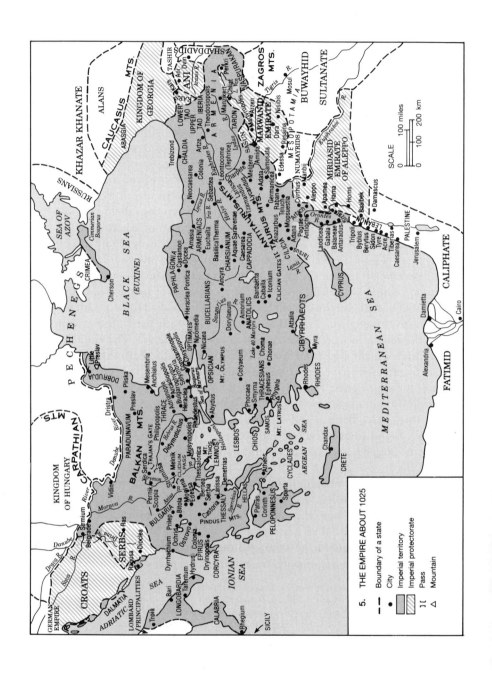

5. THE EMPIRE ABOUT 1025

- Boundary of a state
• City
  Imperial territory
  Imperial protectorate
)(Pass
△ Mountain

SCALE
0   100 miles
0   100   200 km

KHAZAR KHANATE

ALANS

CAUCASUS MTS.

KINGDOM OF GEORGIA

ABASGIA

RUSSIANS

SEA OF AZOV

Cimmerian Bosporus

CRIMEA

Cherson

BLACK SEA
(EUXINE)

PECHENEGS

Trebizond

CHALDIA
Neocaesarea

Amasia
Basilica Therma
Euchaita
Docea
Castamon
Amastris
Heraclea Pontica
PAPHLAGONIA

ARMENIACS

CHARSIANUM

Sebastea
Colonia
Artze
Tephrice
Leontocome
Melitene

Caesarea
CAPPADOCIA

ANTI-TAURUS MTS.

TASHIR
SHADDADIDS

Dvin
ANI
Ani
KARS
Kars

LOWER
UPPER IAO IBERIA
Theodosiopolis
A R M E N I A
SASUN
TARON

Manzikert
Khliat
Archesh
Khoi
Van
APAHUNIK

MARWANID EMIRATE

ZAGROS MTS.

Amida
Martyropolis

Mayyafariqin

BUWAYHID SULTANATE

Tigris R.
Mosul
Nisibis
Dara
Resaina
MESOPOTAMIA
Euphrates R.

NUMAYRIDS
MIRDASID EMIRATE OF ALEPPO

Edessa
Manbij
Cyrrhus
Germanicea
Adata
Samosata
Marash

Aleppo
Hama
Apamea
Hons
Baalbek
Damascus

LEBANON

Laodicea
Gabala
Balaneae
Antaradus
Tripoli
Byblus
Berytus
Sidon
Tyre
Acre
Tiberias
Caesarea
Jerusalem
PALESTINE

CALIPHATE

CYPRUS

MEDITERRANEAN SEA

FATIMID

Damietta
Cairo
Alexandria

CILICIA
Tarsus
Adana
Mopsuestia
Anazarbus
CILICIAN GATES
Podandus
Caesarea
Cybistra
Iconium
Heraclea
Lulon
Faustinopolis
Loulon
ANATOLICS
Amorium
BUCELLARIANS
Ancyra
Dorylaeum
OPTIMATES
Nicomedia
Nicaea

Sangarius R.
OPSICIAN

MT. OLYMPUS
Lake 40 Martyrs
Cotyaeum

CHARSIANUM
Caesarea
Aquae Saravenae
ARMENIACS

Sebastea
Iris R.
Halys R.
Lycandus
CAPPADOCIA
TAURUS MTS.

Cotyaeum
Chonae
Choma
Attalia
CIBYRRHAEOTS
Myra
Rhode
RHODES

Chandax
CRETE

AEGEAN SEA

CYCLADES
Sparta
PELOPONNESUS
Corinth
Patras
HELLAS
Athens
Thebes
MT. LATRUS
SAMOS
Ephesus
Phocaea
Smyrna
CHIOS
LESBOS
MT. ATHOS
Demetrias
Larissa
THESSALY
PINDUS MTS.

Bari
LONGOBARDIA
Tarentum
CALABRIA
Rhegium
SICILY

IONIAN SEA
ADRIATIC
Tripi
DALMATIA
CROATS
GERMAN EMPIRE

Corcyra
CORCYRA
Dryinopolis
EPIRUS
Colonia
Hydrus
Dyrrhachium
Ragusa
Diocleia
SERBS
Ras

Belgrade
Sirmium
KINGDOM OF HUNGARY

Danube
Drava R.
Drina R.
Sava R.
Morava R.

Castoria
Ochrid
Prilep
Ostrovo
Bitola
BULGARIA
Serdica
Pernik
Scopia
Stip
Meinik
Strymon R.
Beroea
Edessa
Thessalonica

Vidin
Morava R.
Naissus
Vardar R.
Axius R.
Sperchius R.
Aliakmon R.

CARPATHIAN MTS.

Danube River

DOBRUDJA

Dristra
Pliska
Little Preslav
Preslav
Mesembria
Anchialus
Develtus
PARADUNAVUM
Preslav
BALKAN MTS.
Philippopolis
Hebrus R.
TRAJAN'S GATE
Adrianople
THRACE
Heraclea
Selymbria
Constantinople
Sea of Marmora
Abydus
Hellespont
CLIDIUM PASS
Philadelphia
Sardis

territory and a Ducate of Sirmium along the Danube.[52] Evidently most of the troops of these ducates were Bulgars. Meanwhile the king of Georgia had stupidly attacked the Ducate of Iberia, provoking a war that he lost to Basil. While the emperor was in Armenia, the king of Vaspurakan voluntarily ceded his kingdom to the empire, and to atone for backing the Georgians the king of Ani had to will his domains to the empire as well.[53] Basil was preparing to reconquer Sicily when he died in 1025, after ruling forty-nine glorious years.

At Basil's death, at the peak of his success, the Byzantine army was stronger than any rival or neighboring force. Since Theophilus's reforms in 840 the army had almost doubled the empire's size, and despite several civil wars it had overthrown no more of its own emperors. Though Basil II's long defensive and retaliatory wars had led to a number of almost accidental annexations, Basil himself cared little for conquests, unlike Nicephorus II and John I. What he really wanted was security, and this he seemed to have achieved. No doubt Nicephorus II, John I, and Basil II had been commanders of great military ability, but the army had shown itself able to rise to the level of its rulers.

THE ARMY'S COLLAPSE

Since by 1028 the only surviving members of the Macedonian house were women past childbearing age, the dynasty was doomed to die out. But during the next thirty-one years the empire was in the hands of two of Basil II's incompetent nieces and the five undistinguished men they married, adopted, or chose. Even these rulers could not wreck the army all at once. With little help from them it retook Edessa, which had been lost during Basil's civil wars, and briefly recaptured eastern Sicily as Basil had intended. The army faced down a serious Bulgar rebellion in 1041, and in 1045 claimed the empire's inheritance of Ani, which was added to the Ducate of Iberia.

Despite these accomplishments, the army was deteriorating and growing increasingly discontented, especially under the bumbling emperor Constantine IX Monomachus. A military rebellion would probably have overthrown Constantine in 1043 if its leader had not suddenly died. Largely to avoid such revolts, the emperors relied more and more on mercenaries and allied auxiliaries, but these were usually few and not necessarily loyal. A band of rebellious Norman mercenaries soon began to take Byzantine Italy for themselves. The Turkish tribes of the Pechenegs and

52. Basil also created three new themes of Dryinopolis, Colonia, and Serbia.
53. The sea raid of a Russian renegade may also have led Basil to create a Theme of Chios, which seems not to have existed when the raid occurred about 1024 but did exist before 1028; cf. Scylitzes, 367–68 and 373.

Uzes arrived in the Balkans as nominally allied troops, but soon started roaming and raiding Byzantine territory. Byzantine Armenia began to be raided by the Seljuk Turks, a major new power to the east.

A profligate spender, Constantine IX debased the coinage, thereby reducing the value of the army's pay by about a fifth.[54] Around 1053 he relieved many thematic soldiers in Armenia of military duties and subjected them instead to a tax. Since Seljuk raids should have kept these men in much better fighting trim than their fellows in themes that had long been peaceful, after this the thematic army cannot have had much military value. The empire's defense now depended mostly on mercenaries, especially the Varangians, and on the tagmata.

In 1057 the neglected army rebelled, overthrew an emperor who had recently served as the minister in charge of military pay, and replaced him with the former commander of the eastern tagmata Isaac Comnenus. But Isaac I concentrated on sorting out the finances rather than reforming the army, and after two years his opponents maneuvered him into abdicating. His successor Constantine X Ducas also devoted his attention to the treasury. Meanwhile the Normans were finishing their conquest of Byzantine Italy, the Pechenegs and Uzes were ravaging the Balkans, and the Seljuk Turks not only raided Armenia but conquered Ani. Then the Seljuks plundered Cappadocia and Cilicia, where no raiders had ventured for over a century.

At this Constantine X's widow, against the wishes of her late husband's relatives, married a capable general, Romanus Diogenes. At his accession in 1068 Romanus IV was the first ruler since Basil II to pay serious attention to the army. What he found was shocking. He called up what was left of the Anatolian themes, and made a valiant effort to whip them into a fighting force. Combining them with mercenaries and the western and eastern tagmata, he defeated a few Turks, though many others evaded him. In 1069 Romanus chased Turkish raiders around Anatolia, but meanwhile the Seljuk sultan captured the Armenian fort of Manzikert.[55]

Some of Romanus's generals wanted to withdraw from Armenia and fall back on Anatolia.[56] But the emperor disagreed, probably realizing that the Anatolian forts were in decay and the Anatolian themes unready to mount an effective local defense. Romanus hoped instead to intimidate

54. See Morrisson, "Dévaluation," whose testing reveals that the nomisma averaged about 75% gold by the end of Constantine's reign, though in his early issues it averaged about 92%, a figure that had long been standard and was nearly the best that Byzantine mints could manage consistently.

55. Perhaps the best account of Romanus's campaigns in the East is in Hild and Restle, *Kappadokien*, 100–105.

56. These generals are said to have included the Magister Joseph Tarchaniotes and the Domestic of the West Nicephorus Bryennius (Bryennius, 105–7), and even Romanus's admirer Attaliates (Attaliates, 136). Some hindsight may however be involved.

the Turks by winning a decisive victory, and in 1071 mustered a great army of thematic, tagmatic, and mercenary troops. He retook Manzikert, attacked the nearby army of the Seljuk sultan, and seemed to be winning the battle. But the disaffected relatives of the late Constantine X spread the rumor in the army that Romanus had been defeated. The soldiers fled, leaving the emperor and those fighting around him to be captured by the sultan.[57]

The sultan released Romanus in return for a treaty ceding the border zone from Antioch to Manzikert. But Romanus's enemies seized power in Constantinople during his absence, defeated him in a civil war, and had him blinded, causing his death. Romanus's general Philaretus Brachamius continued to hold the themes around Melitene as a rebel, evidently with most of the eastern tagmata and perhaps some of the western.[58] Other such rebels held the frontier from Taron to Edessa. The government of Constantine X's son Michael VII held Antioch at the southern end of the frontier and Theodosiopolis at the northern end. But between Taron and Theodosiopolis no one stopped the Turks from pouring in.

Migrating into Anatolia in force, the Turks overwhelmed the Byzantines' disused fortresses. Romanus's half-trained thematic troops seem simply to have dispersed. Giving no aid to the rest of the empire, Philaretus used the eastern tagmata to secure a fiefdom of his own stretching from western Armenia to Cilicia. Despite more debasement of the coinage, Michael's government ran short of money to pay its mercenaries, who repeatedly mutinied. Though the government recruited a new Tagma of the Immortals to replace the eastern tagmata, this was not nearly enough. The remaining western tagmata rebelled three times, and twice were suppressed. The Turks, sometimes called in to help the rebels against the government or to help the government against the rebels, occupied the larger part of Asia Minor.

In 1081 the Domestic of the West Alexius Comnenus seized power at Constantinople with the help of the Varangians and some other mercenaries. The Turks continued advancing in Anatolia, and the Normans of formerly Byzantine Italy invaded the Balkans. Later the same year, the Normans heavily defeated Alexius I near Dyrrhachium, apparently shattering the little that remained of the western tagmata.[59] The last western

57. On the battle, see especially Cheynet, "Mantzikert."
58. After 1071 no eastern tagmata are found in Anatolia proper (except for the Immortals, who had to be recreated about 1075); but when Philaretus nominally ended his rebellion in 1078 he was named Domestic of the East, implying that he then commanded the eastern tagmata.
59. The Excubitors (of the West) are mentioned just before the defeat at Dyrrhachium (Anna Comnena, IV.4.3), but neither they nor the Scholae nor the Hicanati are ever heard of afterward.

tagma mentioned in the sources is the reconstituted Immortals, in 1094.[60] Elements of the eastern tagmata probably survived in the East for some time under Philaretus and his sons, and perhaps even in the new Kingdom of Armenian Cilicia that lasted three hundred years more. But the central government never regained control of them, nor of most of Anatolia.

Alexius gathered new forces, most of them mercenaries, and eventually retook part of Anatolia. In one form or another the empire survived for almost four centuries longer, and continued to have provinces called themes. But the army assembled by Alexius was no longer the direct descendant of the Roman legions, as the old themes and tagmata had been. Nor did the empire ever regain the unquestioned superiority over its enemies that it had lost in the late eleventh century. After almost eight hundred years of adapting to changing conditions surprisingly well, the Byzantine army fell apart, after an extraordinary series of conquests followed by a period of mismanaged peace. Why and how this happened is a difficult question, to which we shall return.[61]

60. For the Immortals, see Anna Comnena, IX.2.2. The Watch is last heard of in 1092: see Zepos and Zepos, *Jus Graecoromanum*, I, 319, referring to a Drungary of the Watch who is probably the historian John Scylitzes; cf. Thurn's edition of Scylitzes, x–xi.
61. See below, pp. 214–19.

CHAPTER TWO

Numbers

How big was the Byzantine army? Even if our knowledge were complete, the question would have many answers. The army's size certainly varied over the almost eight hundred years from 284 to 1081. At any date, the number was different depending on whether it included the navy along with the army, officers along with enlisted men, support staff along with combatants, irregulars along with regulars. Even the figures on the rolls kept by the government and the commanders of individual units cannot have shown all the deaths, retirements, desertions, and enlistments that happened every day. Numbers could be rounded off, though for most purposes this should scarcely matter. Some numbers were also miscopied, though such copyists' errors are often obvious, and sometimes the corrections that should be made to them are obvious as well.

Other problems are more complex. Numbers for armies in ancient and medieval sources could be compiled in at least three different ways. First, the government or commanders could take a census of the men, either by mustering and counting them or by consulting current muster rolls that listed the men's names. For the whole army, such information would be slightly out of date by the time it was collected and compiled, though not seriously so if the records were well kept. A second and easier way was simply to add up the numbers that different units were authorized to have, so that in Roman times each legion could be counted as 5,500 men. Though the resulting total would be somewhat too high if units were under strength, and too low if units were over strength, for most purposes it would be good enough.

A third method was simply to guess. For the government this would not do, and anyone with access to census figures or to the numbers of units and their strengths would normally not need to guess. Many Byzantines who wrote history were themselves officials or officers, and should have had access to official figures. Procopius, for example, the historian of most of Justinian's wars, was the secretary of Justinian's general Belisarius. Since cultured Byzantines formed a small and cohesive group, historians who did not work for the government often had friends and relatives who did. But even an official who was writing about events from long ago and far away might have no relevant figures at hand and be reduced to guessing. Such guesses, usually round numbers, could be much too high or too low.

Another sort of case would be more complex than these three. A Byzantine writer might find some official figures without finding exact information to explain them. Most surviving Byzantine documents have quite rudimentary headings, with only essential names and dates and sometimes not even those.[1] While faithfully transcribing correct numbers, a later writer might well misinterpret them. For example, a figure labeled in a document "army of Constantine the Great" and dated to 312 might actually represent all the soldiers on Constantine's rolls, but might be misunderstood to be the army Constantine actually led into battle against Maxentius in that year. Modern scholars, finding this figure much too high for a battlefield army, might dismiss it as a wild guess, when in fact it was a mislabeled official total.

The total number of soldiers in the empire was always far higher than those who could be mustered for any one battle. Many had to stay home to guard the frontiers and keep order. Seamen were generally not used on land, and the number of available ships restricted the number of troops who could go on naval campaigns. Terrain could limit the usefulness of cavalry, and shortness of time could force generals to leave infantry behind. Any good general knew that a large army of second-rate troops could be worse than a small army of picked men. Besides, campaigning with too large an army led to serious supply problems, as Julian seems to have discovered in Persia. Yet a writer who spent his life in an office and lacked military experience, and who knew how many soldiers were on the rolls but not how many campaigned, might simply assume that any large campaign used all the soldiers on the rolls.

THE PROBLEM OF THE 'NOTITIA DIGNITATUM'

Our first surviving Byzantine statistic is for the army of Diocletian. John the Lydian, a sixth-century bureaucrat, writes that "under Diocletian" the army had 389,704 men and the navy 45,562 men. John adds that when Constantine took over the East (in 324) he increased the size of the army by "as many tens of thousands again," which taken literally would

1. E.g., Constantine VII, *De Ceremoniis*, 651, 661, and 664.

mean another 380,000.[2] But we can be fairly sure that John had no statistic for Constantine's army, or he would have cited it. The most we can reasonably conclude about John's second statement is that he believed Constantine's army was much larger than Diocletian's, perhaps by about double. Since John wrote over two hundred years later, his belief could well be wrong.

Yet the specific figures for Diocletian's army look as if John had found them in the archives, to which he certainly had access. If "under Diocletian" meant that Diocletian was then the only emperor, the figures would belong to the first half of 285, after Diocletian completed his conquest of the whole empire and before he named his first co-emperor. This would have been a likely time for Diocletian to take a census of his troops, and these figures, which seem to include every last man, do look like census figures.

Before Diocletian, the last date for which we can make a good estimate of the army is 235. A. H. M. Jones observed that "in the troubled half century between [235] and Diocletian's accession much must have changed; many units must have been lost and many new formations raised."[3] On the other hand, military necessity would have forced emperors to replace most of their losses, and economic difficulties would not have allowed them to do much more. Ramsay MacMullen considered it impossible to say "with any confidence" whether the army was bigger or smaller in 285 than in 235.[4]

For 235 we know of 34 legions plus the Praetorian Guard, which was about the equivalent of a legion. Taking 5,500 men to the legion, multiplying by 35, and then multiplying by two again to include the auxiliaries, we arrive at 385,000. If we take an average of the highest and lowest possible estimates reckoned by MacMullen with somewhat more precision, we get 388,000; his own most recent estimate is 375,000.[5] Though these are all approximations, they come so close to John's figure of 389,704 that we cannot reasonably dismiss it as either too high or too low. If we cannot confidently say whether the army was bigger or smaller in 285 than in 235, the reason is simply that it was so close to being the same size.

For the navy no useful estimate seems possible for 235, or many years before. But since Procopius says that Justinian sent 30,000 seamen from the East on his African expedition of 532, John's number of 45,562 seamen for the whole empire is not improbably high; nor, if John had any reason

<hr/>

2. John the Lydian, *On Months*, I.27. The Greek implies that John means Constantine doubled only the complete "myriads" (ten thousands) in the army, and not in the navy.
3. Jones, *Later Roman Empire*, 56.
4. MacMullen, "How Big?" 454–55.
5. Ibid., 454, figuring an upper limit of 438,000 and a lower limit of 338,000; cf. MacMullen, "Roman Emperors' Army Costs," 571–72.

for saying that the numbers increased later, need it be improbably low. Few people who know John's work, which reveals a man of middling intelligence with little sense of history, would think that he could falsify so well. On the other hand, John's vague and tidy description of Constantine's additions to the army might easily have been a misunderstanding or invention on his part.

Lactantius, a contemporary who emphasized the burden that Diocletian and his colleagues had forced upon the empire, implies that they more than quadrupled the army between 285 and 305.[6] Though Jones rightly dismissed this as "a fantastic exaggeration," Jones's study of the *Notitia Dignitatum* convinced him that the army "approximately doubled," which would more or less tally with John's reckoning for the later reign of Constantine.[7] Jones also thought that the *Notitia* supported a statement by the sixth-century historian Agathias, another bureaucrat, that under "the emperors of former times" the army had once had 645,000 men. Jones supposed that this number applied to about 395, when the empire was briefly reunited under Theodosius I.[8]

Deducing numerical totals from the *Notitia Dignitatum* is possible in theory, but presents some problems in practice. The document includes a list of all the different sorts of units in the army. As was noted above, these can be dated for the eastern empire to about 395 and for the West to a later date when much of the army of 395 had been destroyed. Since the *Notitia* shows how many of each kind of unit existed, if we can determine the official size of each kind of unit we can work out the official totals easily.

The *Notitia* mentions numbers only for four cohorts and one *auxilium* of infantry and for four *alae* of cavalry. All of these are called *milliariae* ("of a thousand men"), implying that this was exceptional. Evidently it was double the normal strength, because in the early empire standard cohorts and *alae* had had 500 men, and John the Lydian says that in his time cavalry vexillations, which were of more recent formation, had the same number. By reasonable analogies, Jones also reckoned two new sorts of units, cavalry *cunei* and infantry *pseudocomitatenses*, at 500 men each, and supposed that the infantry formations simply called *milites* ("soldiers") were equivalent to cohorts. From various pieces of evidence Jones concluded that by this time legions of the field army numbered 1,000 infantry apiece, since the legions of earlier date had been divided and new legions had been created at the lower strength.[9]

6. Lactantius, *De Mortibus Persecutorum*, 7.2.
7. Jones, *Later Roman Empire*, 59–60; cf. 56–59.
8. Ibid., 679–84; cf. Agathias, V.13.7.
9. Jones, *Later Roman Empire*, 680–82.

Jones's figures for the Army of the East and the Army of Illyricum about 395 can be compared with figures for the same armies in the sixth century given by Procopius. Procopius says that in 531 the Army of the East, then commanded by Belisarius, had some 20,000 men, including both infantry and cavalry.[10] According to Jones's interpretation of the *Notitia*, about 395 the Army of the East had:

	Units and strengths	Total
10	cavalry vexillations of 500 men each	5,000
2	*auxilia* of 500 men each	1,000
9	legions of 1,000 men each	9,000
10	*pseudocomitatenses* of 500 men each	5,000
	TOTAL	20,000 men

This result goes far to justify Jones's whole scheme. During the intervening period of more than a century of relatively infrequent warfare with Persia, the official establishment of the Army of the East seems to have been kept the same.

According to Procopius, in 548 the Army of Illyricum had 15,000 men. Another sixth-century bureaucrat-historian, Marcellinus the Count, gives the same number for the Army of Illyricum in 499.[11] Jones's reading of the *Notitia* for the Army of Illyricum is as follows:

	Units and strengths	Total
2	cavalry vexillations of 500 men each	1,000
9	legions of 1,000 men each	9,000
6	*auxilia* of 500 men each	3,000
9	*pseudocomitatenses* of 500 men each	4,500
	TOTAL	17,500 men

In view of the mauling that this army had suffered at the hands of the Visigoths, Ostrogoths, and Huns between 395 and 499, that the government let replacements fall behind by 2,500 men is likely enough.

For the field armies, therefore, Jones seems to have been on firm ground. In estimating the border troops, however, he made two very questionable assumptions. First, he arbitrarily counted the empire's 27 fleets at 500 men each, though they hardly seem analogous to the cavalry and infantry units of that strength. This would give a total navy of just 13,500 men, far smaller than John the Lydian's figure of 45,562. Second, Jones estimated that unlike the legions of the field army and four legions of the frontier army, which he acknowledged had 1,000 men each, other border legions had about 3,000 men apiece.[12] In reaching this conclu-

10. Procopius, *Wars*, I.18.5.
11. Ibid., VII.29.3; Marcellinus Comes, 95.
12. Jones, *Later Roman Empire*, 680–82.

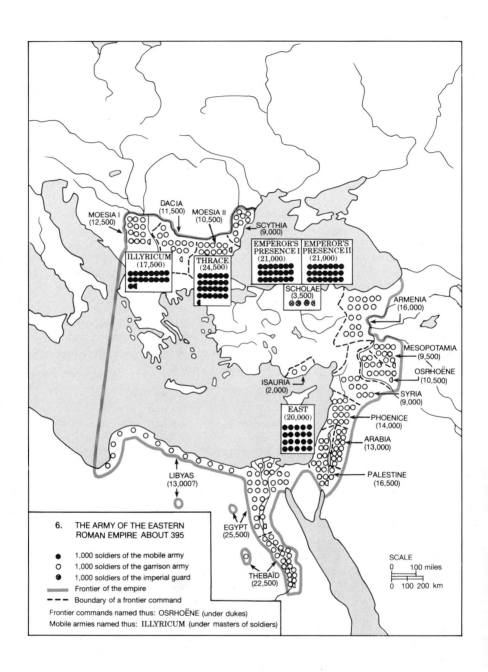

MOESIA I
(12,500)

DACIA
(11,500)

MOESIA II
(10,500)

SCYTHIA
(9,000)

ILLYRICUM
(17,500)

THRACE
(24,500)

EMPEROR'S
PRESENCE I
(21,000)

EMPEROR'S
PRESENCE II
(21,000)

SCHOLAE
(3,500)

ARMENIA
(16,000)

MESOPOTAMIA
(9,500)

OSRHOËNE
(10,500)

ISAURIA
(2,000)

SYRIA
(9,000)

EAST
(20,000)

PHOENICE
(14,000)

ARABIA
(13,000)

LIBYAS
(13,000?)

PALESTINE
(16,500)

EGYPT
(25,500)

THEBAÏD
(22,500)

SCALE

0   100 miles

0   100 200 km

6. THE ARMY OF THE EASTERN
    ROMAN EMPIRE ABOUT 395

●   1,000 soldiers of the mobile army
○   1,000 soldiers of the garrison army
◉   1,000 soldiers of the imperial guard
▬   Frontier of the empire
─ ─ ─   Boundary of a frontier command

Frontier commands named thus: OSRHOËNE (under dukes)
Mobile armies named thus: ILLYRICUM (under masters of soldiers)

sion he relied partly on his interpretation of an Egyptian papyrus that has since been more plausibly reinterpreted to show legions of almost exactly 1,000 men each.[13] Thus unit strengths seem to have been uniform in both field and frontier forces. This would have been quite natural, because the field and frontier armies had been a single force under Diocletian and had still had units transferred from one to the other for many years thereafter.

Jones also overlooked the *Notitia*'s mention of one *auxilium* with 1,000 men, which is less important for changing the total than for supporting Jones's conjecture that *auxilia* normally had 500 men.[14] For some reason Jones was unsure whether his total should include the Scholae, known to have been 3,500 in the East and 2,500 in the West, though there seems to be no good reason for excluding them at this date. Since the page in the *Notitia* that listed the units of the Ducate of Libya is missing, Jones reasonably counted Libya at a rough average of the 14 other eastern frontier armies for purposes of his overall estimate. I have followed his example.[15]

If we revise Jones's figure to count all legions at 1,000 men each, add the Scholae, omit the fleets, and count all other units at 500 men each, we arrive at a total for the whole army of about 500,000 men instead of the 600,000 he calculated. But Jones correctly noted that allowances should be made for the losses in the West. The revised total for the eastern empire alone is 303,000 men, as Table 1 and Map 6 illustrate. If the West had once had about the same number, the total would be back at around 600,000. If Agathias's 645,000 men included 45,000 or so seamen in the fleets, roughly the number given by John the Lydian, the totals would agree well enough. Although these are of course approximations, they show that Agathias's figure cannot be much exaggerated.

THE PROBLEM OF ZOSIMUS

We have another set of figures for this period, interesting but problematic. They appear in another work by a government official, the pagan historian Zosimus, who wrote around the year 500. He gives figures, divided into infantry and cavalry, for the armies of Constantine and his rival Maxentius in 312 and for the armies of Constantine and his rival Licinius in 324. At the latter date he gives numbers for Constantine's seamen (10,000) and ships (200 triaconters and 2,000 transports), and Licinius's ships (a total of 350 triremes). Assuming that the triremes had the

13. Cf. ibid., 1257–59, with Duncan-Jones, "Pay and Numbers."
14. *Notitia Dignitatum*, Or. XLII.23 (Dacia).
15. Jones, *Later Roman Empire*, 682–83. Naturally I adjust Jones's estimates for the other 14 frontier commands by counting all their legions at 1,000 men each.

TABLE I
Eastern Army Units in the Notitia Dignitatum, *ca. 395*

Units	Infantry	Cavalry

I. Scholae: 3,500 men (3,500 cavalry: 100%)

II. Eastern Field Armies: 104,000 men (21,500 cavalry: 20.7%)

ARMY OF ILLYRICUM: 17,500 men

9 legions	9,000	
6 *auxilia*	3,000	
9 *pseudocomitatenses*	4,500	
2 vexillations		1,000
TOTALS	16,500	1,000 (5.7%)

ARMY OF THRACE: 24,500 men

21 legions	21,000	
7 vexillations		3,500
TOTALS	21,000	3,500 (14.3%)

FIRST ARMY IN THE EMPEROR'S PRESENCE: 21,000 men

6 legions	6,000	
18 *auxilia*	9,000	
12 vexillations		6,000
TOTALS	15,000	6,000 (28.6%)

SECOND ARMY IN THE EMPEROR'S PRESENCE: 21,000 men

6 legions	6,000	
17 *auxilia*	8,500	
1 *pseudocomitatensis*	500	
12 vexillations		6,000
TOTALS	15,000	6,000 (28.6%)

ARMY OF THE EAST: 20,000 men

9 legions	9,000	
2 *auxilia*	1,000	
10 *pseudocomitatenses*	5,000	
10 vexillations		5,000
TOTALS	15,000	5,000 (25%)

III. Eastern Frontier Armies: 195,500 men (97,500 cavalry: 49.9%)

DUCATE OF LIBYA: 13,000 men[a]

TOTALS	6,500?[a]	6,500?[a] (50%?)

COUNTY OF EGYPT: 25,500 men

4 legions	4,000	
16 *auxilia*	8,000	
9 cohorts	4,500	
16 *alae*		8,000
2 vexillations		1,000
TOTALS	16,500	9,000 (35.3%)

DUCATE OF THE THEBAÏD: 22,500 men

4 legions	4,000	
10 cohorts	5,000	
1 milites of 1,000 men	1,000	
16 *alae*		8,000
7 vexillations		3,500
2 *cunei*		1,000
TOTALS	10,000	12,500 (55.6%)

TABLE I (*continued*)

Units	Infantry	Cavalry	
DUCATE OF PALESTINE: 16,500 men			
1 legion	1,000		
11 cohorts	5,500		
4 *alae*		2,000	
2 *alae* of 1,000 men		2,000	
12 vexillations		6,000	
TOTALS	6,500	10,000	(60.6%)
DUCATE OF ARABIA: 13,000 men			
2 legions	2,000		
4 cohorts	2,000		
1 cohort of 1,000 men	1,000		
4 *alae*		2,000	
2 *alae* of 1,000 men		2,000	
8 vexillations		4,000	
TOTALS	5,000	8,000	(61.5%)
DUCATE OF PHOENICE: 14,000 men			
2 legions	2,000		
5 cohorts	2,500		
7 *alae*		3,500	
12 vexillations		6,000	
TOTALS	4,500	9,500	(67.9%)
DUCATE OF SYRIA: 9,000 men			
1 legion	1,000		
4 cohorts	2,000		
2 *alae*		1,000	
10 vexillations		5,000	
TOTALS	3,000	6,000	(66.7%)
DUCATE OF OSRHOËNE: 10,500 men			
2 legions	2,000		
2 cohorts	1,000		
6 *alae*		3,000	
9 vexillations		4,500	
TOTALS	3,000	7,500	(71.4%)
DUCATE OF MESOPOTAMIA: 9,500 men			
2 legions	2,000		
2 cohorts	1,000		
3 *alae*		1,500	
10 vexillations		5,000	
TOTALS	3,000	6,500	(68.4%)
DUCATE OF ARMENIA: 16,000 men			
3 legions	3,000		
7 cohorts	3,500		
3 cohorts of 1,000 men	3,000		
11 *alae*		5,500	
2 vexillations		1,000	
TOTALS	9,500	6,500	(40.6%)
COUNTY OF ISAURIA: 2,000 men			
2 legions	2,000		
TOTALS	2,000	0	(0%)

(*continued*)

TABLE I (*continued*)

Units	Infantry	Cavalry	
DUCATE OF SCYTHIA: 9,500 men			
2 legions	2,000		
8 *auxilia*	4,000		
7 *cunei*		3,500	
TOTALS	6,000	3,500	(36.8%)
DUCATE OF MOESIA II: 10,500 men			
2 legions	2,000		
10 *auxilia*	5,000		
7 *cunei*		3,500	
TOTALS	7,000	3,500	(33.3%)
DUCATE OF DACIA: 11,500 men			
2 legions	2,000		
5 *auxilia*	2,500		
1 *auxilium* of 1,000 men	1,000		
2 cohorts	1,000		
1 milites	500		
9 *cunei*		4,500	
TOTALS	7,000	4,500	(39.1%)
DUCATE OF MOESIA I: 12,500 men			
2 legions	2,000		
8 *auxilia*	4,000		
5 milites	2,500		
8 *cunei*		4,000	
TOTALS	8,500	4,000	(32%)
TOTAL EASTERN ARMY:			
303,000 men, 122,500 cavalry (40.4%)			

IV. Armies of Western Illyricum: [b] *63,000 men (28,000 cavalry: 44.4%)*

Units	Infantry	Cavalry	
COUNTY OF ILLYRICUM: 13,500 men			
5 legions	5,000		
13 *auxilia*	6,500		
4 *pseudocomitatenses*	2,000		
TOTALS	13,500	0	(0%)
DUCATE OF PANNONIA II: 16,000 men			
2 legions	2,000		
5 *auxilia*	2,500		
4 cohorts	2,000		
1 milites	500		
1 *ala*		500	
11 vexillations		5,500	
6 *cunei*		3,000	
TOTALS	7,000	9,000	(56.2%)
DUCATE OF VALERIA: 18,500 men			
2 legions	2,000		
6 cohorts	3,000		
5 *auxilia*	2,500		
17 vexillations		8,500	
5 *cunei*		2,500	
TOTALS	7,500	11,000	(59.5%)

TABLE I (*continued*)

Units	Infantry	Cavalry
DUCATE OF PANNONIA I: 15,000 men^a		
4 legions	4,000	
5 cohorts	2,500	
1 tribe of Marcomanni	500?^c	
14 vexillations		7,000
2 *cunei*		1,000
TOTALS	7,000?^c	8,000 (53.3%?)

^a Since the page listing the units in the Ducate of Libya is missing, the figures given here are simply rough averages of the other 14 eastern frontier armies.
^b Western Illyricum was a part of the Western Roman Empire in 395.
^c That the Marcomanni numbered 500 infantry (like a cohort) is simply a guess.

Romans' usual complement of 150 oarsmen apiece plus one captain and two pilots, Licinius would then have had 53,550 seamen, or 54,000 if we round the number to the nearest thousand.[16]

Zosimus's figures can be tabulated as follows:[17]

Emperor and year	Infantry	Cavalry	Army	Seamen	Total
Constantine in 312	90,000	8,000	98,000	—	98,000
Maxentius in 312	170,000	18,000	188,000	—	188,000
Constantine in 324	120,000	10,000	130,000	10,000	140,000
Licinius in 324	150,000	15,000	165,000	[54,000]	[219,000]
TOTAL	530,000	51,000	581,000	[64,000]	[645,000]

Zosimus clearly implies that these were the numbers that fought in the battles of those years; but he never draws a distinction between those numbers and the totals on the various emperors' rolls. MacMullen has pointed out that for field armies such numbers are far too high. While conceding that "such inventions are very puzzling," MacMullen rejects the attempts of several other scholars to consider them as the total number of men on the rolls.[18]

An obvious problem with trying to do this is that by 324 Constantine controlled not only his original share of the empire but that of Maxentius in 312, plus Illyricum. If Zosimus's totals accurately record the official strength of the armies of Constantine and Maxentius in 312, by 324 Constantine should have had some 286,000 men plus the soldiers of Illyricum on his rolls, not just 130,000. It also strains credulity that in 324 Constantine should have had all the triaconters (ships with 30 oars) and transports,

16. For the oarsmen, see Starr, *Roman Imperial Navy*, 53. The captain and two pilots for each ship are found in the later Byzantine navy; see below, p. 91. Though the ships would also have carried soldiers, these were presumably included in the figures for cavalry and infantry.
17. Zosimus, II.15.1 – 2 and II.22.1 – 2.
18. MacMullen, "How Big?" 459 – 60 and n. 37.

while Licinius had all the triremes; each emperor should have had a mixture of transports and warships. But before we throw Zosimus's figures out, we should notice how neatly their supposedly heterogeneous total agrees with Agathias's total of 645,000 for the men on the rolls.

This correspondence suggests that the figures may all belong to one date, and that Zosimus, whose analytic gifts were no greater than those of John the Lydian, may have misapplied the statistics he found in his source. If all Zosimus's figures do belong to one date, it must be 312 rather than 324. In 312 the empire was still divided into four parts with four separate armies; but in 324 it had only two parts and two armies. The former year, when Constantine and Licinius were ranged against Maxentius and Maximin and war was impending, was also a time when any of the four emperors would have been particularly interested in calculating the military resources of all of them. Since the empire was then still juridically one, recent and detailed information about the army should have been available to all four governments.

In 312 the East was admittedly divided not between Constantine and Licinius but between Licinius and Maximin. Yet Zosimus knew, and records in his history, that in 324 Constantine ruled roughly the area in the Balkans ruled by Licinius in 312, and that in 324 Licinius ruled roughly the area in Anatolia, Syria, and Egypt ruled by Maximin in 312. Zosimus might therefore—with some license, but also with a sort of logic—have applied army figures for Licinius in 312 to Constantine in 324, and army figures for Maximin in 312 to Licinius in 324. As for the navy, Zosimus might arbitrarily have divided the totals for 312 to use them for the naval battle of 324, giving Constantine the triaconters and transports and Licinius the triremes. Few who have read Zosimus would think him incapable of such juggling.

This hypothesis can be tested to some extent by comparisons with the army as it appears in the *Notitia* and as it was in 235, when as we have seen it seems to have been about the same size as in 285. In 235 and in the *Notitia* the positions of units are well enough known that we can assign them to the four parts of the empire as they were in 312, when western Illyricum was still part of the East. We may then multiply each legion of 235 by 5,500, and then by 2 to include auxiliaries. In adapting the *Notitia* for 312, we should leave aside not just the 6,000 men of the eastern and western Scholae, which were formed later, but the 42,000 men of the eastern armies in the Emperor's Presence, most of which were transferred from the West in 324 and 388. For the West, the armies in the *Notitia* would have been so badly scrambled by those transfers, and by the disasters after 395, that apportioning them between the domains of Constantine and Maxentius in 312 seems pointless.

The results of such a test appear in this tabulation: [19]

Reference	Egypt, Asia	Balkans	East as in 312	West as in 312	Scholae, transfers	Total
235 (est.)	132,000	121,000	253,000	132,000	—	385,000
Zosimus	165,000	130,000	295,000	286,000	—	581,000
Notitia	171,500	149,000	320,500	145,500	48,000	514,500

When we consider the severe losses that the West had suffered by the date of its part of the *Notitia*, none of these numbers seems far from the mark. Zosimus's figures for Egypt, Syria, and Anatolia are some 25 percent higher than those for 235, and not much lower than those in the *Notitia*. The implied conclusion that Diocletian increased the army in this sector by a quarter is plausible enough.

Zosimus's figures for the Balkans are 7.5 percent above those for 235, while the *Notitia*'s figures add another 15 percent. Yet to conclude that Diocletian and Galerius failed to increase the Balkan armies much is probably wrong, because when Galerius invaded Italy with his Balkan troops in 307 many of them deserted to Maxentius.[20] These men must still have been in Italy in 312, though they presumably returned to their stations later. Allowing for these deserters from the Balkans would also help explain why Maxentius's army in 312 was so much larger than Constantine's, and was in fact the largest in any of the four parts of the empire. If we suppose that about 85 percent of the increase in the army in the Balkans occurred in the time of Diocletian, as seems to have been the case in Asia and Egypt, this interpretation of Zosimus indicates that the deserters numbered about 16,000, so that the East had some 311,000 men before 307.

Even when we transfer 16,000 men from the western total to the eastern, Zosimus's figures seem to show that Diocletian's western colleagues had more than doubled their armies, giving the West about 85 percent as many troops as the East. This would explain why a westerner like Lactantius tended to exaggerate the overall increase. It would also explain why the armies of West and East were generally considered to be of about the same importance during the fourth century, and why Valentinian I could take the West plus all of Illyricum as the senior portion of the empire.

If for the sake of comparison we add the 2,500 western Scholae and the 42,000 men of the eastern praesental armies to the western total computed from the *Notitia*, we arrive at 190,000 men. This is still some 30 percent less than the adjusted total from Zosimus of 270,000 men in 312. The difference would be 80,000 men, roughly Jones's estimate for the losses in

19. The figures for 235 and the *Notitia* are based on Table IX in Jones, *Later Roman Empire*, 1438–45, allowing for the Praetorians and an additional legion in Italy.

20. See Lactantius, *De Mortibus Persecutorum*, 27.3; and Anonymous of Valois, *Origo Constantini*, 7.

the West by the time of the *Notitia*.[21] None of these conclusions seems unacceptable, or even unlikely. In view of an overall increase of 49 percent in the army between 285 and 312, the increase of 40 percent in the navy implied by Zosimus is also to be expected.

But the most striking difference between Zosimus's figures and those of the *Notitia* is the enormous increase in cavalry that seems to follow from them. Calculating the cavalry units in the *Notitia* as in Table 1, the figures for the eastern cavalry would be:

Reference	Egypt and Asia			Balkans		
	Total	Cavalry	%	Total	Cavalry	%
Zosimus	165,000	15,000	9.1	130,000	10,000	7.7
Notitia	171,500	87,000	50.7	149,000	48,000	32.2

This comparison implies that while the total size of the army remained much the same between 312 and 395, a large number of infantry became cavalry during that time.

Yet Zosimus's figures for cavalry are quite close to those that have been estimated for the Roman army in the second century. G. L. Cheesman estimated the cavalry in the second-century auxiliaries at 47,500, which along with 120 more cavalry in each of the 33 legions would give a total of 51,460 for the whole empire. Zosimus's total is 51,000 cavalry. Though Cheesman reckoned another 15,375 men in mixed auxiliary units as "mounted infantry," Zosimus would probably have followed official usage and counted such men among the infantry. Leaving out some cavalry whose stations are unknown, Cheesman found 10,500 cavalry in Egypt and Asia and 13,850 in the Balkans. Along with the legionary cavalry, these would come to 11,940 in Egypt and Asia, rather fewer than in Zosimus, and 15,290 in the Balkans, rather more than in Zosimus. Since the second-century total of 27,230 for the whole eastern empire is close to Zosimus's total of 25,000, some cavalry may well have been shifted from the Balkans to Asia and Egypt in the meantime.[22] Other possible explanations might also be advanced; the numbers are in any case broadly compatible.

While Cheesman's estimates are approximate, and various changes cer-

21. Cf. Jones, *Later Roman Empire*, 683, estimating that the frontier armies of Gaul and Africa, which he reckoned from the *Notitia* at 27,000 men, had originally had as many as 111,000. Both figures are somewhat exaggerated by Jones's counting 3,000 men apiece for frontier legions instead of 1,000.

22. See Cheesman, *Auxilia*, 168 for the totals and 152–64 for Egypt, Asia, and the Balkans. Cheesman considered his totals low, and MacMullen, "How Big?" 452 and n. 2 notes that other auxiliary units have been identified since Cheesman's time; but MacMullen also observes that auxiliary units often disappeared, so that not all of these units would have existed at any given date. These factors would tend to cancel each other out. For the legionary cavalry, see Webster, *Roman Imperial Army*, 116.

tainly occurred during the intervening century and a half, his work gives considerable support to Zosimus's figures for cavalry. The latter imply that the proportion of cavalry remained fairly stable during the third century, that Diocletian's additions to the army were almost all infantry, and that the cavalry expanded greatly during the fourth century. The first conclusion is what we would expect, given the remarkable continuity in the army's numbers. The second conclusion is plausible in view of Diocletian's general reluctance to innovate—except in increasing the size of the army, which would have been easier to do with infantry than with cavalry, and in building forts, which infantry could garrison as well as cavalry.[23]

What evidence is there of a massive expansion of cavalry in the fourth century? Among the units of the Balkan, Asian, and Egyptian forces in the *Notitia*, Jones counted 29 with titles that show that they were raised by Theodosius I between 379 and 395 to replace losses at Adrianople. Fully 20 of these were cavalry units.[24] Jones attributed to Constantine a reorganization of the Balkan frontier that introduced as many as 43 cavalry units of the new type of the *cunei*.[25] These identifiably Theodosian and Constantinian units would by themselves have added 31,500 cavalry to the eastern armies between 312 and 395.

Moreover, many existing units could have been changed from infantry to cavalry during this time without leaving clear traces in the *Notitia*. Most of the change could have been accomplished by making the mixed auxiliary units fully mounted and reclassing the "mounted infantry" as cavalry. We should notice that even in the *Notitia* infantry are still in the majority, and overwhelmingly so in the more important field armies. Yet evidently there is a modicum of truth in the maxim "that typically the Roman fought on foot, the Byzantine on horseback."[26] Though this point can be exaggerated, we cannot reasonably reject Zosimus's figures because they imply that much less of the army was cavalry in 312 than in 395.

Ordinarily when three knowledgeable sources supply information that is consistent, compatible with other sources, and with no evidence against it, we ought to believe it. The balance of probability is therefore that John the Lydian, Zosimus, and Agathias all preserved official figures for the total strength of the army, though Zosimus misused his figures somewhat. In fact, the numbers of Zosimus and Agathias agree so well that both writers look as if they found the same document in the archives, from

23. On Diocletian's conservatism, see Jones, *Later Roman Empire*, 607–8 and 55–60.

24. Ibid., 1429–30.

25. Ibid., 99–100. A forty-fourth Balkan *cuneus*, the *Cuneus Equitum Arcadum* of Scythia, was Theodosian, named for Theodosius's son Arcadius. The *cunei* (including two more in the Thebaïd) are enumerated in Table 1.

26. Bivar, "Cavalry Equipment," 273.

which Zosimus copied the individual figures and Agathias copied the total. Agathias's "emperors of former times" would then be Constantine, Maxentius, Licinius, and Maximin in 312. But since the total seems to have changed very little during most of the fourth century, any date from about 295 to 395 is possible.

Because these totals would represent every last soldier on the rolls, they by no means contradict recorded battlefield figures, like those of an anonymous early biographer of Constantine who says that in 324 Constantine actually fought with 20,000 infantry and cavalry against Licinius with 35,000.[27] Yet MacMullen thinks that the anonymous's numbers[28]

render quite incredible the number ascribed by another source, Zosimus, to Licinius in the year just mentioned: 165,000—incredible in the sense that it does violence to an entire context of other facts easily believed. We may and must set it aside as we set aside Xerxes' army of 1,700,000, or as we must set aside the statement by Lactantius that Diocletian quadrupled the army, or by [John] Lydus, that Constantine doubled it again, or by Agathias, that the whole empire evidently in the second half of the fourth century contained 645,000 soldiers.

Here MacMullen seems to be following Zosimus in confusing battlefield armies with armies on the rolls. No doubt Herodotus exaggerated the army of Xerxes, and Lactantius's and John the Lydian's vague statements about quadrupling or doubling the army ought not to be taken literally. If they are indeed official totals, however, the numbers recorded by Zosimus and Agathias deserve the credence that Jones and others have accorded them.

How far the fourth-century army was kept up to its official strength is a different question. The apparent census figures supplied by John and papyrus figures from Egypt suggest that the army generally was up to strength under Diocletian, with some units even slightly over strength.[29] At other times strengths probably varied along with recent losses and recruitment and the vigilance of the emperors and their officials. Even though the official total can never have been quite the same as the real one, knowing the official total is nonetheless valuable, especially because it determined the payroll.

To sum up the figures for the units that became the Byzantine army, the territories that were eastern after 395 probably had about 198,000 soldiers in 235 (18 legions plus auxiliaries) and about the same number in 285. By 305 Diocletian probably raised this total by around 25 percent, to some 250,000. Around 324 Constantine added the 3,500 eastern Scholae, prob-

27. Anonymous of Valois, *Origo Constantini*, 5.16.
28. MacMullen, "How Big?" 459–60.
29. See below, pp. 88–89.

ably a few thousand frontier troops, and perhaps the equivalent of one praesental army, or 21,000 men. The other praesental army of 21,000 dated from 388, and brought the eastern armies to the 303,000 or so that they had in 395, making an increase of about 50 percent since 285.

Of this total some 104,000 men were field troops, 3,500 were in the Scholae, and about 195,500 were border troops apart from the fleets. If the eastern provinces had about half the navy, they had some 23,000 seamen in 285, perhaps 32,000 in 305, and something like the latter number in 395. The correspondence with Justinian's 30,000 seamen in 532 looks significant. Including the fleets, the grand total for the eastern empire about 395 should have been, in round numbers, 335,000 men. Such figures may not be exact, but for most purposes they should be accurate enough.

From 235 to 285, and from 305 to 395, the whole army seems hardly to have changed in official strength. During the latter period many infantry were replaced with cavalry, often doubtless by mounting the infantrymen. The units destroyed at Adrianople were replaced with new units. Men in other old units were replaced when they died, and some soldiers were transferred within the empire, with some from the West going to the East. After 395 no new mobile armies or frontier ducates were created, and the new guard corps of the Excubitors had just 300 men.[30] Over the entire span of the third and fourth centuries, and even the fifth century in the East, the only major change in the size of the army seems to have been the great increase under Diocletian and his colleagues. As the senior eastern emperor, Diocletian can justly be called the founder of the Byzantine army.

THE PROBLEM OF AGATHIAS

Agathias mentions his total of 645,000 men for the army of former times in order to contrast it with the much smaller total for the army of his own day. Around 559, he says, it barely reached 150,000 men. Agathias specifies that this number included not only eastern troops but the armies in Italy, Africa, and Spain.[31] Since Agathias had evidently been able to find an accurate official figure for the army some two centuries earlier, he should have been able to give a correct figure for the contemporary army as well.

Wittingly or not, however, in his eagerness to dramatize the empire's decline Agathias must be comparing figures that refer to rather different military groups. Agathias's fourth-century total of 645,000 men surely in-

---

30. For the number of the Excubitors, see John the Lydian, *On Magistrates*, I.16.
31. Agathias, V.13.7–8.

cluded the armies of the West, all the border troops, and the fleets. While the armies of the West had of course been lost, along with the Western Roman Empire that they had defended, during his wars Justinian had added new field armies of Armenia, Africa, Italy, and Spain, and frontier ducates in Africa. Justinian seems to have stopped paying the 3,500 Scholae, who had become useless for military purposes, and even with Justinian's additions in Africa the frontier troops probably declined somewhat in numbers between 395 and 559, especially after Justinian stopped paying them in 545.[32] But both frontier troops and Scholae continued to exist, apparently without any vast reduction in numbers, and the same was surely true of the fleets.

The mobile armies alone had some 104,000 men in 395, and we have seen that in Justinian's reign the Army of the East was as large as before, and the Army of Illyricum only a little smaller. If Agathias had included Justinian's frontier troops, his total would leave only about 50,000 men for all of them plus the new field armies. Agathias must therefore be omitting the frontier troops, and no doubt the Scholae as well. Agathias knew that these were no longer the equals of field troops; Procopius wrote in 550 that Justinian had ceased to count the border troops as regular soldiers.[33]

Agathias's 50,000 or so men apart from the old mobile armies should therefore represent the new mobile forces. As noted above, Procopius says that under Justinian the Army of the East had 20,000 men in 531 and the Army of Illyricum 15,000 men in 548.[34] Procopius also says that in 530 the Army of Armenia had just half as many men as a Persian force of 30,000; though Procopius may not have known the exact number of the Persians, he should have known the size of the Army of Armenia, which seems therefore to have numbered 15,000.[35]

As for the Army of Africa, Procopius says that in 533 he and Belisarius sailed for Africa with 15,000 regular troops, of whom 10,000 were infantry and 5,000 cavalry, in addition to 30,000 oarsmen, 2,000 marines from Constantinople, 1,000 barbarian mercenaries, and Belisarius's personal retinue.[36] The oarsmen, marines and mercenaries, and Belisarius's attendants, were clearly not meant to stay in Africa for good. On the other hand, the 15,000 regular troops, equaling the strength of the armies of Illyricum and Armenia, may well have been meant from the first to become the standing Army of Africa.

About the Army of Italy Agathias says that in 554 Narses led 18,000 men

---

32. On Justinian's treatment of the frontier troops and Scholae, see Procopius, *Secret History*, 24.12–22.
33. Ibid., 24.13.
34. See above, p. 47.
35. Procopius, *Wars*, I.15.11.
36. Ibid., III.11.2–19.

to the decisive battle with the Ostrogoths.[37] These cannot have been quite all of Narses' soldiers, since he had to leave some garrisons in the places the Byzantines held in Italy; but such places were few enough at the time, and the battle was so important, that these 18,000 should have been much the largest part of Narses' force. His whole army might thus be estimated at some 20,000. According to Procopius, Belisarius's initial expedition of 535 had had 7,500 men, who were reinforced in stages, after some losses, by some 14,000 men.[38] These numbers again point to a total force of about 20,000, as if Justinian had had that size in mind for the Army of Italy from the beginning. That strength would have equaled the Army of the East and somewhat exceeded the 15,000 men of the armies of Illyricum and Armenia, which had reinforcements nearer to hand, and Africa, which was smaller and easier to defend.

Interestingly, when Tiberius reinforced the Army of the East with his new company of the Federates in 577, it too is said to have numbered 15,000 men.[39] All these figures, like the 30,000 oarsmen of the fleet sent by Justinian to Africa and Agathias's total of 150,000 for the whole army, are divisible by 5,000. The *Strategicon* of Maurice, a military manual that dates from Maurice's reign and may be his work, tends to use the numbers 5,000, 10,000, 15,000, and 20,000 for armies, probably because it reckons normal divisions at 5,000 soldiers.[40] The units of 1,000 and 500 men that made up the fourth-century army fitted neatly into 5,000-man formations, which for that matter were almost the size of an old legion. Such groupings seem to go back to 499, when the Army of Illyricum already had 15,000 men, and they may well date from Zeno's measures to centralize recruitment.[41]

We might therefore guess that the armies for which we lack contemporary statistics, those of Thrace and Spain and in the Emperor's Presence, were also divisible by 5,000 in Justinian's day. If so, the two praesental armies, which can be estimated from the *Notitia Dignitatum* at 21,000 men each around 395, would presumably have been rounded down to 20,000 each. The *Notitia* indicates that the Army of Thrace would have had 24,500 men about 395; but if we round this up to 25,000, no troops remain for Spain from Agathias's total of 150,000. Given the many invasions suffered by Thrace since 395, its army might well have lost several thousand

---

37. Agathias, II.4.10.

38. Procopius, *Wars*, V.5.1–4 (initial force), V.27.1 (1,600 in early 537), VI.5.1–2 (5,600 in late 537), and VI.13.16–18 (7,000 in 538).

39. Theophanes, A.M. 6074, p. 251.

40. Maurice, *Strategicon*, III.8 and 10, with I.4; the latter passage specifies that an army's three divisions should not be larger than 6,000 to 7,000 men apiece, implying a standard division of some 5,000 and a standard army size of perhaps 15,000 men.

41. See above, pp. 47 and 14.

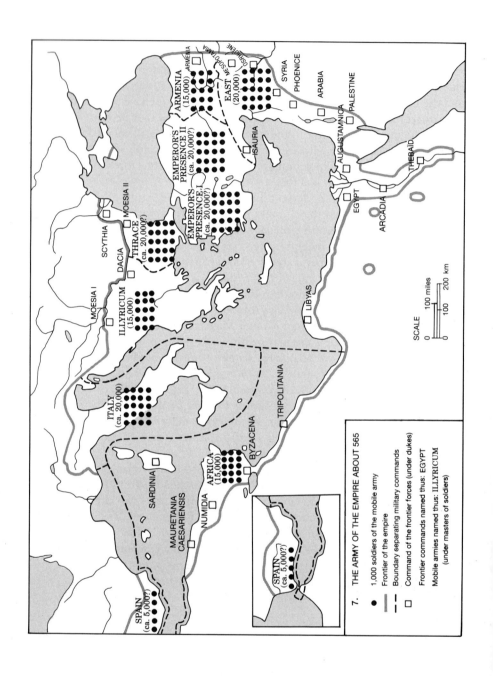

ARMENIA
ARMENIA
(15,000)

MESOPOTAMIA

OSRHOENE

SYRIA

PHOENICE

ARABIA

PALESTINE

EMPEROR'S
PRESENCE II
(ca. 20,000?)

EAST
(20,000)

EMPEROR'S
PRESENCE I
(ca. 20,000?)

ISAURIA

AUGUSTAMNICA

THEBAID

MOESIA II

SCYTHIA

THRACE
(ca. 20,000?)

DACIA

EGYPT

ARCADIA

MOESIA I

ILLYRICUM
(15,000)

LIBYAS

SCALE

0   100 miles

0   100   200 km

ITALY
(ca. 20,000)

TRIPOLITANIA

AFRICA
(15,000)

BYZACENA

SARDINIA

MAURETANIA
CAESARIENSIS

NUMIDIA

SPAIN
(ca. 5,000?)

SPAIN
(ca. 5,000?)

7.   THE ARMY OF THE EMPIRE ABOUT 565

•   1,000 soldiers of the mobile army

    Frontier of the empire

    Boundary separating military commands

□   Command of the frontier forces (under dukes)

    Frontier commands named thus: EGYPT

    Mobile armies named thus: ILLYRICUM
    (under masters of soldiers)

men, like the Army of Illyricum, and fallen to 20,000. This would leave 5,000 men for Spain, which seems reasonable for what must have been much the smallest army.

The resulting totals would be, in 395 and 559:

Unit	Strength 395	Strength 559
praesental army I	21,000	20,000?
praesental army II	21,000	20,000?
Army of the East	20,000	20,000
Army of Thrace	24,500	20,000?
Army of Illyricum	17,500	15,000
Army of Armenia	—	15,000
Army of Italy	—	20,000?
Army of Africa	—	15,000
Army of Spain	—	5,000?
TOTAL	104,000	150,000

Similar considerations led John Haldon to similar results, despite his skepticism about medieval statistics.[42] Despite uncertainties about the numbers with question marks, the overall picture cannot be far wrong. The strengths given here for these armies are illustrated in Map 7.

Even if we follow Agathias in ignoring the frontier troops after 545, before that date they must be taken into account. We cannot easily estimate how many new troops, presumably native Africans, Justinian enrolled in his five African ducates. Since Isauria, the smallest ducate at the date of the *Notitia*, had some 2,000 men, 10,000 would seem to be a minimal total for the five African ducates together, and the real total could easily have been twice that. Yet since the five field armies of 395 had apparently fallen to about 91 percent of their former strength—from some 104,000 to 95,000 men—the border troops should have dropped at least as much, from about 195,500 to perhaps 176,000 men. So for a rough reckoning we might assume that these losses and the new troops in Africa canceled each other out, leaving the total of the border forces approximately the same for the whole empire in 559 as for the East in 395.

Though Agathias omits the navy because it was classed with the frontier forces, after the conquest of Africa, Italy, and Spain it would have been needed more than ever, and unquestionably continued to exist. The 30,000 oarsmen mentioned by Procopius in 532 seem to have been nearly the navy's full strength, since the 2,000 marines on the same expedition would probably not have needed to row themselves, as Procopius says they did, if more regular oarsmen had been available.[43] Since this was the larg-

42. See Haldon, *Byzantium*, 251–53, estimating the total at 154,000 men excluding Spain.
43. Procopius, *Wars*, III.11.16.

est naval expedition Justinian ever sent out at one time, he may well have left the strength of the navy the same afterward, even after founding his naval command of the Quaestor of the Army about 536.[44]

After 565 the Lombard invasion presumably brought considerable losses to the Army of Italy, as forts were lost and their garrisons were not replaced. The armies of Spain and Africa may also have suffered some permanent losses in the later sixth century under the attacks of the Visigoths and Moors. On the other hand, by 578 Tiberius's recruitment of the Federates would have added 15,000 men to the rolls in the East, probably at least as many as had been lost in the West. The empire's field army is therefore likely to have been close enough to 150,000 men up to 602, when the various disasters of the seventh century began.

THE PROBLEM OF AL-JARMĪ

No direct evidence survives for the total size of the army in the seventh century, though we shall see later that an estimate can be made from a payroll figure recorded for 641.[45] For the eighth century one total is given. The chronicler Theophanes Confessor says that in the fall of 773 Constantine V, "mustering the enrolled troops of the themes and the Thracesians and adding the Optimates to the tagmata, made 80,000 [men]." [46] All the themes and the tagmata would be the empire's whole regular army. While Theophanes implies that this is the force that Constantine then led against the Bulgars, for a battlefield army at this date 80,000 is definitely too large. Theophanes seems to have made the same error as Zosimus, assuming that all the men on the rolls actually turned out to fight. On its face, 80,000 is a plausible enough figure for what was left of Justinian's army of 150,000 after the disasters of the seventh century. But Theophanes' figure can also be checked against the size of the army in the subsequent period.

For the ninth century we have the most detailed description of the army as a whole that is available for any part of Roman or Byzantine history. The information is preserved in accounts by three Arab geographers which are often identical and obviously derive from a common source. One of the writers names his source, a certain al-Jarmī. Another Arab work describes Jarmī as a frontier official of the caliphate who was captured by the Byzantines, probably in Theophilus's great raid of 837, returned home in an exchange of prisoners in 845, and then wrote a book on the Byzantine Empire that survived into the next century but is lost today. Thus Jarmī appears to be the source for all three accounts, each of

44. See above, pp. 15–16.
45. See below, pp. 145–47.
46. Theophanes, 447.

which excerpted his work slightly differently. Of the many numbers given, the accounts disagree on only three, and in each of these cases one figure is plainly a miscopying of the other.[47]

When the three accounts are put together, they include descriptions of the army's command structure, pay scale, and individual units, and record the headquarters, the boundaries, and the names and numbers of forts in each theme. Two of the accounts supply numbers for the men in each of 6 tagmata and 14 themes; one gives a total of 70,000 men for the Anatolian themes, allowing us to confirm which of the discrepant figures for three themes are miscopied and which are correct. The third account gives a total of 120,000 men for the whole army, noting that this excluded irregular troops. Although this overall total is 16,000 men higher than the sum of the individual figures mentioned, those figures omit several western themes known to have existed at the time, which can easily account for the remainder. While all the troop strengths reported are in even thousands of men, this follows from the command structure the texts describe, which included officers called drungaries who commanded a unit called a *drungus*, of 1,000 men.[48] Therefore the information attributable to Jarmī appears to be self-consistent.

Everything in it also seems compatible with contemporary Byzantine sources. It agrees almost perfectly with the *Tacticon Uspensky*, an official list of ranks datable to 842 or 843; the one difference is that Jarmī listed Cappadocia as a cleisura and the *Tacticon* lists it as a theme, indicating that the date of Jarmī's list was slightly earlier, before Cappadocia was raised in rank. The ranks of strategi in the *Tacticon* correspond well with the number of men that Jarmī assigned their themes, larger themes generally having strategi with higher ranks.[49] The material derived from Jarmī mentions which themes had more than one subordinate officer called a turmarch; ninth-century Byzantine sources confirm the existence of every turmarch he mentions.[50]

The command structure described by Jarmī is corroborated by both the *Tacticon Uspensky* and the more detailed treatise on ranks by Philotheus, dated to 899. Philotheus observes that the number of places reserved for specified officers of the four senior tagmata at the emperor's Christmas dinners was 204; this is exactly the number of officers needed for units with 4,000 soldiers, the strength that Jarmī attributed to each of these

47. See Treadgold, "Remarks." The material from Jarmī can be found in Ibn Khurdādhbih, 76–84; Qudāmah, 196–99; and Brooks, "Arabic Lists," 72–77 (translating Ibn al-Faqīh).

48. See Treadgold, *Byzantine State Finances*, 15–17.

49. Ibid., 16 and 18–19.

50. Treadgold, "Notes," 280–84.

tagmata.[51] As we shall see, Jarmī's pay scale can be combined with his numbers to calculate a total payroll that is very near to a payroll recorded for about 867.[52] The explanation that I have suggested elsewhere for the extraordinary precision of Jarmī's description, which surpasses even surviving Byzantine state documents, is that he had somehow got access to an official manual prepared to explain Theophilus's military reforms of 840.[53]

Since the information preserved from Jarmī's work does not mention nine western themes listed in the *Tacticon*, it provides no troop strengths for them. One of them, the ephemeral Theme of Crete of about 843, seems not to have existed at the time of Jarmī's list. The other eight themes presumably account for the 16,000 men included in Jarmī's total but not in his individual numbers, so that these western themes should have averaged 2,000 men each. As it happens, several of them were involved in some tenth-century naval expeditions for which a good deal of official documentation survives.

One, the Cibyrrhaeot Theme, was composed of units that according to the documents had 2,240 officers and soldiers in 911, presumably meaning 2,000 soldiers without the officers. Other official figures, probably relating to 921, show that another of these themes, the Peloponnesus, had well over 1,440 men and well under 2,880 men at that date, or in even thousands 2,000. The documents preserved for 911 indicate that another of the eight themes, Cephalonia, was composed of units that together with the Peloponnesus had at least 4,087 soldiers and officers but fewer than 5,000; subtracting the 2,000-odd soldiers and officers of the Peloponnesus, Cephalonia too should have had 2,000-odd soldiers and officers, or 2,000 soldiers without the officers. The documents also seem to show that another of the eight themes, Hellas, had about 2,000 men.[54]

Two more of the eight themes, Dyrrhachium and the Climata, were evidently created when Theophilus sent 2,000 men each to them in 840, so that their armies also had 2,000 men apiece. No direct evidence reveals the strength of the last two themes, Sicily and Thessalonica; but since the *Tacticon Uspensky* ranks each of them between themes that evidently had 2,000 men, that can probably be assumed to be their strength as well, rather than 3,000 for one and 1,000 for the other. Therefore we seem able to compile a complete list of the strengths of the themes in Jarmī's time. This list is given in the third column of Table 2 and illustrated in Map 8.

The list can be compared with the total of 80,000 men reported by

51. See ibid., 270–77.
52. See below, pp. 119–34.
53. Treadgold, "Remarks," 211–12.
54. See Treadgold, "Army," 112–13, 99–100, 100–104, and 116–20.

TABLE 2
Army Units from 773 to 899

Unit	773	809	840	899
	Soldiers and Marines			
THEMES AND CLEISURAE				
Aegean Sea	(Cib.)	(Cib.)	(Cib.)	400
Anatolic	18,000	18,000	15,000	15,000
Armeniac	14,000	14,000	9,000	6,000
Bucellarian	6,000	6,000	8,000	8,000
Cappadocia	(Anat.)	(Anat.)	4,000	4,000
Cephalonia	—	2,000	2,000	1,000
Chaldia	(Arm.)	(Arm.)	4,000	4,000
Charsianum	(Arm.)	(Arm.)	4,000	4,000
Cherson (Climata)	—	—	2,000	2,000
Cibyrrhaeot	2,000	2,000	2,000	1,000
Colonia	(Arm.)	(Arm.)	(Arm.)	3,000
Dyrrhachium	—	—	2,000	2,000
Hellas	2,000	2,000	2,000	2,000
Macedonia	(Thr.)	3,000	5,000	3,000? [a]
Nicopolis	(Ceph.)	(Ceph.)	(Ceph.)	1,000
Opsician	4,000	4,000	6,000	6,000
Paphlagonia	(Arm.)	(Arm.)	5,000	5,000
Peloponnesus	—	2,000	2,000	2,000
Samos	(Cib.)	(Cib.)	(Cib.)	600
Seleucia	(Anat.)	(Anat.)	5,000	5,000
Sicily (Calabria)	2,000	2,000	2,000	2,000
Strymon	(Thr.)	(Mac.)	(Mac.)	2,000? [a]
Thessalonica	—	2,000	2,000	2,000
Thrace	6,000	3,000	5,000	5,000
Thracesian	8,000	8,000	10,000	10,000
SUBTOTAL	62,000	68,000	96,000	96,000
TAGMATA				
Excubitors	4,000	4,000	4,000	4,000
Hicanati	—	4,000	4,000	4,000
Imperial Fleet	0	0	0	4,000
Numera	2,000	2,000	2,000	2,000
Optimates	2,000	2,000	4,000	4,000
Scholae	4,000	4,000	4,000	4,000
Walls	2,000	2,000	2,000	2,000
Watch	4,000	4,000	4,000	4,000
SUBTOTAL	18,000	22,000	24,000	28,000
TOTAL soldiers and marines	80,000	90,000	120,000	124,000
	Oarsmen			
THEMES AND TAGMATA				
Aegean Sea	(Cib.)	(Cib.)	(Cib.)	2,610
Cibyrrhaeot	12,300	12,300	12,300	5,710
Hellas	6,500	2,300	2,300	2,300
Imperial Fleet	19,600	19,600	19,600	19,600
Samos	(Cib.)	(Cib.)	(Cib.)	3,980
TOTAL oarsmen	38,400	34,200	34,200	34,200

NOTE: Anat., Anatolic; Arm., Armeniac; Ceph., Cephalonia; Cib., Cibyrrhaeot; Mac., Macedonia; Thr., Thrace.

[a] The Cleisura of Strymon was split from the Theme of Macedonia about 896, taking probably two drungi (2,000 men) of Macedonia's five. In any case, the number of troops in Macedonia and Strymon combined remained 5,000, so that the subtotal for the themes is not affected.

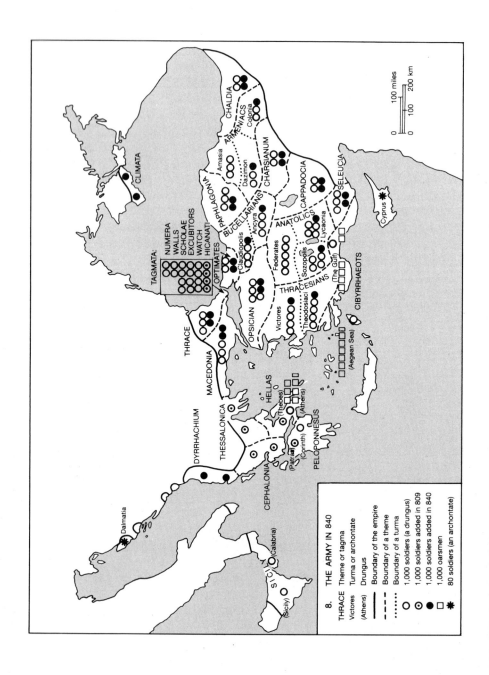

8. THE ARMY IN 840

THRACE   Theme or tagma

Victores   Turma or archontate

(Athens)   Drungus

⎯⎯⎯   Boundary of the empire

– – –   Boundary of a theme

· · · · ·   Boundary of a turma

○   1,000 soldiers (a drungus)

◉   1,000 soldiers added in 809

●   1,000 soldiers added in 840

□   1,000 oarsmen

✳   80 soldiers (an archontate)

TAGMATA:
NUMERA
WALLS
SCHOLAE
EXCUBITORS
WATCH
HICANATI

CLIMATA

CHALDIA

ARMENIACS

Amasia

Dazimon

Colonia

CHARSIANUM

PAPHLAGONIA

CAPPADOCIA

SELEUCIA

Cyprus

BUCELLARIANS

Ancyra

Claudiopolis

ANATOLICS

Lycaonia

Federates

Sozopolis

Theodosiaci

Theodosiopolis

OPTIMATES

THRACESIANS

(The Gulf)

CIBYRRHAEOTS

OPSICIAN

Victores

THRACE

MACEDONIA

(Aegean Sea)

DYRRHACHIUM

THESSALONICA

HELLAS

(Thebes)

(Athens)

(Corinth)

(Patras)

PELOPONNESUS

CEPHALONIA

Dalmatia

SICILY

(Calabria)

(Sicily)

100 miles

100

200 km

Theophanes for 773. As noted above, in 840 Theophilus is reported to have divided his corps of Khurramites, who then totaled 30,000, into fifteen contingents of 2,000 men, which he sent to each of fifteen themes. Since six themes that are known to have existed before 840 had only 2,000 men afterward—Peloponnesus, the Cibyrrhaeots, Hellas, Sicily, Cephalonia, and Thessalonica—they cannot have been included in the distribution. Since apart from these only fifteen military districts existed in 840, including the "theme" of the Optimates and the three cleisurae that were essentially equivalent to themes, these fifteen must be the units that received 2,000 Khurramites apiece.

In fact, the three cleisurae were probably created by Theophilus in 840 for the specific purpose of distributing more Khurramites along the frontier. The Theme of the Climata or Cherson is known to have been created in 840, and Dyrrhachium must have been created at the same time to make up the total of fifteen. To reconstruct the roll of the army as it was before 840, we should first subtract 2,000 men from each of the fifteen units that received Khurramites. Then we should add the strengths of the cleisurae of Cappadocia and Seleucia to the Anatolics, from which they had been separated, and the strength of the Cleisura of Charsianum to the Armeniacs, from which it had been separated. The total would have been 90,000 men before the 30,000 Khurramites began to arrive in 834.[55] This total would have been the same as far back as 809, though before 820 the later themes of Paphlagonia and Chaldia were part of the Armeniacs, to which they should be added.[56] The roster for 809 appears in the second column of Table 2.

We can also reconstruct the army as it was in 773. Before 809 the themes of Peloponnesus, Cephalonia, and Thessalonica and the Tagma of the Hicanati should be subtracted, since they were added by Nicephorus I. Before about 789 the Theme of Macedonia was part of the Theme of Thrace and should be added to it. Since the new units added by Nicephorus totaled 10,000 men, subtracting them gives us the total as it would have been in 773. It was 80,000, as Theophanes says it was.[57] All these changes in the army between 773 and 840 are recorded in Table 2.

By now we can compare this total of 80,000 men in 773 with the total of 150,000 men in 559. Losses in battle, of which there were many during these two hundred—odd years, were by no means the same thing as losses

55. On Theophilus's redistribution of troops in 840, see Treadgold, *Byzantine Revival,* 312–19; and *Byzantine State Finances,* 69–71.

56. Though some have assumed that Paphlagonia had been part of the Bucellarians, this is an error; see Treadgold, "Notes," 286–87.

57. For the details of the reconstruction, see Treadgold, *Byzantine State Finances,* 69–72.

in permanent strength. Given the men and resources, any losses could be replaced. But men and resources were scarce in the seventh century. If units completely disintegrated and the territory they garrisoned was lost, they were likely to disappear altogether. Yet when units suffered limited losses and retained their cohesion, they would probably have been brought back up to strength. If they suffered severe losses and returned as disorganized fugitives, they would most likely have been regrouped with a lower establishment, perhaps a great deal lower.

Some of Justinian's armies can easily be compared with Constantine V's themes. The armies of Byzantine Africa and Spain had of course disappeared along with Byzantine Africa and Spain. All that remained of the 20,000 troops of Byzantine Italy were the 2,000 troops of the Theme of Sicily. This loss was of about the proportion to be expected, because Sicily and Calabria are about a tenth of Italy, and the fall of the isolated remnant of the exarchate in northern Italy in 751 seems not to have permitted any of its troops to be withdrawn to the south.

Remarkably, of the 15,000 troops of Justinian's Army of Armenia, 14,000 seem to have survived the seventh and eighth centuries to become the garrison of the Armeniac Theme, a loss of not quite 7 percent. But then the region of eastern Anatolia where the Army of Armenia was stationed was the area the empire defended most successfully. In 773 the Byzantines still held the northern tip of the Armenian frontier of 565, and even where they had had to withdraw in the south they had not withdrawn very far.

Although Justinian's Army of the East had 20,000 men, after the addition of Tiberius's 15,000 Federates in 578 it would have had 35,000. In 773 the Anatolic Theme had just 18,000 men, a loss of almost 49 percent. Yet such losses are scarcely surprising after first the Persians and then the Arabs had repeatedly defeated the Army of the East and expelled it from its original stations in Syria and Egypt. As for Justinian's Army of Thrace, of its estimated 20,000 men just 8,000 remained in the Thracesian Theme in 773, a loss of 60 percent. But again, this comes as no surprise for an army that had suffered so severely at the hands of the Avars and Slavs, who drove it all the way out of Thrace into Anatolia.

The Opsician Theme is less easily compared with Justinian's two armies in the Emperor's Presence, which totaled some 40,000 men. In 773 the Opsician had only 4,000 men, but by then administrative changes had deprived it of the Bucellarian Theme, probably in 766, the district of the Optimates, perhaps in 743, and the Theme of Thrace, about 681. Yet even if these three units are added to the Opsician, its total would still be just 18,000 men, which would mean a loss of 55 percent since 565. This appears much too high a loss for an army that kept nearly all the territory where it was originally stationed and remained so important into the eighth century that it could often make and unmake emperors.

Another problem is to determine where Constantine V found the troops to form the tagmata, who apart from the Optimates totaled 16,000 men. The vestigial Scholae, Excubitors, and other guards of the earlier period cannot have amounted to more than a handful of usable soldiers. Manpower was short in the eighth century; after the last outbreak of plague between 745 and 748, Constantine had to repopulate Constantinople itself with new settlers from Greece and the Aegean islands.[58] Apart from a failed attempt by Justinian II to conscript captive Slavs, the first well-attested fresh recruits after Tiberius's Federates in 578 were the 10,000 soldiers added by Nicephorus I in 809, and 4,000 of those seem to have been former Mardaïte oarsmen.[59] If Constantine V really recruited 16,000 new men about 743, he would have increased the army by a quarter. This would have been an astonishing achievement at the time, especially without help from immigrants like the Khurramites who fled to Theophilus. Not only are no such immigrants known to have arrived, but most tagmatic soldiers are known to have been native Byzantines.

The solution to the problem is suggested by the case of the Optimates, a tagma created on formerly Opsician territory and evidently with formerly Opsician troops. The original soldiers of the tagmata were probably all, or almost all, former soldiers of the old Opsician Theme. Constantine apparently reduced the power of the Opsician by separating from it not just the Optimates and Bucellarians but the Scholae, Excubitors, Watch, Numera, and Walls. Constantine's obsession with keeping these troops divided, thus minimizing the danger of more revolts, appears in the curious pattern which spread each of the four cavalry tagmata over both Europe and Asia, instead of settling each of them together in a different place. To create the tagmata, Constantine probably moved some Opsician troops into Europe about 743, at least into the lands of the Slavs that he reoccupied; but he may also have assigned the tagmata some troops from what was then the Theme of Thrace.

If this reconstruction is correct, the tagmatic troops were former thematic troops, and not originally different from their comrades in the themes. The soldiers of the tagmata barely outranked those of the themes, were stationed side by side with the thematic troops of Thrace, Macedonia, the Optimates, and the Opsician, and are known to have been paid together with them.[60] Under such circumstances, the tagmata seem almost

---

58. Theophanes, 429; Nicephorus the Patriarch, *Short History*, 68.
59. See below, p. 72.
60. On the ranks of the troops, see Treadgold, "Notes," 285 n. 64. Paying the tagmata together with the themes was a well-established custom by 917; see Symeon the Logothete ("Georgius Monachus"), 881.

certain to have had military lands, as the themes did. Tenth-century legislation assumes that all cavalry had military lands, evidently including the
cavalry tagmata, and even mentions military lands for the marines of the
Imperial Fleet.[61]

Thus before 681 the Opsician Theme should have had not merely
18,000 but 34,000 men, and its losses from the 40,000 men of Justinian's
day would have been just 15 percent, a plausible enough proportion. The
original Opsician force of 34,000 men, of whom 28,000 remained even
after the creation of the Theme of Thrace, would have been almost twice
the size of the next largest theme, the 18,000-man Anatolics. With such
a strength, especially stationed so near the capital, the Opsician Theme
had ample power to stage rebellions. Constantine V divided it for good
reason.

One earlier army and two later themes remain to be accounted for, the
Army of Illyricum and the themes of the Cibyrrhaeots and Hellas. Before
687 both the Cibyrrhaeots and Hellas were part of the Carabisian Theme,
which should therefore have had 4,000 men. The Carabisians seem to
have been one of the original themes. Constans stopped in the territory
that was to become the Theme of Hellas in 662, no doubt to arrange the
transportation of his army to Italy. A late source that incorporates some
earlier material mentions a general who commanded Constans' navy in
Sicily in 668 and was presumably Strategus of the Carabisians.[62]

The Carabisians first acquired oarsmen of their own in 687, when Justinian II took in 12,000 Mardaïtes from the caliphate.[63] The Mardaïtes
were settled in the Aegean islands and on the southern coast of Anatolia
to row for the Cibyrrhaeot marines. These 12,000 were evidently the
adult males, because in 911 the themes that had once made up the Cibyrrhaeots still had 12,300 Mardaïte oarsmen. Perhaps the original 12,000
Mardaïtes received military lands to support their service as oarsmen and
passed the lands on to their heirs; or perhaps their duties were simply
hereditary. The Theme of Hellas seems to have received its own oarsmen
only in 689, when Justinian settled another 6,500 Mardaïtes in its territory. Some of these remained oarsmen for Hellas, but in 809 Nicephorus
apparently used 4,000 of them to garrison his new themes of Peloponnesus
and Cephalonia, where they were known as the Mardaïtes of the West.[64]

The Mardaïtes, however, were oarsmen. Where did the 4,000 Carabisian marines come from? The name Carabisian merely describes their
function as shipmen, and gives no clue to their origin. Constans II, who

61. Zepos and Zepos, *Jus Graecoromanum*, I, 222–23; and Constantine VII, *De Ceremoniis*, 695.
62. Pseudo-Codinus, 251–52.
63. Theophanes, 363 and 364.
64. See Treadgold, "Army," 115–19.

had evidently formed the themes because he had found paying his soldiers so difficult, would hardly have recruited more soldiers as marines, especially because earlier fleets had made do with soldiers from the land army. If Constans formed a corps of marines, he presumably used soldiers he already had.

Which soldiers would have been closest to hand about 660? None seem to have been regularly stationed in southern Anatolia or Greece in Justinian's day, when the Quaestor of the Army may have commanded oarsmen there, but not marines. The southern coast of Anatolia had then been part of the Prefecture of the East, but the Army of the East did its fighting no closer than Syria. The islands of the Aegean, where the Carabisians had their original headquarters on Samos, had been part of the Prefecture of Illyricum, like the territory that became the Theme of Hellas. The Prefecture of Illyricum was defended by the Army of Illyricum.

This raises the question of whether the Avars and Slavs entirely destroyed the old 15,000-man Army of Illyricum around 615, as has usually been assumed.[65] They certainly did overwhelm the army and take almost all of Illyricum; but invaders also took nearly all of Thrace, the East, and Italy, and overwhelmed their armies, yet 40 percent, 51 percent, and 10 percent of those armies seem to have survived. Why should the Army of Illyricum, nearer than Italy to the core of the empire and almost as near as Thrace and the East, have fared so very much worse? It would have been the only Byzantine army to disintegrate entirely while some of its original territory remained Byzantine.

If any troops of the Army of Illyricum escaped, they would presumably have fled south to the islands and the remaining coastal enclaves of Greece. Troops who arrived there would soon have gained some familiarity with seafaring, since the rest of the empire was accessible only by ship. By 659 any remnants of the Army of Illyricum would have been of little use on land. The Avars were far to the north; the Slavs had settled down peacefully in their conquests in Greece, which Constans showed no interest in reoccupying; and no enemy could mount a land attack on the islands. But Constans needed a fleet, both to fight the Arabs, who had just built a fleet of their own, and to carry his expeditionary force to Italy. Such considerations strongly suggest that the 4,000 Carabisian marines represented what was left of the Army of Illyricum. It would have been almost 27 percent of it, somewhat less than survived of the Army of Thrace. These conjectural losses are recorded with the others in Table 3.

Finally, we may reasonably ask who rowed for the 4,000 Carabisian marines between their creation about 660 and their acquisition of Mardaïtes in 687. The fleet with 30,000 oarsmen that Justinian had dispatched

65. E.g., by Toynbee, *Constantine Porphyrogenitus*, 228.

TABLE 3
Army Units in 559 and 773

Unit in 559	Strength	Unit in 773	Strength	Loss, 559–773	Percent loss
Praesental[a]	40,000?	Old Opsician[b]	34,000	6,000?	15%?
East	20,000	Anatolic	18,000	17,000[c]	49%[c]
Armenia	15,000	Armeniac	14,000	1,000	7%
Thrace	20,000?	Thracesian	8,000	12,000?	60%?
Illyricum	15,000	Old Carabisian[d]	4,000	11,000	73%
Italy	20,000?	Sicily	2,000	18,000?	90%?
Africa	15,000	(lost)	0	15,000	100%
Spain	5,000?	(lost)	0	5,000?	100%
TOTALS	150,000		80,000	85,000[e]	52%[e]

NOTE: For the explanation of figures questioned in this table, see the text, pp. 59–63.

[a] Composed of the two armies in the Emperor's Presence, each of about 20,000 men.

[b] Elements of the original Opsician Theme. These were later divided into the themes of the (new) Opsician (4,000), the Bucellarians (6,000), and Thrace (6,000), and the tagmata of the Scholae (4,000), Excubitors (4,000), Watch (4,000), Numera (2,000), Walls (2,000), and Optimates (2,000).

[c] The computation of this loss takes into account the 15,000 Federates added to the Army of the East ca. 577, which expanded its strength to 35,000. If the Federates are disregarded, the loss would be 2,000 (10%).

[d] Elements of the original Carabisian Theme. These were later divided into the themes of the Cibyrrhaeots (2,000) and Hellas (2,000).

[e] The computation of this loss takes into account the 15,000 Federates added to the Army of the East ca. 577. If the Federates are disregarded, the total loss would be 70,000 (47%).

to Africa in 532 and put under the Quaestor of the Army about 536 must have survived in part, or Heraclius and Constans II would have been unable to ship troops to Egypt and Italy. The Imperial Fleet had some 19,600 oarsmen in 911, and evidently also before 870 because it needed that many to row the 4,000 marines it acquired around that date.[66] This would also have been enough oarsmen to row the 4,000 marines of the original Theme of the Carabisians before they received their 18,800 Mardaïte oarsmen. The most plausible answer seems to be that before the Mardaïtes arrived the central fleet did the rowing for the Carabisians.

If Constans II had originally put his Carabisian marines under the commander of the older central fleet, his arrangement would explain some confusing evidence that has led some to think that the Carabisians were never a theme.[67] Around 683, for example, a well-informed source refers awkwardly to a "strategus of the ships [*karabōn*] . . . with the Carabisian marines under his command."[68] When the Mardaïtes arrived in 687, Justinian II would then have attached them to the Carabisians and built new ships for them, freeing the central fleet to carry other soldiers on future naval expeditions. Such a doubling of the empire's navy would also help explain why the Byzantine fleet offered such tardy resistance to the Arab

66. Cf. Treadgold, "Army," 110–12.
67. Cf. Antoniadis-Bibicou, *Études*, esp. 63–98.
68. Lemerle, *Plus anciens recueils*, I, 230–31 (for the text) and 161 (for the date).

raids around Constantinople between 674 and 677, but fought much better during the more formidable Arab siege of Constantinople in 717.

This hypothesis implies that until 687 the navy had about 19,000 oarsmen, the number needed to row 4,000 Carabisians. This would have represented a loss of some 11,000 oarsmen since 559, or around 37 percent of
the total—more or less what might have been expected in view of the
losses suffered by the army in general. By 773, after the arrival of the Mardaïtes, the number of oarsmen would actually have shown a gain in comparison with 559, from some 30,000 to 38,000. The number would then
have decreased to about 34,000 oarsmen in 809, when Nicephorus I
turned the Mardaïtes of the West into marines. Although the empire
could also muster flotillas attached to other themes and if necessary req-
uisition private ships, the latter would have had no regularly paid oarsmen,
while the former were probably rowed by the themes' soldiers, including
the Mardaïtes of the West.

If the reconstruction shown in Table 3 is correct, all 80,000 men of the
army of Constantine V belonged to units descended from those of the
150,000-man army of two centuries before. Since Tiberius had added
15,000 men to Justinian's force, Constantine V's army would have represented only about 48.5 percent of the sixth-century forces. But it represented about 63 percent of the sixth-century armies that were later converted into themes. Since many soldiers from those armies must have been
lost before the themes were created, the themes would have preserved a
much higher proportion of their original strengths than this.

These numbers reveal the approximate scale of what occurred in the
seventh century. It was a military disaster, but not a total military collapse. Most units retained some cohesion, and most men who died must
have been replaced before very long. As soon as the military lands were
introduced in the middle of the seventh century, the state had land to
offer potential replacements. In the ninth century, Jarmī noted that losses
were routinely reported up the chain of command, so that they could
be replaced without delay.[69] This success in replacing so many lost men,
while impressive, was probably no more than the empire needed to do to
survive.

THE PROBLEM OF THE MISSING TOTAL

After al-Jarmī, no further total for the army has reached us for the
ninth, tenth, or eleventh century. We can trace the number of themes
and tagmata through the rank lists known as tactica, of which the *Tacticon
Uspensky* is the first and the treatise of Philotheus the second. Insofar as

69. Qudāmah, 196.

themes were simply divided up, as they often were, the total number of soldiers would hardly have changed. When new themes were added, in some cases we have information about their garrisons. In other cases, their ranks in the tactica can give us at least a rough idea of whether the new themes were larger or smaller than certain others. Nonetheless, the farther we advance from al-Jarmī's total, the worse our estimates will tend to be.

During the rest of the ninth century we are on fairly firm ground. The ephemeral Theme of Crete never became established with its own forces. After the Theme of the Aegean Sea was separated from the Cibyrrhaeot Theme about 843, the documents for 911 show that each of the new themes would have had about 1,000 marines and 6,000 oarsmen. Because the Theme of Colonia had evidently been one of three equal subdivisions of the Armeniacs before it became independent about 861, it would then have had 3,000 men, and the rest of the Armeniacs 6,000. When Dalmatia became a theme about 868 it seems to have received no new troops.[70]

The Imperial Fleet acquired its own marines around 870. According to the documents for 911, that fleet then had about 4,000 marines, the number probably established in 870, and 19,600 oarsmen, the number that as noted above probably went back to the early Byzantine fleet. Since Cyprus was a theme only from about 875 to 882, whatever soldiers it had were not permanent additions to the army. About 882 the Theme of Samos was separated from the Theme of the Aegean Sea, and the documents from 911 show that Samos then had about 600 marines and 4,000 oarsmen, and the Aegean Sea about 400 marines and 2,000 oarsmen. About 896 the Theme of Nicopolis was separated from the Theme of Cephalonia, apparently leaving each theme with one drungus of 1,000 men. Around the same time, the Cleisura of Strymon was split from the Theme of Macedonia; since Strymon remained junior in rank to Macedonia, it probably took 2,000 men, or two drungi, of Macedonia's 5,000 men, or five drungi.[71]

The treatise of Philotheus shows that these were all the new units created between 840 and 899. Only the marines of the Imperial Fleet seem to have permanently increased the size of the army, from 120,000 soldiers to 124,000. All these changes between 840 and 899 are recorded in Table 2. Although minor additions, losses, or transfers could in theory have passed unrecorded in the sources, the sources for this period are relatively good. We have already seen that in the preceding period most units had maintained their strength, while new recruitment had been rare. With the one exception of the creation of the Theme of Samos around 882, the rule that themes should have a round number of thousands of

70. See Treadgold, "Army," 86–87.
71. See ibid., 87–88 and 110–13.

men also seems to have been respected, making minor changes in thematic strength difficult.

Inconveniently for those who would estimate the size of the army in the subsequent period, Leo VI seems to have abandoned that rule about 902. From then on he created new themes and transferred districts from theme to theme without regard for the 1,000-man units known as drungi, maintaining only the 200-man units known as *banda*. When Leo created themes on the border, he combined new recruits and new territory with portions of the soldiers and lands of neighboring older themes, partly compensating those older themes with troops and lands from other neighboring themes.

Thus Leo added bits of the themes of Colonia and Chaldia to his new Theme of Mesopotamia, and combined new territory with the eastern part of the Theme of Charsianum to make the Theme of Sebastea. Then he compensated Charsianum with parts of Cappadocia, the Bucellarians, and the Armeniacs, and compensated Cappadocia with parts of the Bucellarians and the Anatolics. The Anatolics were probably compensated with a bit of the Thracesian Theme, which by 949 seems to have had 9,600 men rather than 10,000.[72] Leo also seems to have compensated the Bucellarians with part of Paphlagonia, since by about 934 the Bucellarians included two ports on the Black Sea that in Jarmī's time were evidently Paphlagonian.[73] These known changes affected all the eastern themes but the Opsician and Seleucia, and even those could easily have been affected by changes that passed unrecorded in the sources. In short, after 902 many of the numbers in Table 2 changed slightly in ways that cannot be fully traced, though most of the changes would have had no effect on the total strength of the army.

Official records survive that list many of the 200-man banda that were transferred and allow us to estimate fairly reliably how many men Leo added to the army. There appear to have been three stages of additions, as follows:

Date and change		*Addition*
901	creation of the Theme of Mesopotamia	2,000 men
902	additions to the Cleisura of Sebastea	1,600
908	creation of the cleisurae of Symposium, Lycandus, and Abara	2,400
	TOTAL	6,000 men

72. Ibid., 125–28.

73. Cf. Brooks, "Arabic Lists," 73, with Constantine VII, *De Thematibus*, VI, listing Heraclea Pontica and Teïum among the cities of the Bucellarians. Brooks's map on p. 68 may also be compared with the map at the end of Pertusi's edition of the *De Thematibus*, though I suspect that Jarmī's boundaries in the south have been distorted somewhat, by him or by his excerptors, because none of the material that survives from his work mentions the existence of the Cibyrrhaeots or the other smaller themes.

Thus the army would have grown from 124,000 to about 130,000 men by 908.[74] Whatever troops Leo added to create the Theme of Longobardia in southern Italy should approximately have equaled the troops lost in Sicily at about the same time. In fact, troops evacuated from Sicily may well have been resettled in Longobardia.

After this no significant additions seem to have been made to the army until the conquest of Melitene in 934, and the flight to the empire of the Arab tribe of the Banū Ḥabīb a year or so later. A reliable Arab source says that the Banū Ḥabīb included 12,000 cavalrymen and their families. These converted to Christianity, and the horsemen joined the Byzantine army and conquered border territories for themselves. The Banū Ḥabīb appear to have formed the garrisons of the five new themes of Melitene, Charpezicium, Arsamosata, Chozanum, and Derzene. Since Charpezicium apparently had 2,400 cavalry in 949, exactly a fifth of 12,000, this was probably the strength of each of the five new themes. They evidently had no infantry at all.[75]

Regardless of how the Banū Ḥabīb were divided, their 12,000 men would have raised the total size of the army to some 142,000. Then in 949 the Byzantines conquered Theodosiopolis and made it a theme. Small though it was, it should have received a minimum of 2,000 recruits, since no earlier Anatolian land theme had had fewer. If that was the strength of the Theme of Theodosiopolis, the army would then have totaled some 144,000 soldiers by 949. As for oarsmen, the documentation for the Cretan expedition of 949 shows little if any change in the navy.[76] Such was the empire's military establishment on the eve of the great conquests of the second half of the tenth century.

For those conquests our only official source is the *Escorial Tacticon*, the last of the rank lists. It was compiled about 971, quite possibly to catalogue the new Balkan themes created in that year by John I. Like other rank lists, it includes no numbers; but in listing the names of the military commanders it supplies a full list of the military commands at the time, both themes and tagmata. For later dates, its list of themes can be supplemented from literary sources, which also supply some numbers and information from which more numbers can be deduced.

The division of the Scholae into separate eastern and western commands about 959 seems to have caused an increase in their strength. An anonymous treatise *On Campaign Organization and Tactics*, which probably dates from around 990, notes that in the emperor's camp the Scholae pitched their tents in two groups of fifteen banda each, one evidently

74. Treadgold, "Army," 93–99.
75. Ibid., 128–30.
76. Ibid., 142 and 144–45.

being the Scholae of the West and the other the Scholae of the East.[77] Thus, though in the time of Jarmī and Philotheus the single tagma of the Scholae had had 4,000 men and twenty 200-man banda, by the date of the treatise each of the two tagmata of Scholae had fifteen 200-man banda, or 3,000 men. This would have come to 6,000 men altogether, an increase of 2,000. Since the *Escorial Tacticon* also mentions Excubitors of the West and East, that tagma was similarly divided, probably with similar additions.[78] These additions, totaling 4,000 men, would have brought the army to perhaps 148,000 in 959.

The next additions were the themes of Crete and Cyprus. The *Escorial Tacticon* lists them one after the other, among themes of the western class, just after Peloponnesus, Nicopolis, and the Cibyrrhaeots, and just before Hellas.[79] At this date Peloponnesus and Hellas should still have had 2,000 men each; Nicopolis and the Cibyrrhaeots, 1,000. Crete and Cyprus ought therefore to have had either 2,000 or 1,000 men; in view of their modest land area and relative defensibility as islands, the smaller number seems more likely. This brings the army to perhaps 150,000 men in 964. Despite some uncertainties, this figure can hardly be off by more than about 5,000 men either way. It may even be exact, since the Byzantine government liked round numbers.

Then the picture becomes more complicated, though two additions are fairly straightforward. The Immortals, the new tagma created by John I, are reliably reported to have been in the vanguard when John's campaign set out in 971. Since another trustworthy source says that the vanguard had 4,000 cavalry, they are presumably to be identified with the Immortals, who therefore had the same strength as the other four cavalry tagmata originally had, and the Watch and Hicanati still did.[80] The Varangian Guard, added by Basil II, is said by a contemporary Armenian source to have numbered 6,000.[81] Though the Varangians were foreign mercenaries rather than a regular tagma, they were an important part of the army, and that they should have had the same number as the expanded Scholae and Excubitors seems reasonable.

From 965 to 1025 a number of themes were subdivided, presumably without affecting the overall strength of the army. But a total of apparently 52 themes and ducates were added in newly conquered territory in the West and East.[82] These certainly varied in size. The Theme of Tarsus

---

77. *On Campaign Organization and Tactics*, 252.
78. *Escorial Tacticon*, 265.
79. Ibid.
80. Cf. Leo the Deacon, 132, with Scylitzes, 295.
81. Stephen of Taron, 164–65.
82. The number of 52 themes follows from my description of the development of the themes in Chapter 1, pp. 35–39 and nn. 44–53, but note that if Oikonomidès's identifi-

is said to have had a garrison of 5,000 cavalry, but it seems to have been exceptionally large; in the *Escorial Tacticon* it outranks all other themes created since 959, except for the Ducate of Antioch.[83] The Theme of Antaradus, created after 971, is said to have had 4,000 men, reportedly Armenians, but it needed a particularly strong garrison because it was just opposite the Fatimid stronghold of Tripoli.[84]

Bulgaria and Iberia, both former kingdoms with powerful armies that became ducates after 971, must have had more troops than this. Yet if all 52 new themes had averaged even as many as 5,000 men, their total strength would have been some 260,000, far more than the whole army in 964, and that is plainly too much. In fact, most of the new themes, especially in the East, were very small in area and not in particularly exposed positions.

About 1053 Constantine IX disbanded what the historian John Scylitzes calls the "Iberian Army" and reckons at some 50,000 men. As a contemporary Drungary of the Watch, Scylitzes should have known what he was talking about.[85] Two other knowledgeable contemporaries, the former officials Michael Attaliates and Cecaumenus, agree with Scylitzes that by demobilizing these soldiers Constantine did catastrophic harm to the empire's eastern defenses.[86] But for the army of the Ducate of Iberia alone, 50,000 men appears to be much too high a figure, and if only the Ducate of Iberia had been disbanded many other themes would have remained to defend the eastern frontier.

Yet Cecaumenus says that Constantine's demobilization covered "Iberia and Mesopotamia," and since those districts were separated from each other by several themes Cecaumenus seems to be thinking of all or most of Byzantine Armenia. Attaliates refers to the demobilized district as "the Iberian land," which was evidently the same as "the land of the Iberians" that he later says began at the border of the themes of Sebastea and Colonia. In another place, Attaliates gives this region beyond Sebastea and Colonia the more common name of the "Armenian themes," which he wanted Romanus IV to abandon because they were devastated and indefensible.[87]

The Armenian themes seem to have comprised about thirty units in

cation of Irenopolis is correct (n. 46), the number would be 53 themes on newly conquered territory.

83. Bar Hebraeus, 171, gives the number for Tarsus; cf. *Escorial Tacticon*, 263–65.

84. Al-Maqrīzī says that Basil II garrisoned Antaradus with 4,000 men in 995 (Forsyth, *Byzantine-Arab Chronicle*, 495); Yaḥyā of Antioch, 443, says that these men were Armenians.

85. Scylitzes, 476; for his position as commander of the Watch, see the title of his work on p. 3. These troops then paid a tax instead of serving.

86. Attaliates, 44–45; Cecaumenus, 152–54.

87. Cecaumenus, 152; Attaliates, 44, 147, and 136.

the empire's new territories in Armenia, north of the new lands in Syria that were under the general command of the Duke of Antioch, or by Constantine IX's time under the Duke of Edessa. The historian Anna Comnena, quoting a treaty made by her father Alexius I in 1108, gives an official list of the themes, by then lost, that had been subject to the dukes of Antioch and Edessa. Their northern tier was Tarsus, Podandus, Anazarbus, Germanicea, Teluch, Edessa, and Limnia, all shown on Map 9.[88]

Since the next ducate to the north was Mesopotamia, the region of the demobilized Iberian Army evidently included everything north of the ducates of Antioch and Edessa and east of the old Anatolian themes—except that the border Theme of Soteropolis, formerly part of Chaldia, seems to have remained subject to the Duke of Chaldia. The other themes were probably called "Iberian" because after the conquest of Iberia in 1000 the general command over them was transferred from the Duke of Mesopotamia to the Duke of Iberia.[89] The boundaries of these Iberian or Armenian themes are marked on Map 9.

We have a good idea of the size of some of these units. They included the five themes garrisoned by the Banū Ḥabīb, which totaled 12,000 men, probably 2,400 apiece. The Armenian themes also included the small themes of Leontocome (formerly Tephrice), Coptus (formerly Euphratia), and Abara (or Amara), all former divisions of the Theme of Sebastea with 800 men each, and Lycandus and Taranta (formerly Symposium), also with 800 men each.[90] John I had separated Coptus from Sebastea and Taranta from Lycandus only about 970, when he separated the other small themes of Romanopolis and Cymbalaeus from the themes of Mesopotamia and Charsianum. The most likely size for those two Armenian themes is also 800 men each. This would have left Mesopotamia, another of the Armenian or "Iberian" themes, with 3,200 men. That would be the same size as Sebastea and Charsianum, which like Mesopotamia had originally had 4,000 men.

88. Anna Comnena, XIII.12.18–19, 21, and 24–25; besides the ducates of Antioch and Edessa, the treaty listed the themes of Sizara, Artach, Teluch, Germanicea, Palatza, Podandus, Tarsus, Mopsuestia, Anazarbus, Laodicea, Gabala, Balaneae, Antaradus, and Limnia, all of which existed in 1025, plus the themes of St. Elias, Borze, Pagrae, Zumē, Maraceōs, and Aëtus, which seem to be later divisions and additions. All of these were under the Duke of Antioch except for Edessa itself, Limnia, and Aëtus. For the locations, see Honigmann, *Ostgrenze*, 125–29.

89. This is probably the solution to the problem identified by Cheynet, "Du stratège de thème au duc," 185–86, who notes that in 1047 Leo Tornices held a command at Melitene that is described as being Iberian or in Iberia, though Tornices was plainly not Duke or Strategus of Iberia and Melitene was certainly not part of Iberia.

90. See Treadgold, "Army," 128–30. Coptus, as Euphratia had been, was the small region between Tephrice and Abara, and Taranta, as Symposium had been, was the small region bounded by Lycandus, Larissa, and Abara; cf. Hild and Restle, *Kappadokien*, 209 (Coptus) and 290–91 (Taranta).

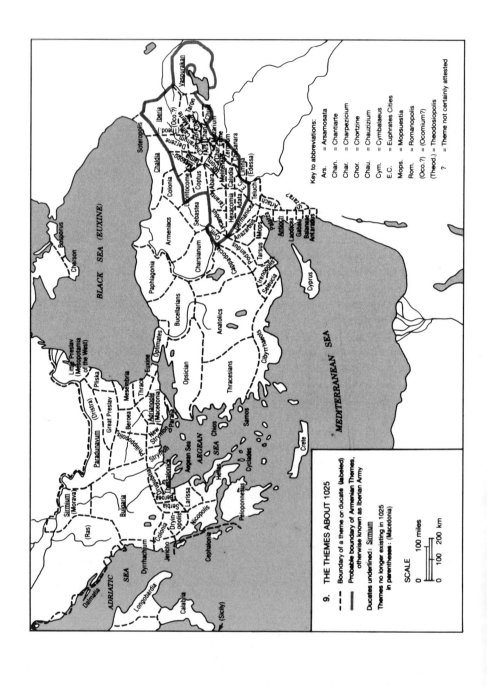

Key to abbreviations:

Ars. = Arsamosata
Chan. = Chantiarte
Char. = Charpezicium
Chor. = Chortzine
Chau. = Chauzizium
Cym. = Cymbalaeus
E.C. = Euphrates Cities
Mops. = Mopsuestia
Rom. = Romanopolis
(Oco.?) = (Ocomium?)
(Theod.) = Theodosiopolis
? = Theme not certainly attested

BLACK SEA (EUXINE)

MEDITERRANEAN SEA

AEGEAN SEA

ADRIATIC SEA

9.   THE THEMES ABOUT 1025

– – – – –   Boundary of a theme or ducate (labeled)

————   Probable boundary of Armenian Themes,
         otherwise known as Iberian Army

Ducates underlined: Sirmium

Themes no longer existing in 1025
in parentheses: (Macedonia)

SCALE

0   100 miles

0   100   200 km

In fact, we cannot go far wrong if we assume that every small eastern theme had 800 men, since they are unlikely to have had more men than considerably older themes like Leontocome and Lycandus, and no land theme is known to have had a smaller garrison than 800. As for Taron, the *Escorial Tacticon* ranks it after the two domestics of the Excubitors, who evidently commanded 3,000 men each, and the Theme of Theodosiopolis, which I have conjectured at 2,000 men; it then ranks before the Theme of Melitene, which as one of the five themes of the Banū Ḥabīb probably had 2,400 men.[91] Although admittedly ranks in the *Escorial Tacticon* correspond to size of command only in a general way, Taron can still be reasonably estimated at 3,000 men.

Thus we can make fairly well-supported estimates for all the thirty-one themes of the 50,000-man "Iberian Army" except Iberia and Vaspurakan. Subtracting the other themes leaves a total for these two of some 15,000, which is plausible enough. Iberia was the more important, and by this time it incorporated the former Theme of Theodosiopolis of perhaps 2,000 men. After 1045 Iberia also included the former Kingdom of Ani; but since Constantine IX cared so little for all these troops that he decommissioned them less than ten years later, when he annexed Ani he may simply have dismissed its army, which after all had just been fighting him. In any case, we might guess something like 10,000 men for Iberia and 5,000 men for Vaspurakan.

This would give us the following distribution, which ought to be more or less correct:

Unit	Strength
Iberia (ducate)	10,000?
Vaspurakan	5,000?
Mesopotamia	3,200
Taron	3,000?
Derzene, Chozanum, Arsamosata, Charpezicium, and Melitene (2,400 men each?)	12,000
Leontocome, Coptus, Romanopolis, Abara, Taranta, Lycandus, Cymbalaeus, Hexacomia, Adata, Caludia, Euphrates Cities, Chasanara, Zermium, Erkne, Muzarium, Chantiarte, Chuët, Chortzine, Chauzizium, Cama, and Melte (800 men each?)	16,800?
TOTAL "Iberian Army"	50,000

We may now venture rough estimates for the other themes on the rolls in 1025. The ten other small eastern themes (Mopsuestia, Palatza, Laodicea, Gabala, Balaneae, Sizara, Artach, Teluch, Germanicea, and Limnia) dated from about the same time as the Armenian themes and had com-

91. *Escorial Tacticon*, 265.

manders with similar ranks; they may also be reckoned at 800 men each. Anazarbus had a somewhat higher rank, after Taron (3,000?) and Melitene (2,400), and before Peloponnesus (2,000) and Nicopolis (1,000), so that it might be estimated at 2,000 men.[92] The strengths of Tarsus and Antaradus are recorded, as we have seen, and Antioch might be estimated at about 5,000 men, like Tarsus.

As for the western themes, the land themes of the West seem to have continued to conform to the rule that themes should have round thousands of men; none is known to have been smaller than 1,000. The eleven new small western themes, which anyway were rather larger in area than the new small eastern themes, therefore seem likely to have had 1,000 men apiece. This would account for the themes of Colonia, Dryinopolis, Serbia, Beroea in Greece, Drugubitia, Philippopolis, Beroea in Thrace, Mesembria, Great Preslav, Pliska, and Little Preslav (formerly the Mesopotamia of the West). But the three western ducates of Bulgaria, Sirmium, and Paradunavum (formerly Dristra) were definitely larger.

All we know of the size of the army of independent Bulgaria is that in 1014 Basil II captured and blinded about 15,000 of its soldiers.[93] Though a good many soldiers remained and continued to resist for four more years, the 15,000 soldiers formed enough of the total to leave Bulgaria crippled after they were blinded. Basil seems to have incorporated most of the rest of the Bulgarian army into his ducates of Bulgaria and Sirmium, and his themes of Colonia, Dryinopolis, and Serbia.

The latter three themes probably totaled some 3,000 men, having 1,000 men apiece like other small western themes. For purposes of a rough estimate, we might count Bulgaria at 10,000 men, like Iberia, and Sirmium at 5,000 men, like Tarsus, Antioch, and Vaspurakan. This would make the Bulgarian army of 1014 at least 18,000 strong after it lost 15,000 men. Though that army could easily have been bigger, Basil may also have dismissed some Bulgar soldiers, and others may have chosen not to serve him. Finally, taking 5,000 men as the usual strength of a ducate, we might count Paradunavum at that figure as well.

The total of these numbers, which range from recorded statistics to very rough estimates, would be as follows:

Unit	Strength
army in 964	150,000?
Immortals	4,000
Varangian Guard	6,000
Bulgaria	10,000?
Iberia (besides 2,000 already counted in Theodosiopolis)	8,000?
Tarsus	5,000

92. Ibid., 265–69.
93. Scylitzes, 349.

Unit	Strength
Antioch, Sirmium, Paradunavum, Vaspurakan (5,000 each?)	20,000?
Antaradus	4,000
Taron	3,000?
Anazarbus	2,000?
11 new small themes of western type (1,000 each?)	11,000?
31 new small themes of eastern type (800 each?)	24,800?
TOTAL for 1025	247,800?

This total can hardly be considered exact, but it suggests that in 1025 the empire had something like 250,000 soldiers. The margin for error might be some 20,000 men either way. After the reconquests of Crete and Cyprus, which seem not to have expanded the permanent naval establishment significantly, the Byzantines seem to have maintained their navy at about its old strength.[94] After 1025 keeping track of changes in the regular army seems pointless, since the troops of the themes began to lose most of their effectiveness and probably fell under strength, though a few new themes were added, like Edessa in 1031. Mercenaries were also becoming important at the time, and they are difficult to estimate. Their numbers must have varied from year to year, and in any case would have been smaller than the ample margin for error of any overall estimate.

Yet most of the soldiers of the themes remained on the rolls, because Constantine IX was able to tax those in the Armenian themes around 1053, and Romanus IV was able to call up even those in the Anatolian themes in 1068 and to make an attempt to train them. All the tagmata remained effective units in 1069, when Attaliates says that Romanus IV brought east "the five western tagmata," plainly meaning the Scholae, Excubitors, Watch, Hicanati, and Immortals.[95] These would probably have included 3,000 men each from the Scholae and Excubitors and 2,000 men each from the Watch, Hicanati, and Immortals, for a total of 12,000 soldiers. The strength of the tagmata of the East would have been about the same. Though these tagmatic troops were usually dispersed among the themes, they remained powerful until the eastern tagmata became rebels and the western tagmata succumbed to the chaos of the late eleventh century.

The foregoing discussion has uncovered a surprising amount of good

94. Though the expedition to Crete in 960–61 included 307 warships, while the Imperial Fleet and the themes of the Cibyrrhaeots, Samos, and the Aegean Sea had 240 or so ships in 949, the difference is probably to be accounted for by requisitioned private ships and the flotillas of other themes (Treadgold, "Army," 142–43). Three hundred or so ships seem to have remained the maximum the empire dispatched throughout the ninth and tenth centuries, since that number is mentioned both by the Arab chronicler Ṭabarī for 852 (Vasiliev, *Byzance et les Arabes*, I, 315) and by Leo the Deacon (129) for 971.

95. Attaliates, 123. This seems a strong argument against counting as regular tagmata the stratelatae, satraps, and Megathymi discussed by Kühn, *Byzantinische Armee*, 247–50.

evidence for the size of the Byzantine army. Yet these results by no means imply that all numbers in medieval sources are correct. Many obviously exaggerated figures for battlefield armies have been left out of account, like the 100,000 men who according to Theophanes marched against the Arabs in 778.[96] Presumably Theophanes meant to include some irregulars, since he had just said that the empire had a total of 80,000 regular troops five years before; but 100,000 still looks like a guess, a large round number used for an army that Theophanes or his source simply knew was large.

Since even accurate battlefield figures can include irregulars, servants, and camp followers, and always omit regular soldiers occupied elsewhere, none is of any real use for estimating the total size of the regular army. A large battlefield figure means very little unless it can be corroborated and related to specific units of the army. A small battlefield figure, even if corroborated, may provide a very low minimum for the size of the whole army, but gives no indication of what the maximum might be. Unfortunately, some historians have chosen to ignore almost all the evidence for the total size of the army because it suggests totals much higher than a few low figures for armies on the battlefield. This tendency to confuse the different kinds of numbers seems to be compounded by a vague feeling that guessing too low is more "cautious" than accepting a higher figure, even if the low estimate is an arbitrary modern guess and the higher figure is recorded by a medieval source in a position to know.

In practice, the sources are more likely to give wrong totals for armies on the battlefield than for the empire's whole military force. The idea of the total number of men in the army, as distinguished from those who actually fought at a given time and place, is a fairly sophisticated one for a medieval author. It is essentially an abstraction: though the men existed, no one could ever have seen them all at the same time. Any writer who gives a figure for such a total is likely either to be well informed himself or to be borrowing the concept and the total from another well-informed source.

The figures cited here present a coherent and self-consistent picture. The evidence for them is as good as that for much of the rest of Byzantine and other ancient and medieval history. Like our standard accounts of historical events, and particularly their chronology, the numbers include some imprecisions and probably some outright errors, and can doubtless be improved upon by further research. But if our standards for evidence are so high that we refuse even to consider such statistics, we should also despair of learning most other details of what the world was like before the year 1000.

96. Theophanes, 451.

CHAPTER THREE

Structures

Just as the number of soldiers on the rolls was different from the number of soldiers who took part in any battle, so the organization of the army on paper differed from its formation on the battlefield. The units that appear in the *Notitia Dignitatum*, or in al-Jarmī's description, scarcely ever went into battle in full strength unaccompanied by other troops. A large command like the Ducate of Syria or the Anatolic Theme could provide a fighting force from its own components alone, and often more than one, as when it sent detachments to oppose enemy raids. But major expeditions generally consisted of detachments from different units. Though men from the same unit would usually be grouped together as far as possible, all the detachments had to obey the expeditionary commander and to adapt themselves to the task of the expeditionary force.

DIOCLETIAN'S REGIMENTS

When Diocletian divided up the old Roman legions of 5,500 men, he kept most of their command structure as it had been. He seems to have made no changes in the size or structure of the old infantry cohorts and cavalry *alae*. Legions, cohorts, and *alae* continued to have officers called tribunes, centurions, and decurions as late as the sixth century. In the early empire every cohort of the infantry, whether part of a legion or independent, had been commanded by a tribune. The tribune's subordinate officers were 6 centurions, each commanding a century of 80 infantry, and 60 decurions, each commanding 8 infantry including the decurion himself. (Originally, as the names imply, centurions had commanded 100 men and decurions 10, but the numbers had been changed during the early

Republic.) Every *ala* of the cavalry had also been commanded by a tribune, but his subordinate officers were 16 decurions, each commanding a *turma* of 30 cavalry including himself, with no centurions or centuries. Diocletian's new legions of 1,000 men would therefore have had two cohorts, each actually of 480 infantry plus officers, while independent cohorts and *alae* of 500 men actually had 480 infantry or cavalry plus officers.[1]

Additional officers of these regiments are named in papyri and in a military manual of the late sixth century, the *Strategicon* of the emperor Maurice. The papyri give considerable importance to the vicarius, the lieutenant commander of a regiment, who served as the real commander when the nominal tribune was an absentee. One papyrus notes that a sixth-century cohort had eight senior officers (*ordinarii*), including the top-ranking primicerius (the tribune's chief of staff), the adjutor (the regiment's clerk), and six others, probably the six centurions. Other officers mentioned in papyri are the centurions, draconarii (standard bearers), actuarii and optiones (quartermasters), and the regiment's surgeon, campidoctor (drill sergeant), and drummer.[2] The *Strategicon* adds heralds, who like the draconarii came two to a regiment, plus a cape bearer for the commander and a regimental trumpeter.[3]

The official establishment of an infantry regiment of the old type therefore seems to have consisted of the following 501 men, not necessarily in quite this order of rank:

1	tribune
1	vicarius
1	primicerius
1	adjutor
6	centurions (commanding 80 men each)
1	campidoctor
1	actuarius
1	optio
1	surgeon
2	heralds
2	draconarii
1	cape bearer
1	trumpeter

1. See Watson, *Roman Soldier*, 22 (for cohorts) and 24–25 (for *alae*). On many points of military organization up to the seventh century, Grosse, *Römische Militärgeschichte*, though partly outdated, still supplies useful references to the sources.

2. Jones, *Later Roman Empire*, 626 (for actuarii and optiones), 634 (for centurions and decurions), and 674–75 (for the other officers).

3. Maurice, *Strategicon*, I.3, I.5, III.1, and XII.7.

> 1   drummer
> 60   decurions (commanding 8 men each including themselves)
> 420   common soldiers

Since Diocletian's time, each legion would have had two cohorts with this many men, plus the prefect who commanded the legion and at least a cape bearer for him. In practice, of course, most regiments would be slightly over or under strength. Papyri covering the years from 297 to 300 seem to show one legion of about 998 men and two cohorts of another legion with about 572 and 506 men respectively. A third legion has one cohort of about 554 men and another of about 439; but to the latter we should probably add a detachment of about 78 men, evidently an 80-man century, making 517 men in all. Soldiers from an independent cohort seem to come to about 164 men, but these probably represented only two of the cohort's centuries, four more being stationed elsewhere.[4] These numbers would not include the servants, who were sometimes slaves and sometimes relatives and attended almost all officers and a few of the common soldiers.[5]

An *ala*, a cavalry regiment of the old type, would presumably have had the same sorts of officers as a cohort except for the centurions and decurions. As in earlier times, the *ala* should still have had 16 decurions with commands of 30 men apiece including themselves. Though in the early empire *alae* had no centurions, by Byzantine times cavalry centurions had been introduced. Maurice's *Strategicon* refers to cavalry centurions, or hecatontarchs ("commanders of a hundred"), who were subordinates of the cavalry tribunes.[6] A papyrus written for a commander of an *ala* in the mid-fourth century already refers to a centurion (hecatontarch) who evidently belonged to that cavalry regiment.[7]

The official command of a cavalry centurion in the fourth century was probably 120 men. The papyri from 297 to 300 cited above show groups of cavalry from an *ala* that seem to number 121 and 116 or 118 men, evidently a quarter of the total strength.[8] Probably Diocletian created cavalry centurions to command just such detachments of cavalry as these when he distributed some *alae* among different forts. The official establishment of an *ala* would accordingly have been 499 men, including 4 centurions, 16 decurions, 464 troopers, and the other 15 officers listed above for a cohort.

Such were the older regiments. The new sorts of regiments—the infan-

---

4. Duncan-Jones, "Numbers and Pay," 546–49.
5. Jones, *Later Roman Empire*, 647.
6. Maurice, *Strategicon*, I.3.
7. *Abinnaeus Archive*, no. 80, p. 163.
8. Duncan-Jones, "Numbers and Pay," 546–49.

try *auxilia* and *pseudocomitatenses*, the cavalry vexillations and *cunei*, and the Scholae—had no officers called centurions or decurions, but a number of new ranks. St. Jerome gives a list of ranks for a cavalry regiment, which other sources show held good for infantry regiments as well. From the top to the bottom rank, the list is:

> tribune (*tribunus*)
> primicerius
> senator
> ducenarius
> centenarius
> biarchus
> circitor
> semissalis
> soldier (*eques, miles*)
> recruit (*tiro*)

These ranks clearly represent a hierarchy, and in fact most of them were used by analogy for grades in the bureaucracy.[9]

Yet the officers of these new regiments must also have had real functions, even if no one has yet clarified what all of them might be. The tribune and primicerius we already know from the older regiments. The recruit was a man who had not yet reached the rank of soldier; the soldier was an ordinary private and the semissalis was a more senior soldier who, at least originally, received pay and a half.[10] For other officers the evidence is not clear. The late fourth-century military writer Vegetius, describing the Roman legions as they had once been but no longer were, says that a ducenarius had once commanded 200 men, a centenarius had once commanded 100 men, and a circitor had been an inspector of the sentries, though the title of circitor "has now become a military rank."[11] This tells us little about actual conditions in Vegetius's time. A contemporary tombstone describes an officer who was both a biarchus and a draconarius, or standard bearer.[12] The double title shows that this rank and function, though compatible, were not equivalent.

The key to the problem is probably that almost every field army and frontier ducate had both older and newer regiments, so that they must have been ready to fight alongside each other or even combined with each other. Under such circumstances all regiments must have had virtually interchangeable command structures. The *Strategicon* of Maurice makes

9. Jones, *Later Roman Empire*, 633–34 and nn. 57 and 58.
10. Ibid., 633–34.
11. Vegetius, II.8 and III.8.
12. Hoffman, *Spätrömische Bewegungsheer*, I, 75.

no distinction between the old and new types of regiment, both of which continued to exist, but only between cavalry and infantry. The *Strategicon* mentions only tribunes, centurions, and decurions—with the alternative names of counts, hecatontarchs, and decarchs—all of whom the general commander could arrange on the battlefield however he wished. Even the newer regiments seem therefore to have had men who performed the functions of centurions and decurions.

The likely explanation would run as follows. Most centurions in these regiments held the rank of centenarius, as the similar name implies. But just as a semissalis had the same function as a common soldier but out-ranked him, so a decenarius had the same function as a centenarius or centurion but held a slightly higher rank. The next rank up, that of sena-tor, would be appropriate to a senior officer, an adjutor or perhaps a cam-pidoctor or actuarius. The two lower ranks of biarchus and circitor would be appropriate to decurions or junior officers, including draconarii and heralds. Though the number in each rank would vary according to how long the men had served, the number with each function would have stayed more or less the same, as in regiments of the older type. The system described by Jerome thus seems to conceal a basic uniformity under vari-ous old and new names.

About the fleets our information is meager. The only eastern fleets in the *Notitia* are low-ranking units of the Danube frontier ducates. The eastern empire must have had some sort of central fleet, since it never had trouble shipping troops west. It sent an enormous though unsuccessful expedition against the Vandals in 468, and a spectacularly successful ex-pedition against the Vandals in 532. But the early Byzantine navy was, like the earlier Roman one, mainly a vehicle for carrying armies. The only naval officers it needed were captains and pilots—probably, as in later Byzantine times, one captain and two pilots per vessel.[13] The reason that we hear of no other naval officers may well be that there were none.

Besides the staffs of the regiments, the commanders of the field armies and the frontier ducates had central bureaus of their own for administra-tive purposes. The *Notitia* shows that these were headed by a chief staff officer (*princeps*) and included a disciplinary officer (*commentariensis*), two head accountants (*numerarii*), clerks (*scrinarii*), and secretaries (*exceptores*). The Master of Soldiers of the East also had billeting officers (*mensores*). The staffs of masters of soldiers grew large, and in 441 they had to be capped at 300 men for each of the five eastern field armies. The frontier dukes had smaller staffs with officials of the same sorts, plus an official who transmitted petitions to the civil administration (*a libellis*).[14] In 534 Justin-

13. Leo VI, *Naumachica*, I.8, p. 20.
14. Jones, *Later Roman Empire*, 597–98.

ian set up five ducates for Africa with identical staffs, presumably modeled on similar staffs in the eastern ducates, each numbering 41 men.[15]

Such was the army proper. The imperial bodyguard of the Scholae was organized into cavalry regiments of the new type, each called a Schola.[16] In the East there were seven Scholae of 500 men each, making 3,500 men. Their senior officers were called domestics or protectors, and together with an extra adjutant for the tribune they apparently numbered ten to a Schola.[17] Besides the adjutant, these ten domestics were perhaps the Schola's vicarius, primicerius, adjutor, four cavalry centurions, campidoctor, and actuarius. An official called the Count of the Domestics supervised not only the domestics in the Scholae but other domestics, who were dispatched to serve as officers in units of the regular field armies and frontier ducates, and were sent on various other missions as well.[18] The Scholae enjoyed higher pay and higher status than the rest of the army, so that even their ordinary soldiers seem to have held the rank of circitor and kept at least one servant as a squire.[19]

The privileges of the Scholae, and the frequent use made of their members for civilian missions, gradually caused them to lose their fighting edge—except for the First Schola, which seems actually to have guarded the emperor. But even the First Schola declined after Leo I created the new elite guard of the Excubitors. Since the Excubitors had only 300 men, they cannot have been a full cavalry regiment of the regular sort.[20] Their officers, called scribons, were perhaps equivalent to cavalry decurions, so that the Excubitors had ten scribons commanding 30 men apiece including themselves.[21]

Relying on the Excubitors, Zeno allowed the Scholae to degenerate into parade-ground troops, and put places in them up for sale as prestige items for the rich. Justinian first sold 2,000 new positions in the Scholae, then dismissed the new recruits, and finally forced the 3,500 men of the original Scholae to give up their pay for long periods. By his time the government was probably making more money from the Scholae than it paid them in salaries. They became merely decorative, their old functions taken over by the Excubitors.[22]

15. *Justinian Code*, I.27(2).19–34.
16. From meaning a guardroom in the imperial palace, the name came to mean the guards in it; see Frank, *Scholae Palatinae*, 14–15.
17. Ibid., 52–58.
18. Ibid., 81–97.
19. Ibid., 56 (for the rank); and Jones, *Later Roman Empire*, 647 (for the servants).
20. John the Lydian, *On Magistrates*, I.16.
21. On the scribons, see Jones, *Later Roman Empire*, 658–59; in the ninth century they were senior officers of the Tagma of the Excubitors (see below, p. 102).
22. Frank, *Scholae Palatinae*, 201–19.

We have already seen that during the fourth century, while the overall size of the army remained much the same, the proportion of cavalry rose dramatically. Yet the *Notitia Dignitatum* shows that by 395 the cavalry were far more numerous among the frontier troops, whose status was markedly inferior to that of the field soldiers. Table 1 indicates that only some 20.7 percent of the field army was cavalry, compared with about 49.9 percent of the frontier forces. This is the reverse of what we would expect if the cavalry were the most important troops on the battlefield.

By the late fourth century, the frontier forces' main duties were not campaigning but patrolling and policing.[23] Such tasks could require a high degree of mobility, which was best achieved if many of them were mounted. The field armies, though they needed to have a cavalry arm and in particular cavalry scouts, usually marched rather slowly on their great expeditions. Around 395 the brunt of battles still seems to have been borne by the infantry, as in Roman times. To say that Byzantine soldiers of this period usually fought on horseback is therefore inaccurate, and at best an exaggeration.

MAURICE'S REGIMENTS

By the sixth century the army changed considerably. The changes went well beyond Justinian's removal from the payroll of the frontier forces, and virtually of the Scholae. As already noted, the *Strategicon* of Maurice still describes an army officered by hecatontarchs and decarchs, the terms already used as the Greek equivalents of centurions and decurions in the fourth century. But the *Strategicon* specifies that its hecatontarchs had commands of 100 men and its decarchs commands of 10 men, unlike any hecatontarchs or decarchs in the fourth century. It also mentions some entirely new officers: pentarchs, with commands of 5 men, and tetrarchs, leaders of rear guards whose title implies a command of 4 men.[24]

This terminology is self-consistent. It means that the decarch commanded 10 men including himself, the pentarch, and the tetrarch, while the pentarch commanded 5 men including himself, and the tetrarch commanded 4 men including himself. The two subordinates' commands add up to 9 rather than 10 men because the command of a pentarch or tetrarch naturally could not include their own commander, the decarch. The *Strategicon*'s battle diagrams bear these numbers out, showing hecatontarchs at the head of 10 lines of 10 men, with each line having a decarch in first

23. On the frontier troops' policing duties, see Isaac, *Limits of Empire*, esp. 89–99 and 161–218.
24. Maurice, *Strategicon*, I.3.

place, a pentarch in second place, and a tetrarch in the tenth and last place.[25]

Beyond this, the *Strategicon* says that the army's regiments (*banda*), commanded by a tribune or count, should vary between 200 and 400 men, so as to prevent the enemy from reckoning the army's size by counting the standards each bandum carried. The author later describes a sample regiment or bandum with 310 men, who include a tribune, standard bearer, cape bearer, and trumpeter. Such regiments are then grouped under chiliarchs, who despite a title that implies a command of a thousand (*chilias*) commanded between 2,000 and 3,000 men. The commands of these chiliarchs are then grouped into divisions (*merē*) under merarchs, who were to command no more than 6,000 or 7,000 men and on average commanded perhaps 5,000.[26]

Obviously these are battlefield formations, and in other places the author shifts troops into different patterns, sometimes mixing cavalry and infantry, with files varying from 2 deep to 16 deep. The *Strategicon*'s regiment of 200 to 400 men under a tribune, with its own standard, must be a regular 500-man regiment, minus 100 to 300 men not used on the campaign. The *Strategicon*'s chiliarchs seem to be commanders of the 1,000-man legions; since legions accounted for fewer than half the men in the eastern field armies at the time of the *Notitia*, on the battlefield the chiliarchs had to command at least 2,000 men, most of whom would not have been from their legion. This much is compatible with the military system of the fourth century.

Yet in the *Strategicon* the hecatontarchs who command 100 men, instead of 80 or 120, and the decarchs who command 10 men, instead of 8 or 30, seem to be different from the centurions and decurions of the fourth century and earlier. The pentarchs, who command 5 men, and tetrarchs, who command 4 men, are unlike any officers in the traditional system. While the *Strategicon* defines the tribune as the commander of a battlefield regiment of variable size, it defines the hecatontarch and decarch specifically as commanders of 100 men and 10 men. It also states that "until the present" all decarchies in all divisions have consisted of 10 men, even on the battlefield. Though the author recommends that in the future decarchies should vary from 5 to 10 men to confuse enemy spies, here he is clearly referring only to battlefield formations, not to regular establishments.[27]

The commands of centurions and decurions seem therefore to have been standardized, at least in the field armies, at 100 men and 10 men for both cavalry and infantry at some date. This was perhaps the same date

25. Ibid., III.1–4.
26. Ibid., I.4 and III.2–4.
27. Ibid., II.6.

when the field armies were standardized at multiples of 5,000 men. Five thousand men is the approximate size of a division (*meros*) in the *Strategicon*, which corresponds to no formation in the earlier army—though it is close to the 5,500-man strength of the legions before Diocletian. The date when this division was introduced seems to have been before 499, and I have already suggested that it came in the reign of Zeno, who reorganized recruitment after dismissing many barbarian troops.[28]

The aim of this whole organizational reform was probably to make the units easier to combine into different formations of the type found in the *Strategicon*. The change in the size of the commands of the decarchs was probably made in the Excubitors as well, since they remained an important unit as late as the seventh century, before they finally declined like the Scholae.[29] Whether the reform of the sizes of units was applied to the deteriorating Scholae and border troops is uncertain; but most likely it was, since they were still officially parts of the army in the late fifth century. Table 4 shows how the reform changed the command structure.

The change was a fairly easy one to make, though it probably involved adding a few men, perhaps only by upgrading recruits to soldiers. While the old regiments had theoretically numbered 501 for infantry and 499 for cavalry, the new regiments would theoretically have numbered 520 for both:

1	tribune
1	vicarius
1	primicerius
1	adjutor
5	hecatontarchs (commanding 100 men each)
1	campidoctor
1	actuarius
1	optio
1	surgeon
2	heralds
2	draconarii
1	cape bearer
1	trumpeter
1	drummer
50	decarchs (commanding 10 men each including themselves)
50	pentarchs (commanding 5 men each including themselves)
50	tetrarchs (commanding 4 men each including themselves)
350	common soldiers

28. See above, pp. 14 and 61.
29. Cf. Haldon, *Byzantine Praetorians*, 139 and 161–64.

TABLE 4
Development of Command Structures, pre-290 to post-959

	Size of command				
	To ca. 290		Ca. 290–480		Ca. 480–660
Officer	Infantry	Cavalry	Infantry	Cavalry	(all troops)
legate of legion	5,500				5,000?[a]
(merarch)[b]	(legate)	—	—	—	(merarch)
prefect of legion			1,000		1,000
(chiliarch)	—	—	(prefect)	—	(chiliarch)
tribune (count)	500	500	500	500	500
centurion					
(hecatontarch)	80	—	80	120	100
—	—	—	—	—	—
decurion (decarch)	8	30	8	30	10
pentarch	—	—	–ᴄ	—	5

[a] See pp. 93–95.
[b] "Meriarch" is the later (but less correct) form of "merarch."

This total would again omit servants, who seem to have become more common since the army's pay had increased. The author of the *Strategicon* requires all cavalrymen to have squires, though if they are unusually poor he is willing to let as many as four of them share a squire.[30]

The legions and other regiments survived the reform, commanded by their chiliarchs or tribunes, and they were joined by some categories of troops introduced since the time of the *Notitia*. Besides the Federates, introduced in 578 by Tiberius, the *Strategicon* mentions the Optimates ("Best Men"), an elite cavalry corps, and the Illyriciani and Vexillations, cavalry ranking higher than ordinary cavalry but lower than the Optimates.[31] Though the *Notitia Dignitatum* mentions some Illyriciani among the cavalry of the eastern border ducates, the *Strategicon*'s Illyriciani were evidently mobile troops, either recruited after 395 or transferred from the border ducates into the field army.[32] In the *Notitia* vexillations are a type of cavalry regiment, but in the *Strategicon* they are evidently particular cavalry regiments, like the Optimates or Illyriciani.

Since the *Strategicon* speaks of divisions (*merē*) of Federates, Illyriciani, and Vexillations but only regiments (*banda*) of Optimates, the Optimates probably numbered at least 1,000 men but fewer than 5,000, while the others numbered at least 5,000. The Federates, with 15,000 men, would

30. Maurice, *Strategicon*, I.2.
31. Ibid., I.2 (Federates), I.3 (Optimates), I.4 (Optimates), II.6 (Federates, Vexillations, Illyriciani, Optimates), II.11 (Optimates, Federates), III.6 (Federates), III.7 (Optimates), and III.8 (Vexillations, Federates, Illyriciani).
32. *Notitia Dignitatum*, Or. XXXI–XXXVII.

TABLE 4 *(continued)*

Officer	Size of command				
	Ca. 660– 840 (themes)	Ca. 743– 902 (tagmata)	Ca. 840– 902 (themes)	Ca. 902–59 (themes and tagmata)	From ca. 959 (themes and tagmata)
turmarch (topoteretes, meriarch)[b]	2,000– 5,000	2,000	1,000– 5,000	800– 2,400	800– 3,000
drungary (chiliarch)	1,000	—	400– 1,000	400– 1,000	400–1,000 (themes only)
count	—	200	200	200	200
hecatontarch (centarch)	100	40	40	100	100
pentecontarch (tribune)	50	—	—	50	50
decarch	10	10	10	10	10
pentarch	5	5	5	5	5

have had three divisions. In the eighth century, 2,000 Optimates remained; perhaps this was the original number, since the praesental armies of which they had been a part had suffered fairly light casualties. We shall see that the Federates and two fourth-century regiments, the Theodosiaci and the Victores, continued to exist in the ninth and tenth centuries.[33] Many other units whose names happen not to be mentioned in the later sources must have survived as well.

The frontier troops did not survive the seventh century, but they did survive the loss of their pay in 545, and are still found up to the Persian conquest. Their pay had long been so meager that they had had to find other means of supplementing it. They still received some rations or ration allowances, and enjoyed some legal privileges, often including lands that they cultivated.[34] Dukes who commanded border troops continued to be appointed in Syria and Egypt, even by Heraclius when he recovered them from the Persians. After conquering Syria, the Arabs maintained four military provinces there that apparently continued the ducates of Palestine, Arabia, Phoenice, and Syria.[35] The border troops may have be-

33. See below, pp. 99–100.
34. See Jones, *Later Roman Empire*, 661–63, 671–73, and 678; and below, pp. 171–72.
35. The existence of these provinces—the *ajnād* (sg. *jund*) of Palestine, Jordan, Damascus, and Homs (Emesa)—was first pointed out by Shahid, "Heraclius and the Theme System," and "Heraclius and the Theme System: Further Observations." Though Shahid argued persuasively that the *ajnād* continued Byzantine military districts, his contention that they were equivalent to themes seems incompatible with the other evidence for the themes' development. (The *ajnād* were first identified with the ducates by Haldon, *Byzantium*, 215 n. 27.) I doubt that Phoenice had two commanders in the sixth century, as Shahid indicates in his later article (1989: 216 n. 25). Though Procopius, *Wars*, I.13.5 and II.8.2,

come little more than a militia used for emergency police duty, something like the National Guard in the United States; but they nonetheless kept the same military organization and officers as before.

Though the precepts in the *Strategicon* must be referring only to the fully professional soldiers of the field armies, the author's main concern is with cavalry. While he stresses the importance of infantry tactics, he observes that they were a neglected subject in his day, and he himself says that a general is better off with more cavalry than infantry, especially because cavalry can always dismount and fight on foot.[36] Though cavalry made up barely a fifth of the field armies in the late fourth century, new cavalry seem to have been added in the meantime, and doubtless included the Optimates, Vexillations, Illyriciani, and some of the Federates. On the other hand, Justinian seems to have assigned the field Army of Africa 10,000 infantry and 5,000 cavalry, or only a third cavalry.[37] We shall see that the proportions of cavalry and infantry in the mobile forces during Maurice's reign can be estimated by looking at later developments.

FROM LEGION TO THEME

The *Strategicon* of Maurice gives the last account of military organization before the creation of the themes. Our first glimpse of military organization afterward comes in a text from the *Miracles of St. Demetrius* that mentions events to be dated between 678 and 685, and most probably between 682 and 684. The story refers to "centarchs, pentecontarchs, and decarchs" assigned as officers of irregular troops raised in an emergency at Thessalonica.[38] Though Thessalonica was not part of a theme at that time, the local authorities seem to have organized their irregulars on the pattern of regular soldiers in the themes, because the *Life of St. Philaretus*, referring to a mustering of thematic troops that occurred about 785, refers to chiliarchs, hecatontarchs, and pentecontarchs.[39]

Presumably the former text omits chiliarchs because Thessalonica mustered fewer than a thousand irregulars, while the latter text omits decarchs

---

16.17, and 19.22, speaks of two commanders of "soldiers in Lebanon," in the latter two passages he describes their areas of concern as "Phoenice and Syria," which may well have been their commands, since Homs is as near to Mt. Lebanon as Damascus is. While the later *jund* of Homs extended into Mesopotamia, just before the Arab conquest in 638 Osrhoëne still had a commander with full powers who was probably its duke (Theophanes, 340). There is of course no reason why the empire could not sometimes have shifted the boundaries of its ducates, or the caliphate the boundaries of its *ajnād*.

36. Maurice, *Strategicon*, XII B preface, VIII.2 (85).
37. See above, p. 60.
38. Lemerle, *Plus anciens recueils*, I, 224 (translation) and 230 (text); and II, 161 (date).
39. See *Life of Philaretus*, 125–27; for the date, see Treadgold, *Byzantine State Finances*, 137 n. 299.

because they were such junior officers. Both texts omit the still more junior pentarchs, but pentarchs and tetrarchs reappear in a text of the early tenth century, and are unlikely to have ceased to exist in the meantime. The centarchs of the *Miracles* are clearly the same as the hecatontarchs of the *Life of Philaretus* or centurions of the earlier period. Chiliarchs, hecatontarchs, and decarchs are already found in the *Strategicon*, and went back all the way to the legionary prefects, centurions, and decurions. But the pentecontarchs, "commanders of fifty men," are new, and may well date from the foundation of the themes. This may also be the date when the tribunes disappeared, leaving no officer between the chiliarchs commanding a thousand men and centarchs commanding a hundred men.

Ranking above the chiliarchs were the strategi, corresponding to the old masters of soldiers of the field armies that had become the themes. But there was also an officer ranking between the strategus and chiliarch, the turmarch. Although the scanty sources for the seventh and eighth centuries fail to mention turmarchs, they were evidently the descendants of the merarchs who headed the divisions (*merē*) of some 5,000 men in the *Strategicon*. Around 900 Philotheus and the *Tactica* of Leo VI give the turmarch serving with the strategus the title of meriarch, a variant of merarch.[40] In 840 the commands of turmarchs seem to have varied from 5,000 to 2,000 men, and the total number of turmarchs was evidently 26.[41]

In the ninth century the senior turmarch of the Anatolic Theme was the Turmarch of the Federates.[42] His men were of course the descendants of the Federates that Tiberius had attached to the Army of the East before it became the Theme of the Anatolics. The Optimates of the *Strategicon* are to be identified with the Optimates whom Constantine V separated from the Opsician Theme and settled in their own district in Bithynia. Their decline in status from an elite cavalry corps to a mere baggage corps is an indication that they had fallen into disgrace, perhaps because they had been particularly eager supporters of the rebel Artavasdus in 741–43.

In 949 the Theme of the Thracesians had, in order of rank, a Turmarch of the Theodosiaci, a Turmarch of the Victores, a Turmarch of the Seacoast, and a meriarch.[43] The Theodosiaci dated from the reign of Theodosius I. They appear in the *Notitia Dignitatum* as the third-ranking regiment in the Army of Thrace, and at that time were a vexillation with the full title of Equites Theodosiaci Juniores.[44] Evidently this regiment's name

40. See Oikonomidès, *Listes*, 108–9 and n. 65.
41. Cf. Treadgold, "Notes," 280–84. I count 3 turmarchs each for the Anatolics and the Armeniacs, 2 each for the Thracesians and Bucellarians, and 1 each for the other 16 themes and cleisurae.
42. Ibid., 280–83.
43. Treadgold, "Army," 125–26.
44. *Notitia Dignitatum*, Or. VIII.27.

had later been applied to the whole division of which it became a part. The Latin name of the Victores shows that they too went back to the early Byzantine period; probably they were the auxilium of Victores listed in the *Notitia* as part of the first praesental army, and if so they were transferred to the Army of Thrace at some time after 395.[45]

The Thracesians' other turmarch and meriarch must date from after 840, since at that date Jarmī assigned the Thracesians only two turmarchs.[46] In 840, according to the information from Jarmī, each turmarch commanded 5,000 men, the apparent command of one of the *Strategicon*'s meriarchs.[47] But before the Thracesians received 2,000 Khurramites in 840, each turmarch had presumably commanded 4,000 men. Both turmae had thus taken their names from one of their original regiments, and this was probably the pattern in other themes, though no other original names of turmae seem to appear in the sources. The turmarch was the superior of his turma's chiliarchs, now more often called drungaries.

Like his predecessor the master of soldiers, the strategus of a theme had his own staff. Besides the theme's turmarch or turmarchs, it included an adjutant known as the count of the tent and an officer called the domestic, who was probably in charge of the theme's scouts, surveyors, and medics. Next came the chartulary in charge of the theme's muster roll, the protocancellarius heading a half-dozen or so clerks, and the protomandator heading the theme's heralds or mandators. Table 5 illustrates the phases of the organization of the themes, using the Thracesians as an example.

Until 840, one of the centarchs with his 100 men formed the strategus's personal guard, the spatharii. When the centarchs' commands were reduced to 40 men apiece in 840, the strategus was assigned two companies of guards, called the spatharii and the hetaeria, for a total of 80. When the centarch's command rose to 100 men again around 902, that again became the number of the strategus's guard. Interestingly, as late as 949 those guards were infantry, not cavalry.[48] Strategi could also call up the civilian population to serve as irregular troops, either in forts under commanders called "protectors of the forts," or in the field under commanders called "drungaries of the foot."[49]

Naval themes were organized in the same way as other themes, with turmarchs, drungaries, centarchs, and so on, for their marines. But for

45. Ibid., Or. V.63. These are the only Victores listed in the East, though three others are listed in the West (ibid., Oc. V.185 and 215 and VII.17).

46. Treadgold, "Notes," 283–84.

47. Treadgold, *Byzantine State Finances*, 18–19.

48. See Treadgold, *Byzantine Revival*, 29–31, though in the chart the commands of centarchs should add up to 9 and not 10, and the centarch of the spatharii should command infantry, not cavalry; see Treadgold, "Army," 104–6 (on the decarchs) and 126 (on the guards).

49. Treadgold, *Byzantine State Finances*, 33–34.

TABLE 5
Development of the Thracesian Theme, 660 to post-936

Rank	Ca. 660–840	Ca. 840–902	Ca. 902–36	From ca. 936
		Number in rank		
strategus	1 (1:8,000)	1 (1:10,000)	1 (1:9,600)	1 (1:9,600)
turmarchs	2 (1:4,000) [a]	2 (1:5,000) [b]	4 (1:2,400) [c]	4 (1:2,400) [d]
count of the tent	1	1	1	1
chartulary	1	1	1	1
domestic	1	1	1	1
drungaries [e]	8 (1:1,000)	10 (1:1,000)	24 (1:400)	24 (1:400)
counts	—	50 (1:200)	48 (1:200)	48 (1:200)
protocancellarius	1	1	1	1
protomandator	1	1	1	1
protobandophorus	—	—	—	1
protodomestics	—	—	—	24
protocentarchs	—	—	—	24
centarchs	80 (1:100) [f]	250 (1:40) [g]	96 (1:100)	96 (1:100)
pentecontarchs	160 (1:50)	—	192 (1:50) [h]	192 (1:50) [h]
decarchs	800 (1:10)	1,000 (1:10)	960 (1:10)	960 (1:10)
common soldiers	7,200	9,000	8,640	8,640
TOTALS	8,256	10,318	9,970	10,019

[a] Turmarchs of the Theodosiaci and Victores.
[b] Turmarchs of the Theodosiaci and Victores.
[c] Turmarchs of the Theodosiaci, Victores, and Seacoast; and Meriarch.
[d] Turmarchs of the Theodosiaci, Victores, and Seacoast; and Meriarch.
[e] Also known as chiliarchs.
[f] Including the centarch of the spatharii, commander of the strategus's bodyguard. Of these centarchs, 64 (including the centarch of the spatharii) commanded infantry, and 16 commanded cavalry.
[g] Including the centarch of the spatharii and the count of the hetaeria, commanders of the strategus's two bodyguards. Of these centarchs, 200 (including the centarch of the spatharii and count of the hetaeria) commanded infantry, and 50 commanded cavalry.
[h] Including the centarch of the spatharii and the count of the hetaeria, commanders of the strategus's two bodyguards. Of these pentecontarchs, 144 (including the centarch of the spatharii and count of the hetaeria) commanded infantry, and 48 commanded cavalry.

their oarsmen the naval themes had captains of ships, confusingly called centarchs, and pilots, called protocarabi ("heads of ships") though each ship had two of them. The Mardaïte oarsmen of the Cibyrrhaeots had their own commander, the Catepan of the Mardaïtes of Attalia, appointed directly by the emperor like a strategus. This catepan was supposed to obey the Strategus of the Cibyrrhaeots, but the two occasionally quarreled over their jurisdictions.[50] Until the ninth century the central fleet at Constantinople seems to have had no marines of its own, and simply transported troops from other units, as earlier Byzantine fleets had done. The central fleet did have an admiral, the Drungary of the Imperial Fleet, with a staff and oarsmen, and presumably centarchs and protocarabi, for its ships.[51]

50. Cf. Constantine VII, *De Administrando Imperio*, 50, pp. 240–42.
51. See Treadgold, *Byzantine State Finances*, 32–33.

In the eighth century Constantine V organized the tagmata somewhat differently from the themes. Tagmatic officers had a bewildering variety of names that recall their origins in the early Byzantine period, but conceal an identical command structure. The tagmata had no equivalents of the themes' turmarchs, chiliarchs, or pentecontarchs. Instead they had officers called topoteretae who commanded 2,000 men each and counts (scribons for the Excubitors) who commanded 200 men each. In the tagmata Constantine V reduced the commands of centarchs, some of whom received different titles, from 100 to 40 men. The tagmatic regiments of 200 men were called standards or banda, like the regiments of 200 to 400 commanded by tribunes in the *Strategicon*; and also like those predecessors, they had two standard bearers and two heralds apiece.[52]

Since themes and tagmata often fought together, on the battlefield both of them probably continued to use banda, five of which could easily be formed from the thousand-man commands of the drungaries. Since the tagmata were supposed to be ready to go into battle as a whole, they, unlike the themes, had banda built into their command structure. They also had a small staff of officers, with the two subordinate commanders called topoteretae, apparently one for the part of the tagma settled in Europe and one for the part settled in Asia. Then came a chartulary to keep the tagma's muster roll, and a protomandator in charge of its heralds. In two tagmata the protomandators had the special titles of proximus ("first secretary") or acoluthus ("attendant").

The heralds and standard bearers of the tagmata, unlike those of the themes, had the rank of junior officers. Many also had special titles derived from the standards they carried, like sceptrophori ("scepter carriers") or draconarii ("dragon carriers"), or taken from officers of the old Scholae and Excubitors, like protectors and senators. These officers were nonetheless drawn from the ranks, and were included in their tagma's complement of 4,000 men.[53] All the members of the cavalry tagmata had squires. Of the infantry tagmata, the Numera and Walls, as garrison units, had no standard bearers, and the Optimates, as a support unit, had no standard bearers or heralds, though they had a protocancellarius to help administer their miniature theme.[54] Table 6 illustrates the development of the tagmata, using the Scholae as an example.

Probably from the time of Constantine V himself, the leading officers of each tagma, except for the Optimates, were invited to dine with the emperor on one of the twelve days of Christmas. Each tagma's officers filled the imperial banquet hall of the Nineteen Couches, where an extra

52. Leo VI, *Tactica*, IV.10 and IV.35, cols. 701D and 705D.
53. See Treadgold, "Army," 104–6.
54. See Treadgold, *Byzantine Revival*, 27–28, though there the command of a decarch should again add up to 9, not 10; cf. Treadgold, "Army," 104–6.

TABLE 6
Development of the Tagma of the Scholae, 743 to post-959

Rank	Ca. 743–902	Ca. 902–36	Ca. 936–59	From ca. 959
	Number in rank			
domestic	1 (1:4,000)	1 (1:4,000)	1 (1:4,000)	2 (1:3,000) [a]
topoteretae	2 (1:2,000) [b]	2 (1:2,000) [b]	2 (1:2,000) [b]	2 (1:3,000) [c]
chartulary	1	1	1	2
drungaries	—	4 (1:1,000)	10 (1:400)	—
counts	20 (1:200)	20 (1:200)	20 (1:200)	30 (1:200)
centarchs	100 (1:40)	40 (1:100)	40 (1:100)	60 (1:100)
tribunes	—	80 (1:50)	80 (1:50)	120 (1:50)
protomandator	1	1	1	2
protobandophorus	—	—	1	2
bandophori	40	40	40	60
mandators	40	40	40	60
decarchs	400 (1:10)	400 (1:10)	400 (1:10)	600 (1:10)
common soldiers	3,520	3,520	3,520	5,280
TOTALS	4,125	4,149	4,156	6,180

[a] One domestic of the East and one domestic of the West.
[b] One in Thrace and one in Bithynia.
[c] One topoteretes of the East and one topoteretes of the West.

two couches had to be brought in to accommodate them. They reclined at their tables in the ancient fashion along with twelve other dignitaries, including their commander, and twelve paupers invited out of charity. Until 959 the officers of all four cavalry tagmata had the numbers shown for the Scholae in Table 6. Table 7 lists the rather complicated titles of the tagmatic officers and gives their equivalents in the themes.

The guest lists of the four cavalry tagmata for the emperor's Christmas banquets were as follows: [55]

2	topoteretae
1	chartulary
20	counts (scribons)
100	centarchs (domestics, draconarii)
1	protomandator (proximus, acoluthus)
40	standard bearers (protectors, eutychophori, sceptrophori, axiomatici, draconarii, sceuophori, signophori, senators, bandophori, laburesii, semiophori, ducinators)
40	mandators (thurori, legatarii, diatrechontes)
204	officers total

Dining with the emperor was naturally a special mark of favor, shared only by the highest officials of the bureaucracy.

55. For a more detailed explanation of the guest lists, see Treadgold, "Notes," 273–77.

TABLE 7
Officers of the Tagmata, ca. 743 to 902

Equivalent in the themes	Scholae	Excubitors	Watch	Hicanati
strategus	domestic	domestic	drungary	domestic
turmarch	topoteretes	topoteretes	topoteretes	topoteretes
chartulary	chartulary	chartulary	chartulary	chartulary
count	count	scribon	count	count
centarch	domestic	draconarius	centarch	centarch
count of the hetaeria	—	—	—	—
protocan- cellarius	—	—	—	—
protomandator	proximus	protomandator	acoluthus	protomandator
bandophorus	protector	draconarius	bandophorus	bandophorus
	eutychophorus	sceuophorus	laburesius	semiophorus
	sceptrophorus	signophorus	semiophorus	semiophorus
	axiomaticus	senator	ducinator	ducinator
mandator	mandator	mandator	mandator	mandator
	—	legatarius	legatarius	legatarius
	—	—	thurorus	—
	—	—	diatrechon	—

The army underwent more changes in the ninth and tenth centuries. In 840 Theophilus altered the organization of the themes to make it resemble the tagmata's more closely. Though he retained the themes' turmarchs and drungaries, he introduced from the tagmata the 200-man banda commanded by counts, and as in the tagmata he reduced the commands of centarchs from 100 to 40 men. Since the reduced commands of the centarchs made the pentecontarchs' commands of 50 men redundant, Theophilus abolished the rank of pentecontarch, which seems never to have existed in the tagmata. In practice, Theophilus probably promoted all his pentecontarchs to centarch, since he had been careful to leave the total number of officers the same, at 31 per 1,000-man drungus.[56] Theophilus's main purpose in this reform was doubtless to make the themes easier to combine with the tagmata on expeditions. But his reform also made the themes more effective for purposes of defense, as we shall see.[57]

When Basil I recruited marines for the Imperial Fleet about 870 he gave them an organization comparable to those of the four cavalry tagmata. It too appears in Table 7. The marines of the Fleet had no standard bearers, which on shipboard at least they did not need. Their commander, the Drungary of the Fleet, ranked lower than the commanders of cavalry tagmata but higher than those of infantry tagmata, and had a bodyguard

56. It had formerly been 1 drungary, 10 centarchs, and 20 pentecontarchs; Theophilus made it 1 drungary, 5 counts, and 25 centarchs.
57. See below, pp. 109–10.

TABLE 7 (*continued*)

Equivalent in the themes	Fleet (after ca. 870)	Numera	Optimates	Walls
strategus	drungary	domestic	domestic	count
turmarch	topoteretes	topoteretes	topoteretes	topoteretes
chartulary	chartulary	chartulary	chartulary	chartulary
count	count	tribune	count	tribune
centarch	centarch	vicar	centarch	vicar
count of the hetaeria	count of the hetaeria	—	—	—
protocan- cellarius	—	—	protocan- cellarius	—
protomandator	protomandator	protomandator	—	protomandator
bandophorus	—	—	—	—
	—	—	—	—
	—	—	—	—
	—	—	—	—
mandator	mandator	legatarius	—	legatarius
	—	mandator	—	mandator
	—	—	—	—
	—	—	—	—

headed by a count of the hetaeria. Since the fleet already had ships and oarsmen before 870, it would likewise have had centarchs and protocarabi to be captains and pilots for them.

About 902 Leo VI made another major change in the command structure. His *Tactica* summarize the officers for a force of 4,000 picked men as follows: [58]

2	turmarchs (i.e., one for each turma, 2,000 men)
4	drungaries/chiliarchs (one for each drungus, 1,000 men)
20	counts (one for each bandum, 200 men)
40	centarchs/hecatontarchs (one for each 100 men)
80	tribunes/pentecontarchs (one for each 50 men)
400	decarchs (one for each 10 men)
800	pentarchs (one for each 5 men)
1,346	officers total

In practice Leo sometimes modified this scheme. Of course it could vary on the battlefield, where Leo notes that the count's bandum could be enlarged from 200 men to as many as 400, the drungus to as many as 3,000, and the turma to as many as 6,000.[59] In some themes Leo reduced the 1,000-man command of the drungary to 400, permitting himself to

58. Leo VI, *Tactica*, XVIII.149, col. 988A, with XVIII.143 and 145, cols. 981C and 985B for Leo's characterizations of the whole force.
59. Ibid., IV.41–45, cols. 708C–709A.

create themes, cleisurae, and turmae that did not divide evenly into thousands. Turmarchs now had commands that could be as small as 800 men, though some were still as large as 2,400.[60] Drungaries now had variable commands in the themes; but they seem to have been introduced into the tagmata with their original command of 1,000 men.[61] Leo increased the command of a centarch from 40 back to 100 men. He also created a new officer he called a tribune, commanding 50 men.[62]

The purpose of this final change must have been to expand the cavalry. In the middle of the tenth century the *Military Precepts* of Nicephorus II specify that a bandum of cavalry, evidently meaning the cavalry within a 200-man bandum, had 50 men.[63] This was the command of a tribune, a name that Leo VI may have chosen because he knew that in earlier times tribunes had been the most senior officers who could command units that were all cavalry. But no tribunes had existed in the later ninth century, just before Leo's reform. Since the nearest equivalent to a tribune had then been the 40-man unit of a centarch, that was presumably the level at which cavalry and infantry units had become distinct before 902. Thus Leo seems to have raised the proportion of cavalry in most themes from a fifth to a quarter, no doubt by supplying some of the infantry with horses.

Like a theme, a turma, and before 902 a drungus, a bandum of a theme was not only a body of soldiers but the district where those soldiers were settled on their military lands. Since no military district smaller than a bandum existed, the lands of cavalry and infantry must have been interspersed around their bandum. Before Theophilus created the territorial bandum in 840, cavalry and infantry must have been settled throughout their 1,000-man drungus. Yet they fought in such different ways that they cannot have belonged to the same units. The smallest units were then the 50-man commands of the pentecontarchs, which were the same size as the later cavalry banda. If the proportion of thematic cavalry was a fifth before 840, as it appears to have been afterward, each drungus would have had four cavalry pentecontarchs, who presumably served under two cavalry centarchs.

The proportion of one-fifth cavalry almost certainly did hold good for the themes before 840. The alternatives are to assume either that some centarchs then commanded a mixture of cavalry and infantry, which would have been impractical, or that cavalry before 840 were as few as a tenth or as many as three-tenths. A fraction as low as a tenth seems impossible, in view of the obvious importance of cavalry in the sixth century. But a fraction as high as three-tenths would mean that Theophilus

60. See Treadgold, "Army," 93–99, 107–9, and 125–28.
61. See ibid., 106 and 130–34.
62. Ibid., 89–91.
63. Nicephorus II, *Military Precepts*, 12.

cut the cavalry in half, though he had vast sums of money and his reforms made the army more mobile and efficient. Therefore Theophilus seems to have left the ratio of cavalry to infantry as it had been, settling his Khurramites in such a way that each bandum had the same ratio as the whole theme.

The number of cavalry in the whole army, however, was not simply the number of soldiers in the themes divided by five—or after 902 by four. The tagmata were either all cavalry or all infantry. Naval themes had no cavalry among their marines; for this purpose, the naval themes were the Cibyrrhaeots and Hellas, the original naval themes, and Peloponnesus, Cephalonia, and Nicopolis, which had been settled with the Mardaïtes of the West. After 934, though apparently not before, some new themes on the eastern frontier were all cavalry. The cavalry proportion of a fifth should nonetheless apply to themes descended from the old mobile armies of the East, Armenia, and Thrace. It did not apply to themes descended from the Army of Illyricum, if that is indeed the origin of the Cibyrrhaeots and Hellas, and may not have applied to the Opsician Theme before the tagmata were separated from it.

If this reconstruction is correct, the Anatolic, Armeniac, and Thracesian themes should have had armies that were 20 percent cavalry from the time of their creation. Strikingly, in the *Notitia Dignitatum* cavalry form 20.7 percent of the eastern mobile armies, as Table 1 shows. A quarter of the Army of the East was cavalry, which should have been more than enough to give the Anatolics a fifth. Though the Army of Armenia did not yet exist at the time of the *Notitia*, it may well have had about the same proportion of cavalry as the Army of the East, which it often joined in fighting the Persians. While the Army of Illyricum was just 5.7 percent cavalry, no theme descended from it seems to have had any cavalry whatever. Though the Army of Thrace was only 14.2 percent cavalry, it had suffered losses of 60 percent, and probably more of its cavalry than of its infantry escaped the Avars and Slavs.

In the *Notitia* the two praesental armies are 28.6 percent cavalry. After Constantine V divided the Opsician Theme, the cavalry in its components would have been as follows:

Unit	Strength	Cavalry
Scholae, Excubitors, Watch	12,000	12,000
Numera, Walls, Optimates	6,000	0
Opsician, Bucellarians, Thrace	16,000	3,200
TOTAL	34,000	15,200 (44.7%)

Though Constantine V may well have upgraded some infantry to cavalry when he founded the cavalry tagmata, such an increase would have been partly offset by his degrading the Optimates from cavalry to support troops. The possibility therefore remains that the proportion of cavalry in the original Opsician Theme could have been three-tenths (30%) under three cavalry centarchs, or even two-fifths (40%) under four cavalry centarchs. Thus a good many more cavalry might have been added to the praesental armies during the two centuries after 395, and then have become part of the original Opsician Theme.

Nevertheless, despite the impression given by Maurice's *Strategicon*, the mobile armies of the sixth century must have been well over half infantry. Even if we disregard the similarity between the 20.7 percent of the mobile armies that were cavalry in 395 and the 20 percent of the themes that were cavalry later, assuming any large increase in cavalry between the fourth and sixth centuries, except in the praesental armies, would lead to the highly improbable conclusion that the mobile armies lost many more cavalry than infantry in the seventh century.

We can now form an approximate idea of how Constans II settled the mobile armies around 660 when he turned them into the themes. The empire's remaining territory in Anatolia, Thrace, and Greece was divided into drungi, regions with enough imperial estates or vacant land to support 1,000 soldiers, 200 of whom would be cavalry with presumably larger allotments. The praesental armies may have had somewhat more cavalry, so that in the Opsician Theme the number of cavalry in a drungus could have been 300 or 400. The remnants of the Army of Illyricum, which had never had much cavalry, were probably settled in drungi without cavalry in the Carabisian Theme to serve as marines. These armies and their divisions were probably settled in territories that corresponded more or less to the stations they then occupied. Distinctions among the old regiments were apparently disregarded. Most regiments would have been depleted and scrambled in the chaos of the earlier seventh century, though some of their names were still attached to the divisions.

Michael Hendy and others have supposed that the borders of the original themes mostly corresponded with existing provincial boundaries. Such an arrangement would obviously have been convenient for administrative purposes. The boundaries of both provinces and themes at the time are uncertain enough that such an hypothesis cannot be disproved, though it clashes somewhat with the little evidence we have.[64] Yet if the available land failed to fit the old provincial boundaries, other boundaries could have been used. What would have mattered most was not adminis-

---

64. See Hendy, *Studies*, 623, with his maps on pp. 102 and 105. Hendy's boundaries are highly schematized, and even so he must divide the province of Phrygia Salutaris between the Opsician and Anatolic themes, Caria between the Cibyrrhaeots (originally the Carabisians) and the Thracesians, Galatia I between the Bucellarians (originally the Opsician) and the Anatolics, and Isauria between the Cibyrrhaeots (originally the Carabisians) and Seleucia (originally the Anatolics).

trative convenience, or even strategic considerations, but simply getting the troops set up on land grants so that they could support themselves as quickly as possible.

THE ARMY OF CONQUEST

As it turned out, the themes functioned rather well for defensive purposes. The troops, originally settled in about 80 drungi covering most of the empire, were near at hand wherever the enemy might strike, and had an obvious reason to want to keep lands that belonged to them. After Nicephorus I and Theophilus expanded the themes and Theophilus made the banda into districts, the troops were settled in about 480 banda covering even more territory in much smaller commands. When the enemy invaded, the soldiers often fled, to the nearest fort or to an even safer place farther away; but after the invaders left, the soldiers returned to the stations that were their homes. The Arabs thus found Anatolia easy to raid regularly, but almost impossible to conquer permanently.

For offensive purposes the themes were less good. Mustering them at all required sending heralds all over each theme to almost as many different places as there were soldiers, then waiting for the men to assemble. Although the frequent Arab and Bulgar raids insured that many thematic soldiers had experience defending forts, the soldiers had less experience marching or riding, and less interest in campaigning far from their homes. In regions that had been free from invaders for some time, which later came to cover much of the empire, the soldiers naturally tended to get out of training.

Theophilus improved the themes' offensive capabilities. His creation of the banda helped tighten supervision of the soldiers by making senior officers responsible for every 200 men instead of a thousand. In comparison with drungaries, the counts of the banda could call up their men on much shorter notice for drilling, offensive campaigns, or even an improvised defense against a sudden invasion. As long as thematic soldiers were called up periodically for campaigns, they were kept trained for battle. On major expeditions thematic troops campaigned together with troops from the tagmata, who provided an example of greater experience and even better training. As more professional soldiers, the troops of the tagmata ranked ahead of those of the themes, but only just ahead.

Since the tagmata were primarily field troops, the emperors needed bodyguards as well, probably as early as the time when the Excubitors were absorbed by the tagmata. Therefore Constantine V may well have created the bodyguard known as the Imperials, which served under a commander known as the Protospatharius of the Imperials or of the Hippodrome. According to a text derived from al-Jarmī, in 840 these guardsmen of the Hippodrome numbered 400—that is, two banda.[65] To the Imperials some other guards were added, perhaps soon after 840, under the command of the Hetaeriarch ("Head of the Guards"). These new guardsmen were organized into the Great Hetaeria, the Middle Hetaeria, and the Third Hetaeria. The Third Hetaeria consisted of two companies of foreign mercenaries, one of Khazars and another of Phargani, the latter evidently Turks from Farghana in Central Asia who are first attested in 855.[66] At least by the tenth century, the first two hetaeriae and the two companies of the Third Hetaeria seem each to have formed a bandum of 200 men, making a total of 1,200 guards along with the Imperials. These guardsmen could be used for various missions, military expeditions included.[67]

Besides the Optimates, who helped carry baggage on expeditions, the empire had three other support units. The Protostrator managed the Imperial Stables, and kept horses and arms for the emperor and his guards. When the emperor campaigned, the Logothete of the Herds requisitioned horses and mules for the imperial baggage train, while the Count of the Stable distributed them.[68] The procedures for equipping the emperor's baggage train were elaborate, and involved contributions from various dignitaries and even monasteries.[69] The Protospatharius of the Basin was in charge of the emperor's galley and barges, which could also join naval expeditions.[70]

Such was the organization of the army that won its first real victories against the Arabs under Michael III, Basil I, and Leo VI. About 902, as we have seen, Leo VI raised the cavalry complement of a 200-man bandum from 40 to 50 in the themes—except for the Cibyrrhaeots, Hellas, Peloponnesus, Cephalonia, and Nicopolis, which had no cavalry. Including the new banda that Leo added to the themes along the eastern frontier, the cavalry would have increased by 5,900 men:

	Before Leo VI		After Leo VI	
Units	Total	Cavalry	Total	Cavalry
themes	96,000	17,600 (18.3%)	102,000	23,500 (23.0%)
tagmata	28,000	16,000 (57.1%)	28,000	16,000 (57.1%)
TOTAL	124,000	33,600 (27.1%)	130,000	39,500 (30.4%)

65. Ibn Khurdādhbih, 81.

66. Symeon the Logothete ("Georgius Monachus"), 815. At such an early date, when the name was new and presumably reflected the guardsmen's origin fairly accurately, these "Phargani" seem unlikely to have been Varangians, as suggested by A. Kazhdan, *Oxford Dictionary of Byzantium*, II, 925.

67. See Treadgold, "Army," 121–23.

68. See Oikonomidès, *Listes*, 337–39, though on p. 338 I would agree with J. B. Bury that the Protostrator's armophylaces were in charge of arms rather than chariots; cf. Bury, *Imperial Administrative System*, 117–18, 111, and 113–14.

69. Constantine VII, *Three Treatises*, 96–120.

70. Constantine VII, *De Administrando Imperio*, 51, pp. 248–56.

This increase in the cavalry would have been helpful for offensive warfare, but it fell far short of making the cavalry the principal component of the army.

Leo's other contribution was to divide the 1,000-man drungus, the descendant of the old legion, and to make the 200-man bandum the basis of military organization. This change sacrificed nothing of importance, and was convenient for making annexations. Dividing themes by banda rather than by drungi allowed new frontier themes to be assigned parts of several adjoining themes to make the new units larger and give them a number of experienced soldiers. An organization based on banda also permitted the creation of frontier districts smaller than 1,000 men. Before Leo's changes, small conquests had presented an administrative problem, because they could only be garrisoned by creating at least one new drungus of 1,000 men or by spreading men from adjoining drungi thinner on the ground. Irene and Nicephorus I seem to have used the latter method when they expanded their holdings in Thrace, which the Bulgars soon managed to conquer. After Leo had himself created two drungi for his new Theme of Mesopotamia about 901, he appears to have seen the problem and devised his reforms to solve it.[71]

Leo's reforms, after leading to some modest annexations by 908, had less immediate effect than might have been expected, because the empire became bogged down in political infighting and war with the Bulgars. But by 926 the empire began attacking the Arabs in earnest, and in 934 it resumed its expansion by taking Melitene, long the seat of the strongest Arab emirate to the empire's east. This success induced the 12,000 cavalry of the Banū Ḥabīb to desert to the Byzantines. The five new themes that Romanus I evidently used the Banū Ḥabīb to garrison, and largely to conquer, were of a different type from earlier themes. The organization of one of them, the Charpezician Theme, can be deduced from an official document of 949, and the same structure probably applied to all five themes.

The organization of the Theme of Charpezicium follows from the fact that it was all cavalry. It therefore had banda of 50 cavalry, without the 150 additional infantry of regular themes. Its official strength was 2,400 men, one-fifth of the 12,000 cavalry of the Banū Ḥabīb, who seem to have been distributed equally among their five themes. The emperor flattered his new Arab subjects by giving their junior officers inflated titles. Thus the commanders of 100 men were called greater turmarchs instead of centarchs, the commanders of 50 were called lesser turmarchs instead of pentecontarchs, and the commanders of 10 were called drungaries instead of decarchs.

71. See Treadgold, "Army," 93–99.

The documented organization of Charpezicium was therefore as follows:[72]

1	strategus
1	meriarch
1	count of the tent
1	domestic
24	greater turmarchs (centarchs)
48	lesser turmarchs (pentecontarchs)
240	drungaries (decarchs)
2,160	common soldiers
2,476	men total

Each of these five themes should also have had a chartulary, protocancellarius, and protomandator, like other themes, although the document from 949, probably assuming their existence, does not mention them.

The date of these new themes, about 936, may also be the time when the other themes and tagmata acquired a few officers that they are known to have had in 949 but not in 911. No evidence seems to exist of other military reforms in the interval, and an emperor who had been as lavish with titles for Arabs as Romanus I may have bestowed a few more titles on Byzantines. By 949 the older themes had new protobandophori, protodomestics, and protocentarchs. The tagmata also had protobandophori and gained more drungaries, one for each 400 men instead of one for each 1,000. The protobandophorus, one to a theme or tagma, was the chief of the theme's standard bearers or bandophori. But the themes had not merely one protodomestic and protocentarch apiece but one for each 400 men, which by this time was the usual command of a drungary.[73]

Probably the protodomestics supervised scouts, surveyors, and medics for each 400-man drungus, since there were no lower-ranking domestics for them to supervise as their title might imply. In other words, protodomestics ranked not above but below the domestic of the theme, and performed the same duties for the drungaries as the domestic of the theme did for the strategus. By analogy, the protocentarchs are more likely to have been adjutants for the drungaries than chiefs for the centarchs, who already had counts to command them. Despite gaining these subordinates, the drungaries of the tenth century were in danger of duplicating the functions of the counts, who had commands half as large as theirs. Later in the century the rank of drungary appears to have been abolished, while the rank of count remained.[74]

72. Ibid., 128–30.   73. Ibid., 126–28 and 130–33.
74. The description of an army camp in the late tenth-century treatise *On Campaign Organization and Tactics*, 252, mentions the topoteretes, counts, and domestics of the Scholae, but no drungaries.

The 12,000 Banū Habīb, whose descendants would have kept up their numbers in the future, increased the Byzantine cavalry by more than twice as much as Leo VI's reforms had done. From about 936, the empire had some 51,500 cavalry, perhaps 36 percent of a new total of 142,000 soldiers. Though the composition of the Theme of Theodosiopolis created in 949 is not known for certain, in the absence of another windfall like the desertion of the Banū Habīb Theodosiopolis was most likely a theme of the usual type, with perhaps 500 cavalry and 1,500 infantry. On the other hand, the expansion of the cavalry tagmata of the Scholae and Excubitors around 959 should have increased the cavalry by 4,000 men. As the great conquests began, the cavalry would thus have totaled some 56,000 men, about 38 percent of the army.

When Nicephorus Phocas attacked Aleppo in 962, he is said to have had 30,000 cavalry and 40,000 infantry, numbers well within the empire's capacity at the time.[75] Nicephorus liked cavalry, as is evident not only from his creating a class of them with heavy armor but from his garrisoning at least his Theme of Tarsus with 5,000 cavalry and no infantry.[76] Besides Tarsus, some of the other 25 or so new themes created in Nicephorus's reign are likely to have consisted entirely of cavalry, particularly in the Cilician plain, which was well suited to cavalry warfare. Yet the army Nicephorus led into Cilicia was after all more than half infantry.

Two military treatises written at Nicephorus's order give extensive treatment to infantry warfare. One, *On Skirmishing*, stresses the value of infantry for fighting on rough ground and in ambushes.[77] The other treatise, *Military Precepts*, describes an army of 8,000 regular cavalry, 504 or 384 heavy cavalry of Nicephorus's new sort, and 16,000 infantry. The work assumes that the infantry will bear the brunt of any defense, and describes a new infantry battlefield formation called the taxiarchy. This unit, commanded by a taxiarch or chiliarch, had 1,000 men, like the old drungus, and was commanded by the usual centarchs, pentecontarchs, and decarchs. But it was divided into specialized companies of 400 heavy infantry, 300 archers, 200 lancers, and 100 pikemen.[78]

Thus the 200-man bandum, though it continued to exist as a military district, ceased to be a formation on the battlefield. There the basic for-

75. Canard, *Histoire*, 811.

76. See below, p. 174; and above, pp. 79–80 and n. 83.

77. *On Skirmishing*, III.2 and XI.1, pp. 154 and 182 in Dennis's edition and 41 and 73 in that of Dagron and Mihăescu. On Nicephorus's military works, see Dagron and Mihăescu, *Traité sur la guérilla*, 153–75.

78. Nicephorus II, *Military Precepts*, 13–14 (16 cavalry parataxeis of 500 men each), 10 (the heavy cavalry), 1–2 (11,200 infantry apart from the light infantry consisting of 4,800 archers), 19 (16 infantry taxiarchies in a camp), 1 (the officers of a taxiarchy), and 3 (the specialized companies of a taxiarchy). On the arms and armor used by the various soldiers, see Kolias, *Byzantinische Waffen*.

mations were 100-man centarchies for infantry and 50-man cavalry banda for regular cavalry. The 504 or 384 heavy cavalry had a single special formation in a wedge of twelve rows—each larger than the one before—but its men seem to have been drawn from ten or eight cavalry banda. Since Nicephorus gave infantry such a major part in warfare, most of his new themes probably included infantry, especially because many of them were in Armenia, a country suited to mountain fighting and ambushes.

John I also liked cavalry, since he created the new cavalry tagma of the Immortals at the beginning of his reign. The army he led against the Russians in Bulgaria in 971 seems to have included 17,000 cavalry and 15,000 infantry, plus a rear guard of uncertain size and composition.[79] Since cavalrymen were not very useful in the rear guard, most of it was probably infantry, so that the whole army would have been rather less than half cavalry. There is no particular reason to think that John's new themes in the Balkans, several of which were in the Balkan Mountains, had more cavalry than the quarter that had been usual for themes for some time.

John evidently created the overarching commands of dukes, each with jurisdiction over a number of small border themes. In the West his Duke of Thessalonica was the commander for northern Greece, while his Duke of Adrianople—the new title of the Strategus of Macedonia—was the commander for Thrace as far north as the Danube. In the Dobrudja John also created a Catepan of the Mesopotamia of the West, who seems to have been a naval official for fleets on the Danube and the Black Sea. The Theme of the Mesopotamia of the West had its own strategus, who ranked much lower than the catepan and was presumably subject to the Duke of Adrianople.[80] In the East, John gave only a little wider authority to the Duke of Chaldia created by Nicephorus II, who seems to have had charge of no more than the themes of Colonia and Soteropolis in addition to Chaldia.[81] But John gave the Duke of Mesopotamia authority over all

79. Leo the Deacon, 132, notes that after the Immortals, for whom he gives no number, came 15,000 infantry and 13,000 cavalry, plus the rear guard and baggage train. Scylitzes, 295, says that the army's vanguard numbered 5,000 infantry, apparently chosen from the 15,000, and 4,000 cavalry, presumably the Immortals.

80. This seems to be the only adequate means of explaining why the *Escorial Tacticon*, 263 and 269, lists a Duke of Mesopotamia, a Catepan of the Mesopotamia [of the West], and a Strategus of the Mesopotamia of the West, a difficulty not explained by Oikonomidès, *Listes*, 354. (The term "Mesopotamia of the West" seems to refer to the Danube Delta; cf. Oikonomidès, *Listes*, 363 and n. 409.) The mention of strategi as well as dukes of Thessalonica, Chaldia, and the eastern Mesopotamia in the *Escorial Tacticon*, 263 and 265, can be explained by supposing that the old strategi continued to exist when the new dukes were added (unlike the strategi of Antioch and Macedonia, replaced by the dukes of Antioch and Adrianople); yet the Mesopotamia of the West was an entirely new command. Though catepans later became equivalent to dukes, the catepans of Paphlagonia and of the Mardaïtes were certainly naval officials, and so was the Catepan of Italy, at least in part; cf. Ahrweiler, *Byzance et la mer*, 110–11.

81. Kühn, *Byzantinische Armee*, 184–85 and n. 5.

the new Armenian themes, and the Duke of Antioch authority over all the Syrian and Cilician themes to the south.[82]

The dukes of Thessalonica, Adrianople, Mesopotamia in the East, and Chaldia all had ducates that had formerly been themes of the traditional type—that is, three-quarters infantry. The Duke of Mesopotamia did have charge of the five themes of the Banū Ḥabīb, which were all cavalry. But the same duke also controlled several earlier themes that were chiefly infantry, and various newer themes that were probably of the same sort. The Duke of Antioch had jurisdiction over the Theme of Tarsus, which was all cavalry, and over several other themes that may well have been all cavalry. But then the garrison of Antioch itself could easily have consisted only of cavalry. For a duke with an immediate command that was mostly infantry to have authority over many other themes that were all cavalry seems inappropriate, since the men with whom he was most familiar would have played only a secondary role in the campaigns he led. Although the Byzantines may not have thought in this way, and we would not necessarily know if the garrisons of the ducates had been upgraded to be all cavalry, the hypothesis may be suggested that most themes under the Duke of Antioch were all cavalry, while most themes under the other dukes had the usual mixture of cavalry and infantry.

Infantry definitely remained important under Basil II. The treatise *On Campaign Organization*, probably written for him, envisages a campaigning force of between 12,000 and 16,000 infantry, and between 9,000 and 9,200 cavalry. This work describes taxiarchies like those of Nicephorus II, except that it lists 500 heavy infantry instead of 400 and omits the 100 pikemen.[83] Basil's new themes in the Balkans appear to have been of the usual type, combining a majority of infantry with a minority of cavalry. On the other hand, Basil did inaugurate the Varangian Guard, a force of 6,000 cavalry.

The Varangians were also foreign mercenaries, though at the time they must not have seemed to represent a very sharp break with Byzantine military tradition. The Byzantines had been hiring small bodies of Russian mercenaries for expeditions as early as 911.[84] The emperors had also been maintaining permanent companies of foreign mercenary guards, the Turkish Khazars and Phargani, since the mid-ninth century. The Varangians had the same number of men as the expanded tagmata of the Scholae and Excubitors. The Varangian Guard may at first have been considered to be the equivalent of a cavalry tagma, making three tagmata of 6,000

82. See above, pp. 35–36 and 80–81.

83. *On Campaign Organization*, 246 (the organization of a taxiarchy, with 16 taxiarchies equaling 16,000 infantry), 268 (12 taxiarchies equaling 12,000 infantry), 274 (8,200 or 8,000 cavalry, plus 1,000 cavalry attending the emperor).

84. See Treadgold, "Army," 112.

each (Scholae, Excubitors, Varangians) and three tagmata of 4,000 each (Watch, Hicanati, Immortals) for a total of 30,000 cavalry.

But the Varangians proved to be a rather different sort of company. They lacked military lands and the distractions and independence those brought with them; Varangian soldiers were also frequently replaced by new recruits from Russia, and elsewhere. In consequence, the Varangian Guard was easy to keep in training, and generally remained loyal to the emperors who paid it and formed its only strong connection with the empire. Especially for weak emperors whom the rest of the army disliked, such mercenaries seemed to give better value for the money than thematic or even tagmatic troops. In the eleventh century the emperors increasingly hired Normans, Germans, Turks, and other foreigners, who served under their own officers in units with their own organization. These appear usually to have been cavalry, and by this time cavalry were finally becoming what they had never been before, the empire's main fighting forces. The mercenaries, often sent out to border regions, began to replace the Byzantine army rather than merely to complement it.

While the themes declined, the 24,000 Byzantine soldiers of the five cavalry tagmata continued to be an active part of the army. By themselves they were enough to provide cavalry for any but the largest expeditions. Their western and eastern branches of 12,000 men each, commanded by the domestics of the East and West, could also handle many missions alone. Yet as a rule they seem to have been divided up into various contingents and used along with other troops. Like the mercenaries, many of them were sent to border regions. There they and the mercenaries were put under the command of the dukes; and dukes became more numerous during the eleventh century.[85] Tagmatic and mercenary troops seem entirely to have replaced the thematic soldiers of the Armenian or Iberian themes whom Constantine IX disbanded.

Even when stationed far from Constantinople, the tagmata could still be called up for expeditions. Romanus IV led many of them to the battle of Manzikert as late as 1071, and as late as 1081 Alexius I led some of the western tagmata to the battle of Dyrrhachium. Romanus IV was even able to call up the thematic troops of Anatolia. The thematic troops of the Armenian or Iberian themes still did enough military service up to the 1050's so that Constantine IX could ask them to pay taxes in order to be excused from serving. The Bulgarian thematic troops in the Balkans helped defeat the Uzes as late as 1065.[86] In 1069 Romanus IV seems not to have included the thematic troops under the dukes of Antioch and

85. See Cheynet, "Du stratège du thème au duc," 181–94; and Kühn, *Byzantinische Armee*, 158–242.
86. Scylitzes Continuatus, 115.

Edessa in his drills, probably because they needed no more drilling, since fighting with the nearby Turks and Arabs had kept them in trim. Even after 1081, the troops of the dukes of Antioch and Edessa, along with the eastern tagmata, sustained Philaretus Brachamius in the east.

The rest of the themes succumbed to demobilization and to too long an interval of peace. Themes continued to serve as the empire's provinces for centuries to come, and as geographical subdivisions banda even survived down to the fall of the last Byzantine state, the Empire of Trebizond, in 1461.[87] The heads of these administrative divisions and subdivisions on occasion even tried to organize the population for purposes of defense. But after the eleventh century themes and banda were no longer bodies of regular troops.

The themes and tagmata that were the lineal descendants of the mobile armies of the fourth century, and of the far older Roman legions, disappeared before the year 1100. Of course the themes and tagmata had changed greatly over the centuries, as the empire itself had done. Yet soldiers and commanders must have continued to feel that their units were part of an institution that was very old indeed, and they probably had some idea that it went back to the glorious days of Constantine I, and before him to "the older Rome." Although the army had suffered many defeats, the knowledge that it had survived them all must have been a source of confidence to its men. Moreover, military service would have been hereditary in the families of many soldiers for as long as they or anyone else could trace. That millennial tradition, once lost, was irrecoverable.

87. On the survival of the bandum, see Bryer, "Rural Society," 53; and the map of administrative boundaries of the Empire of Trebizond ca. 1432 in Bryer and Winfield, *Byzantine Monuments*, I, ii.

CHAPTER FOUR

Pay

As St. Paul asked rhetorically, "Who would pay money to serve in the army?"[1] The life of a Byzantine soldier suited many men, but it was not such a pleasure as to make up for inadequate pay. Military service was usually regarded as respectable, but not so prestigious, except perhaps in the highest ranks, that its glory outweighed poor wages. In the fourth century the government had to resort to conscription to fill out the rolls. Even with compulsion, however, soldiers had to be supported well enough to keep them fit to fight and properly equipped. Under the system of volunteer enlistment that prevailed by the early sixth century, men had to be paid enough to make them choose soldiering rather than civilian employment, which was in most cases safer.

Several modern scholars have supposed that during the sixth century basic pay for a soldier was one annona a year, or 5 nomismata, although no source says this explicitly.[2] If it were right, when Heraclius cut military pay in half in 616, soldiers would have received 2½ nomismata a year. With the introduction of the themes, presumably for reasons of financial necessity, military pay seems to have been lowered still further to less than a living wage, the difference being made up by granting military lands. Yet 2½ nomismata would hardly have been a living wage in the first place.

Unskilled laborers in the provinces typically earned 3 nomismata a year at the time, perhaps in addition to room and board. According to Procopius, prostitutes in Constantinople were barely able to survive on yearly earnings of 4 or 5 nomismata. In Egypt a carpenter could make 16 nomismata a year, and a caulker 18 nomismata. Common soldiers, however, supported families and sometimes kept slaves, who cost 10 nomismata or

1. I Corinthians 9.7.
2. Hendy, *Studies*, 166; Haldon, *Byzantine Praetorians*, 113, 115, and 120–22.

more apiece.[3] Something therefore seems to be wrong with the reckoning of 5 nomismata for the pay of common soldiers. Probably the best way of checking this number is to start in the ninth century, when we have some explicit evidence for military pay, and to work forward and backward from there.

THE PAY SCALE OF THEOPHILUS

The indirectly preserved text of al-Jarmī, apparently drawn from a Byzantine government manual prepared at the time of Theophilus's military reform of 840, describes a number of grades of military pay.[4] It lists officers' salaries in pounds of gold in a descending scale of 40, 36, 24, 12, 6, and "as low as one pound," and soldiers' pay of 18 or 12 nomismata, which would be a quarter and a sixth of a pound of gold respectively.[5] Expressed in coins, these grades would be 2,880, 2,592, 1,728, 864, 432, 72, 18, and 12 nomismata. A little later on, the Arabic text says that "officers" received "from three pounds of gold to one pound," evidently meaning 3, 2, and 1, while "soldiers" received 1 nomisma the first year, 2 the second, 3 the third, and so on up to 12 nomismata in the twelfth and all later years.[6] Three pounds would be 216 nomismata, 2 pounds 144 nomismata, and 1 pound 72 nomismata. The detail in this information is impressive, the clarity less so.

Yet any inconsistency is only apparent, and probably the result of summarizing by the Arab geographer who used Jarmī's work. An official salary list, datable to about 910 and preserved by the emperor Constantine VII himself, gives the grades for the different strategi and cleisurarchs as 40, 30, 20, 10, and 5 pounds of gold.[7] These salaries clearly correspond to the 40, 36, 24, 12, and 6 pounds of gold reported by Jarmī, which except for the highest grade must have been lowered somewhat during the preceding 70 years. Since Constantine specifies which strategi received which salaries—the cleisurarchs all received the lowest sum—we can determine their salaries in 840 by substituting Jarmī's grades into Constantine's pay scale.

The three remaining officers' salaries of 3 pounds, 2 pounds, and 1 pound must apply to subordinates of the strategi and cleisurarchs. The top three ranks of subordinate officers mentioned by Jarmī are turmarchs, drungaries, and counts. Since the centarchs, whom Jarmī ranks next, are absent from the list of subordinate officers of a strategus in the treatise

---

3. For these wages and prices, see Morrisson, "Monnaie et prix," 251–60.
4. See above, pp. 64–65.
5. Ibn Khurdādhbih, 84.
6. Ibid., 85.
7. Constantine VII, *De Ceremoniis*, 696–97.

of Philotheus, they seem not to have ranked as commissioned officers.[8] Thus for these lowest-ranking officers Jarmī supplies three pay grades and three ranks to go with them, so that the turmarchs presumably received 3 pounds, the drungaries 2 pounds, and the counts 1 pound.

The higher of Jarmī's two salaries for "soldiers," 18 nomismata, must be that of the centarchs, junior officers who appear only in Philotheus's comprehensive rank list of government employees, just five places ahead of the common soldiers of the themes. Since even that list has no separate entry for the decarchs, Jarmī's lowest grade, the decarchs seem to have shared the rank and pay of regular soldiers.[9] For regular soldiers, according to Jarmī, full pay was 12 nomismata, though they only began to receive it in their twelfth year of service. Twelve years' experience may well have been the usual prerequisite for promotion to decarch.

So far we have eleven grades of pay, counting full pay of 12 nomismata and newer recruits' pay of 1 to 12 nomismata as different grades. But the summary of Jarmī's work that has reached us never mentions some officers recorded by Philotheus, including the seven staff officers of the themes, the ships' officers of the Cibyrrhaeots and the Imperial Fleet, and some special officers of the tagmata.[10] Their pay should have corresponded to their rank, if we are to judge from a report by Liudprand of Cremona, a Lombard ambassador of the Frankish king of Italy.

In 950 Liudprand was invited to attend the annual payment of officials and officers in Constantinople, which occurred during the three days before Palm Sunday. For hours Liudprand watched Constantine VII pass out salaries, starting with the highest sums for the highest ranks and gradually descending to the lowest sums for the lowest ranks. Those who earned less than one pound of gold were left to be paid by the Grand Chamberlain during Holy Week.[11]

Since Liudprand's description shows that pay followed rank, the rank lists both of Philotheus for 899 and of the *Tacticon Uspensky* of 842-43 should in theory be convertible into pay scales that would supply the missing salaries. The *Tacticon* is virtually contemporary with Jarmī's information, being at most three years later. Though its final section is defective, its deficiencies can be completed with considerable confidence from the last part of Philotheus's comprehensive list, because a comparison of the lists shows that the status of low-ranking officers and officials had hardly changed in the intervening half-century.[12]

8. Philotheus, 109–11.
9. See ibid., 161, where I would retain the reading of the manuscript and put the soldiers of the tagmata before the soldiers of the themes; see Treadgold, "Notes," 285 n. 64.
10. Cf. Philotheus, 109–13, 115, 117, and 119–21.
11. Liudprand of Cremona, *Antapodosis*, VI.10, 157–58.
12. See Treadgold, "Notes," 284–85.

The *Tacticon* and Philotheus's treatise are divided into sections corresponding to the Byzantine court titles of patrician, protospatharius, spatharocandidatus, and so on. Both lists accordingly mention the highest military officers twice or even three times, first in the place of precedence the officer would have if he held one or another court title, later in the place determined by his military rank alone, without a court title. In reconstructing the pay scale all the earlier mentions ought to be omitted, because they reflect the court title rather than the military rank. The last position should be the one determined by the military rank as such. When such a position falls among officials with a given court title, the military rank must by itself have conferred a status corresponding to that title.

The ranks listed by Jarmī appear in their order of precedence in both the *Tacticon Uspensky* and Philotheus. In both lists the rank of strategus corresponds to the titles of patrician and protospatharius, and the rank of cleisurarch corresponds to the titles of spatharocandidatus and dishypatus. Then the rank of turmarch corresponds to the title of spatharius, and the rank of drungary corresponds to the titles of hypatus through vestitor. The military ranks lower than drungary correspond to officials the lists call *apratoi*, in this case meaning those with no court title.[13]

The salaries of the strategi can already be determined by comparing Jarmī's pay list with that given by Constantine VII. In both the *Tacticon* and Philotheus, the same section that includes the strategi—that for patricians and protospatharii—includes the commanders of the tagmata. This is natural enough, because themes and tagmata were of similar size and organization. Since the Domestic of the Scholae appears after the Strategus of the Anatolics and before the Strategus of the Armeniacs, both of whom were paid 40 pounds of gold, that was evidently the domestic's salary as well.[14] Since the other commanders of the tagmata come after all the strategi but still fall within the section for patricians and protospatharii, these lower-ranking tagmatic commanders evidently received the lowest salary for a strategus, 12 pounds of gold.[15] These salaries are listed as grades I through IV in Table 8.

Similarly, all the military officers among the spatharocandidati and dishypati probably earned 6 pounds of gold, like the cleisurarchs who are listed among them. All the officers among the spatharii probably earned

13. On the meanings of *apratos* (pl. *apratoi*), see Oikonomidès, *Listes*, 290.
14. The precedence of the strategi and domestics must be determined from the first mention of the strategi in the *Tacticon Uspensky*, 47.14–49.2, since the second mention at 51.12 refers only to the generals "according to their commands" without naming them; cf. the first mention and summarized second mention in Philotheus, 137.20–22 and 143.20–23.
15. See *Tacticon Uspensky*, 51.12 (strategi), 51.15 (Domestic of the Excubitors), 51.32 (Drungary of the Watch), 53.2 (Domestic of the Hicanati), and 53.7–9 (Domestic of the Numera, Domestic of the Optimates, and Count of the Walls).

TABLE 8

Military Pay Scale in 842

GRADE I: 40 pounds of gold (2,880 nomismata)
Strategus of the Anatolics   Domestic of the Scholae   Strategus of the
Armeniacs   Strategus of the Thracesians

GRADE II: 36 pounds of gold (2,592 nomismata)
Count of the Opsician   Strategus of the Bucellarians   Strategus of
Macedonia

GRADE III: 24 pounds of gold (1,728 nomismata)
Strategus of Cappadocia   Strategus of Paphlagonia   Strategus of Thrace
Strategus of Chaldia[a]

GRADE IV: 12 pounds of gold (864 nomismata)[b]
Strategus of Peloponnesus[a]   Strategus of the Cibyrrhaeots   Strategus of
Hellas[a]   Strategus of Sicily[a]   Strategus of Cephalonia[a]   Strategus of
Thessalonica[a]   Strategus of Dyrrhachium[a]   Strategus of the Climata [i.e.,
Cherson][a]   Domestic of the Excubitors (51.12)   [Protospatharius] of the
Hippodrome [of the Imperials] (51.29)   Drungary of the Watch (51.32)
Logothete of the Herds (53.1)   Domestic of the Hicanati (53.2)   Domes-
tic of the Numera (53.7)   Domestic of the Optimates (53.8)   Count of
the Walls (53.9)   Protostrator (53.14)   Drungary of the Fleet (53.16)
acting strategi of themes (53.17)   Count of the Stable (53.20)

GRADE V: 6 pounds of gold (432 nomismata)
Cleisurarch of Charsianum (55.5)   Cleisurarch of Seleucia[d] (55.6)   Drungary of the Aegean Sea [of the Cibyrrhaeots] (57.10)   Drungary of the Gulf
[of the Cibyrrhaeots][e] (57.10a)   Duke of Calabria [of Sicily] (57.14)

GRADE VI: 3 pounds of gold (216 nomismata)[f]
spatharii of the Spatharicium [of the Imperials] (57.27)
turmarchs [of the land themes] 59.12   topoteretae [of the tagmata] (59.14)

GRADE VII: 2 pounds of gold (144 nomismata)[g]
turmarchs of the naval themes (61.21)   imperial strators (61.22)   counts
of the Scholae (61.25)   counts of the tent of the themes (61.26)   candidati
[of the Imperials] (61.29)   scribons [of the Excubitors] (63.1)   domestics
of the Scholae (63.3)   domestics of the themes (63.4)   imperial mandators
[of the Imperials] (63.7)   Chartulary of the Scholae (63.17)   chartularies
of the themes (63.18)   counts of the tent of the naval themes (63.19)
drungaries of the themes (63.20)

GRADE VIII: 1 pound of gold (72 nomismata)[h]
counts of the themes (157.11)   counts of the Watch (157.12)   Chartulary
of the Watch (157.13)   Chartulary of the Fleet (157.15)   Chartulary of
the Stable (157.16)   counts of the Hicanati (157.17)   Chartulary of the
Hicanati (157.18)   Epeictes of the Stable (157.19)   tribunes of the Numera (157.20)   Chartulary of the Numera (157.21)   counts of the Optimates (157.22)   Chartulary of the Optimates (157.23)   tribunes of the
Walls (157.24)   Chartulary of the Walls (157.25)   Proximus of the Scholae (157.27)   centarchs of the Watch (157.28)   centarchs of the
Hicanati (157.29)   protectors of the Scholae (159.1)   vicars of the
Numera (159.2)   vicars of the Walls (159.3)   draconarii of the Excubitors (159.4)   Acoluthus of the Watch (159.6)   Protomandator of the Excubitors (159.7)   Protomandator of the Hicanati (159.8)   [centarchs of
ships and] protocarabi (159.9)   protonotarii of the Herds (159.10)

TABLE 8 *(continued)*

GRADE IX: ½ pound of gold (36 nomismata)[i]

bandophori of the Watch (159.11)   bandophori of the Hicanati (159.12)
eutychophori of the Scholae (159.13)   sceuophori of the Excubitors (159.14)
laburesii of the Watch (159.15)   sceptrophori of the Scholae (159.16)
signophori of the Excubitors (159.17)   semiophori of the Watch (159.18)
semiophori of the Hicanati (159.19)   axiomatici of the Scholae (159.20)
senators of the Excubitors (159.21)   ducinators of the Watch (159.22)
ducinators of the Hicanati (159.23)   mandators of the Scholae (159.24)
protocancellarii of the themes (159.25)   Protomandator of the Numera (159.29)   Protomandator of the Walls (159.30)   protomandators of
the themes[j] (159.33)   mandators and legatarii of the Excubitors (159.33a)
mandators and legatarii of the Watch (159.34)   mandators and legatarii of the
Hicanati[k] (159.35)   mandators of the Numera (161.9)   mandators of the
Walls (161.10)   centarchs of the strategi of the themes [i.e., centarchs of the
spatharii and counts of the hetaeria] (161.13)   protectors of the forts [for irregular troops] (161.15)

GRADE X: ¼ pound of gold (18 nomismata)[l]

centarchs of the banda [of the themes] (161.16)   drungaries of the foot [for
irregular troops] (161.18)

GRADE XI: ⅙ pound of gold (12 nomismata)

soldiers of the tagmata [including decarchs and oarsmen][m] (161.22)   soldiers
of the themes [including decarchs and oarsmen] (161.21)

GRADE XII: ¹⁄₁₂–⅙ pound of gold (1–12 nomismata)

soldiers and oarsmen with up to 12 years' service

NOTE: References are to page and line numbers of the editions of the *Tacticon Uspensky* and Philotheus. The words in square brackets are explanatory additions.

[a] The salary listed for this strategus includes 12 pounds that he collected directly from the revenues of his theme.

[b] This grade corresponds to *Tacticon Uspensky* 51.12–53.21. Here I omit civilians, retired officers, and the drungaries of the Aegean Sea and the Gulf (53.18–19)—of whom the former is repeated at 57.10, where the latter must be accidentally omitted—and the Duke of Chaldia (53.4), at this date an obsolete rank (Treadgold, "Notes," p. 280).

[c] This grade corresponds to *Tacticon Uspensky* 53.22–57.20. Here I omit civilians, retired officers, and the turmarchs of the themes (55.7–8, 55.16–57.3) and Fleet (57.16) and topoteretae of the tagmata (55.9, 57.6–9, 57.17–18), who are repeated later (59.12, 59.14, 61.21); I also make the corrections to the published text listed in Treadgold, "Notes," p. 288.

[d] See Treadgold, "Notes," pp. 280–83.

[e] Missing from this place in the *Tacticon Uspensky*, but supplied by comparing 57.10 with 53.18–19.

[f] This grade corresponds to *Tacticon Uspensky* 57.21–61.6. Here I omit civilians, retired officers, and the counts of the tent of the themes and Fleet and the chartularies of the themes and tagmata (59.3–4, 59.10, 61.1–3, 61.6), who are repeated later (61.26, 63.2, 63.17–19, 63.22).

[g] This grade corresponds to *Tacticon Uspensky* 61.7–63.20. Here I omit civilians, retired officers, and the first mention of the chartularies of the themes (63.2), who are repeated later in the same section (63.18).

[h] At this point the text of the *Tacticon Uspensky* becomes defective (see Treadgold, "Notes," pp. 284–85), and must be supplied from Philotheus. This grade corresponds to Philotheus 157.11–159.10; here I omit civilians and the counts of the Imperial Fleet (157.14), who would not yet have existed in 842.

[i] This grade corresponds to Philotheus 159.11–161.15. Here I omit civilians and make the corrections to the text listed in Treadgold, "Notes," p. 288.

[j] See Treadgold, "Notes," p. 285 n. 63.

[k] See Treadgold, "Notes," p. 288.

[l] This grade corresponds to Philotheus 161.16–20. Here I omit civilians.

[m] See Treadgold, "Notes," p. 285 n. 64.

3 pounds, like the turmarchs who are listed in their section of the list. Then all the officers with the lowest court titles—the hypati through the vestitors, or the "hypatovestitors" in Byzantine court slang—probably earned 2 pounds, the salary of the drungaries listed among them.[16] These salaries are listed as grades V through VII in Table 8. At this point the text of the *Tacticon Uspensky* becomes defective, and Philotheus must be used instead.

The grades that include the counts, earning 1 pound of gold, and the centarchs, earning 18 nomismata, are divided in Philotheus's list by three entries for officials described as *apratoi*. Yet at this low level all the officials were *apratoi*, because none of them had the status needed for a court title, as anyone familiar with court practice would have known without being told. At first glance Philotheus seems to have no reason for including the word *apratoi* in these three places, though nowhere else among the lowest-ranking officials and officers.[17]

Philotheus, however, has marked the end of each of his four preceding sections by describing some officials either as *apratoi* or as *dia poleōs kai exōtikoi* (meaning men "in the city [of Constantinople] and in the provinces" who held purely nominal court titles).[18] The officials so described clearly belong in those places, because as men without real court titles they ranked last in each category. But afterward Philotheus seems to have used the word *apratoi*, which was accurate but unnecessary for describing such lowly officials, simply as a marker for the end of one section and the beginning of another.

In fact, here the word *apratoi* marks off three grades of pay. The first includes the counts, earning 1 pound of gold; the second includes the junior staff officers of the themes; and the third includes the centarchs, earning a quarter-pound of gold or 18 nomismata. Apparently the summary of Jarmī's work left out not just the junior staff officers but the grade of pay that belonged to them. Since this grade fell between 1 pound and one-quarter pound of gold, it was presumably one-half pound, or 36 nomismata. At the end of the list Philotheus does not distinguish the decarchs and soldiers who earned full pay of 12 nomismata from those who received less; the reason may quite possibly be that the distinction had lapsed by his day, so that all of them earned the same amount. But Jarmī

16. On the "hypatovestitors," see *Tacticon Uspensky*, 61.7, with Oikonomidès's translation and n. 44.

17. Philotheus, 157.9–14, 159.10, and 161.15.

18. See ibid., 147.25–26 (*dia poleōs* . . . *kai exōtikoi*) at the end of Grade IV; 151.13–14 (*dia poleōs*; supply *kai exōtikoi* as suggested by Oikonomidès in n. 115) at the end of Grade V; 155.8–9 (*dia poleōs kai exōtikoi*) at the end of Grade VI; and 157.9–10 (*apratoi*) at the end of Grade VII. On the phrase *dia poleōs kai exōtikoi*, see Oikonomidès, *Listes*, 299.

makes clear that in 840 soldiers with up to twelve years' service earned from 1 to 12 nomismata, which made a sort of Grade XII.

The complete pay scale in 840 has been reconstructed in Table 8. It has twelve grades: 40, 36, 24, 12, 6, 3, 2, 1, ½, ¼, ⅙, and ¹⁄₇₂–⅙ pounds of gold. The Byzantine treasury's love of the number 12 and its multiples shows not only in the number of pay grades but in their amounts. It also shows in the whole currency system of 24 folles to the miliaresion, 12 miliaresia to the nomisma, and 72 nomismata to the pound of gold.[19] One may even suspect that a few Khurramites were dismissed or a few new recruits added to them in 840 to make the total number of soldiers an even 120,000, or 12 myriads.

Philotheus lists the soldiers of the tagmata just ahead of the soldiers of the themes. While both sorts of soldiers fell within the same pay grade, the state provided the tagmata, like imperial bodyguards, with free rations (*sitēresia*) and fodder (*chortasmata*). Since at least in principle these were paid in kind, and not annually but monthly, they were not a part of the regular military payroll.[20] They closely resembled the rations and fodder known as *annonae* and *capitus* in the sixth century, when they were valued at 5 nomismata per annona and 4 nomismata per capitus.[21]

We shall see that the 5-nomismata annona remained in use until the early ninth century, while horses presumably ate about as much in the ninth century as in the sixth. The value of the rations and fodder of the tagmata and guards should therefore have been about 9 nomismata a year. The state also supplied the tagmata and guards with arms, uniforms, and horses, which soldiers in the themes had to provide for themselves.[22] Thus tagmatic soldiers were appreciably better off than thematic soldiers, even if their military lands were comparable. Imperial guardsmen were far better off, since those ranking as spatharii earned 3 pounds of gold apiece and those ranking as candidati or imperial mandators earned 2 pounds.

While Philotheus includes naval officers in his list, he omits oarsmen— unless he is counting them among the soldiers. If he is, soldiers and oars-

---

19. See Grierson, *Catalogue*, III.1, 14–19.
20. See Haldon, *Byzantine Praetorians*, 314. On p. 307 Haldon states that the tagmata received not only their rations and fodder by the month but their salaries as well. But the only evidence he mentions for this (in n. 928 on p. 577) is a passage formerly considered anonymous but now recognized as part of Cecaumenus's *Strategicon* (see Lemerle, *Prolégomènes*, 5–8). In this passage, Cecaumenus (276–78) advises the emperor to have his soldiers "receive their *sitēresia* every month without interruption, and the *chortasmata* and their salaries entire." Here the phrase "every month" explicitly refers only to the *sitēresia*, though for the sake of convenience the *chortasmata* are likely to have been issued monthly as well. But Symeon the Logothete ("Georgius Monachus"), 881, shows that in the tenth century by long-established custom the tagmata were paid along with the themes—that is, annually—and Cecaumenus says nothing to contradict this.
21. See below, pp. 149–50.
22. Haldon, *Byzantine Praetorians*, 318–23.

men should have been paid the same. Though Jarmī cannot be including the oarsmen along with the soldiers in his total of 120,000 men, their status seems not to have been much lower than that of soldiers. The Mardaïtes of the West were easily converted from oarsmen to soldiers in 809, and presumably in cases of need soldiers could row and oarsmen could fight as infantry. Constantine VII specifically includes oarsmen in his own scale for campaign pay on the expedition to Crete of 949. Although campaign pay differed from regular annual pay, being lower and less sharply graded by rank, it does seem to preserve the distinctions between pay grades.

Constantine's pay scale may be compared with the regular scale as reconstructed in Table 8:

Rank	Campaign pay in 949[23]	Annual pay in 842
turmarchs	30 nom.	3 lbs. (216 nom.)
counts of the tent	20 nom.	2 lbs. (144 nom.)
chartularies of themes	20 nom.	2 lbs. (144 nom.)
domestics of themes	20 nom.	2 lbs. (144 nom.)
drungaries	20 nom.	2 lbs. (144 nom.)
counts	6 nom.	1 lb. (72 nom.)
ships' officers	4 nom.	1 lb. (72 nom.)
soldiers	3 nom.	1−12 nom.
oarsmen (Mardaïtes)	3 nom.	1−12 nom.(?)

Of these nine groups, only the counts and ships' officers have the same annual pay in Table 8 and different campaign pay in 949. Yet we know that ships' officers did not earn less than a pound of annual pay even in 949, because one year later Liudprand observed that Constantine VII paid protocarabi in person, and says that in order to be paid by the emperor one had to earn at least a pound.[24] Perhaps the ships' officers received less campaign pay because they were not expected to see combat after landing on Crete. Since such a consideration probably did not apply to the oarsmen, who on their arrival would have been needed to fight alongside the soldiers, oarsmen probably had the same pay as soldiers. Soldiers in any case had the lowest pay grade in the scale, and even newly recruited oarsmen could scarcely have been paid less than 1 nomisma.

Pay of 1 to 12 nomismata depending upon length of service must have been difficult for Byzantine paymasters to compute, since they are most unlikely to have had an actuarial table to consult. We also lack an actuarial table for Byzantium, but life tables have been compiled from tombstones for Roman Spain and Roman Africa, and from parish records for medieval

---

23. Constantine VII, *De Ceremoniis*, 662.
24. Liudprand of Cremona, *Antapodosis*, VI.10, p. 158.

England. If the people in these tables had enrolled in the Byzantine army at age 18, retired at age 60, and drawn the salaries described by Jarmī, they would have received an average of 9.5 to 10 nomismata a year. To allow for deaths in battle, late enlistments, early retirements, and promotions to officer rank, this figure needs to be lowered slightly. Elsewhere I have adopted a rough average of 9 nomismata a year.[25]

This average is worth comparing with a campaign payroll preserved by Constantine VII. It applies to 1,000 men of the Scholae from Thrace and Macedonia who went on the expedition against Crete of 911. For 1,037 men including both soldiers and officers, the sum given is 10,176 nomismata, an average of about 9.8 nomismata per man.[26] This looks very much like campaign pay of 9 nomismata per soldier with some additional pay for the officers. These 1,037 men were presumably the 1,036 belonging to one drungus, plus a commander, possibly the Domestic of the Scholae himself but more likely his subordinate topoteretes of Thrace and Macedonia.

I have reconstructed the payroll elsewhere as follows, in what seems to be the only plausible way of arriving at the recorded totals:[27]

Number in rank	Rate	Total
1 topoteretes (or domestic)	144 nom.	144 nom.
1 drungary	72 nom.	72 nom.
5 counts	36 nom.	180 nom.
10 centarchs	24 nom.	240 nom.
20 pentecontarchs	24 nom.	480 nom.
10 bandophori	12 nom.	120 nom.
10 mandators	12 nom.	120 nom.
980 soldiers with decarchs	9 nom.	8,820 nom.
1,037 men total		10,176 nom. total

This was very generous campaign pay. The counts, for example, received a quarter of the 144 nomismata that would have been their annual salaries in 840, while the mandators received a third of the 36 nomismata that would have been their annual salaries in 840. The soldiers received the whole of what seems to have been their average annual wage in 840. Though we know that the officers' pay scale had changed somewhat in the meantime, any significant pay increase for the over 150,000 soldiers and oarsmen would have been very expensive, and any important decrease would have caused widespread discontent.

What seems most likely is that soon after 840 the government abandoned the cumbersome procedure of paying soldiers according to years of

25. Treadgold, *Byzantine State Finances*, 24.
26. Constantine VII, *De Ceremoniis*, 655.
27. Treadgold, "Army," 106.

service and decided simply to pay all of them 9 nomismata, an eighth of a pound of gold, which was probably the average the treasury had appropriated per soldier from the start. Recruits gained a good deal by the change, veterans lost very little, and paymasters could dispense with the trouble of figuring out how many years each man had served. The fact that Philotheus's list fails to distinguish veteran soldiers from recruits seems to indicate that the change had been made by 899.

We may now compute the army payroll as it was in 842. When combined with the numbers supplied by Jarmī for the soldiers and those supplied by Constantine VII for the oarsmen in 911, the pay scale indicates a payroll for the themes and tagmata of some 1,441,404 nomismata, or 20,019½ pounds of gold. The calculations appear in tables 9 and 10.

We have a means of confirming both the pay scale in Table 8 and the payrolls in tables 9 and 10. The total of 20,019½ pounds of gold may be compared with a figure supplied by Theophanes Continuatus, an official history commissioned in the next century by Constantine VII, and the Pseudo-Symeon, a rather strange work that draws on some good sources. Both authors, obviously using the same source, state that around 867 Michael III, who had exhausted the treasury by his extravagance, melted down 20,000 pounds of gold ornaments from the throne room and used it to meet his army payroll.[28] The agreement with the total payroll calculated from Jarmī is far too close to be a coincidence.

In fact, the closeness is almost uncanny, and it becomes even more so for 840. At that date, according to Jarmī, Cappadocia was commanded not by a strategus, as in 842, but by a cleisurarch.[29] The cleisurarch's salary would have been 6 pounds of gold rather than the 24 pounds of gold of the later strategus, so that in 840 the payroll would have been 18 pounds less, or about 20,001½ pounds. One and a half pounds would amount to the pay of just 12 oarsmen, and the number of oarsmen, even though they rowed the same number of marines, could easily have increased by this tiny number between 840 and 911 as new ships were introduced with somewhat different designs.[30]

For those who study the army from the bottom up, the idea that the army payroll could somehow have evolved to be almost exactly 20,000 pounds of gold in 840 will seem preposterous. But Byzantium was run from the top down, and the payroll in 840 was the result not of evolution but of the orders of one man, the emperor Theophilus. He alone appropriated money for the payroll, in whatever number took his fancy, and

28. Theophanes Continuatus, 173; Pseudo-Symeon ("Symeon Magister"), 659.
29. See Brooks, "Arabic Lists," 75 with n. 3.
30. And, of course, I may still have made some minor errors in computing the payroll, as I did in my *Byzantine State Finances*, 12–31. Cf. Treadgold, "Army," 104–6.

TABLE 9
Payroll of Selected Themes and Tagmata in 842

Unit and rank	Number in rank	Salary (nom.)	Total pay (nom.)
ANATOLIC THEME			
strategus	1	2,880 nom.	2,880 nom.
turmarchs	3	216	648
count of the tent	1	144	144
chartulary	1	144	144
domestic	1	144	144
drungaries	15	144	2,160
counts	75	72	5,400
centarch of the spatharii	1	36	36
count of the hetaeria	1	36	36
protocancellarius	1	36	36
protomandator	1	36	36
centarchs [a]	373	18	6,714
soldiers with decarchs	15,000	9	135,000
TOTALS	15,474		153,378 nom.
ARMENIAC THEME			
strategus	1	2,880 nom.	2,880 nom.
turmarchs	3	216	648
count of the tent	1	144	144
chartulary	1	144	144
domestic	1	144	144
drungaries	9	144	1,296
counts	45	72	3,240
centarch of the spatharii	1	36	36
count of the hetaeria	1	36	36
protocancellarius	1	36	36
protomandator	1	36	36
centarchs [a]	223	18	4,014
soldiers with decarchs	9,000	9	81,000
TOTALS	9,288		93,654 nom.
THRACESIAN THEME			
strategus	1	2,880 nom.	2,880 nom.
turmarchs	2	216	432
count of the tent	1	144	144
chartulary	1	144	144
domestic	1	144	144
drungaries	10	144	1,440
counts	50	72	3,600
centarch of the spatharii	1	36	36
count of the hetaeria	1	36	36
protocancellarius	1	36	36
protomandator	1	36	36
centarchs [a]	248	18	4,464
soldiers with decarchs	10,000	9	90,000
TOTALS	10,318		103,392 nom.
OPSICIAN THEME			
count	1	2,592 nom.	2,592 nom.
turmarch	1	216	216

(*continued*)

TABLE 9 (*continued*)

Unit and rank	Number in rank	Salary (nom.)	Total pay (nom.)
count of the tent	1	144	144
chartulary	1	144	144
domestic	1	144	144
drungaries	6	144	864
counts	30	72	2,160
centarch of the spatharii	1	36	36
count of the hetaeria	1	36	36
protocancellarius	1	36	36
protomandator	1	36	36
centarchs[a]	148	18	2,664
soldiers with decarchs	6,000	9	54,000
TOTALS	6,193		63,072 nom.
BUCELLARIAN THEME			
strategus	1	2,592 nom.	2,592 nom.
turmarchs	2	216	432
count of the tent	1	144	144
chartulary	1	144	144
domestic	1	144	144
drungaries	8	144	1,152
counts	40	72	2,880
centarch of the spatharii	1	36	36
count of the hetaeria	1	36	36
protocancellarius	1	36	36
protomandator	1	36	36
centarchs[a]	198	18	3,564
soldiers with decarchs	8,000	9	72,000
TOTALS	8,256		83,196 nom.
THEME OF CAPPADOCIA			
strategus	1	1,728 nom.	1,728 nom.
turmarch	1	216	216
count of the tent	1	144	144
chartulary	1	144	144
domestic	1	144	144
drungaries	4	144	576
counts	20	72	1,440
centarch of the spatharii	1	36	36
count of the hetaeria	1	36	36
protocancellarius	1	36	36
protomandator	1	36	36
centarchs[a]	98	18	1,764
soldiers with decarchs	4,000	9	36,000
TOTALS	4,131		42,300 nom.
THEME OF CHALDIA[b]			
CLEISURA OF CHARSIANUM[c]			
THEME OF PAPHLAGONIA			
strategus	1	1,728 nom.	1,728 nom.
turmarch	1	216	216
count of the tent	1	144	144
chartulary	1	144	144
domestic	1	144	144
drungaries	5	144	720
counts	25	72	1,800
centarch of the spatharii	1	36	36

TABLE 9 (*continued*)

Unit and rank	Number in rank	Salary (nom.)	Total pay (nom.)
count of the hetaeria	1	36	36
protocancellarius	1	36	36
protomandator	1	36	36
centarchs [a]	123	18	2,214
soldiers with decarchs	5,000	9	45,000
TOTALS	5,162		52,254 nom.

THEME OF THRACE [d]

CLEISURA OF SELEUCIA [e]

THEME OF MACEDONIA [f]

THEME OF PELOPONNESUS
strategus	1	0 nom. [g]	0 nom. [g]
turmarch	1	144	144
count of the tent	1	144	144
chartulary	1	144	144
domestic	1	144	144
drungaries	2	144	288
counts	10	72	720
centarch of the spatharii	1	36	36
count of the hetaeria	1	36	36
protocancellarius	1	36	36
protomandator	1	36	36
centarchs [a]	48	18	864
soldiers with decarchs	2,000	9	18,000
TOTALS	2,069		20,592 nom.

THEME OF CEPHALONIA [h]

THEME OF THESSALONICA [i]

THEME OF DYRRHACHIUM [i]

THEME OF THE CLIMATA [i]

THEME OF SICILY [j]

CIBYRRHAEOT THEME
strategus	1	864 nom.	864 nom.
Drungary of the Aegean Sea	1	432	432
Drungary of the Gulf	1	432	432
turmarch	1	144	144
count of the tent	1	144	144
chartulary	1	144	144
domestic	1	144	144
counts	10	72	720
centarchs of ships	67	72	4,824
protocarabi	134	72	9,648
centarch of the spatharii	1	36	36
count of the hetaeria	1	36	36
protocancellarius	1	36	36
protomandator	1	36	36
centarchs [k]	48	18	864
soldiers with decarchs	2,000	9	18,000
oarsmen	12,300	9	110,700
TOTALS	14,570		147,204 nom.

(*continued*)

TABLE 9 (*continued*)

Unit and rank	Number in rank	Salary (nom.)	Total pay (nom.)
THEME OF HELLAS			
strategus	1	0 nom.[g]	0 nom.[g]
turmarch	1	144	144
count of the tent	1	144	144
chartulary	1	144	144
domestic	1	144	144
drungaries	2	144	288
counts	10	72	720
centarchs of ships	10	72	720
protocarabi	20	72	1,440
centarch of the spatharii	1	36	36
count of the hetaeria	1	36	36
protocancellarius	1	36	36
protomandator	1	36	36
centarchs[k]	48	18	864
soldiers with decarchs	2,000	9	18,000
oarsmen	2,300	9	20,700
TOTALS	4,399		43,452 nom.
TAGMA OF THE SCHOLAE			
domestic	1	2,880 nom.	2,880 nom.
topoteretae	2	216	432
chartulary	1	144	144
counts	20	144	2,880
domestics	100	144	14,400
proximus	1	72	72
protectors	10	72	720
eutychophori	10	36	360
sceptrophori	10	36	360
axiomatici	10	36	360
mandators	40	36	1,440
soldiers with decarchs	3,920	9	35,280
TOTALS	4,125		59,328 nom.
TAGMA OF THE EXCUBITORS			
domestic	1	864 nom.	864 nom.
topoteretae	2	216	432
chartulary	1	144	144
scribons	20	144	2,880
draconarii[l]	100	72	7,200
protomandator	1	72	7,200
draconarii[m]	10	72	720
sceuophori	10	36	360
signophori	10	36	360
senators	10	36	360
mandators	40	36	1,440
soldiers with decarchs	3,920	9	35,280
TOTALS	4,125		50,112 nom.
TAGMA OF THE WATCH			
drungary	1	864 nom.	864 nom.
topoteretae	2	216	432
chartulary	1	72	72
counts	20	72	1,440
centarchs	100	72	7,200

TABLE 9 (*continued*)

Unit and rank	Number in rank	Salary (nom.)	Total pay (nom.)
acoluthus	1	72	72
bandophori	10	36	360
laburesii	10	36	360
semiophori	10	36	360
ducinators	10	36	360
mandators	40	36	1,440
soldiers with decarchs	3,920	9	35,280
TOTALS	4,125		48,240 nom.
TAGMA OF THE HICANATI[n]			
TAGMA OF THE NUMERA			
domestic	1	864 nom.	864 nom.
topoteretes	1	216	216
chartulary	1	72	72
tribunes	10	72	720
vicars	50	72	3,600
protomandator	1	36	36
mandators	20	36	720
soldiers with decarchs	1,980	9	17,820
TOTALS	2,064		24,048 nom.
TAGMA OF THE WALLS[o]			
TAGMA OF THE OPTIMATES			
domestic	1	864 nom.	864 nom.
topoteretae	2	216	432
chartulary	1	72	72
counts	20	72	1,440
centarchs	100	36	3,600
protocancellarius	1	36	36
soldiers with decarchs	4,000	9	36,000
TOTALS	4,125		42,444 nom.

[a] Except for the centarch of the spatharii and the count of the hetaeria, already listed above.

[b] The Theme of Chaldia differed from the Theme of Cappadocia only in the salary of its strategus, which was 864 nomismata.

[c] The Cleisura of Charsianum differed from the Theme of Cappadocia only in the salary of its cleisurarch, which was 432 nomismata.

[d] The Theme of Thrace had the same payroll as the Theme of Paphlagonia.

[e] The Cleisura of Seleucia differed from the Theme of Paphlagonia only in the salary of its cleisurarch, which was 432 nomismata.

[f] The Theme of Macedonia differed from the Theme of Paphlagonia only in the salary of its strategus, which was 2,592 nomismata.

[g] The strategus collected his pay of 864 nomismata from his theme's revenues.

[h] The Theme of Cephalonia had the same payroll as the Theme of Peloponnesus.

[i] The themes of Thessalonica, Dyrrhachium, and the Climata differed from the Theme of Peloponnesus only in having turmarchs paid 216 nomismata.

[j] The Theme of Sicily differed from the Theme of Peloponnesus in the addition of the Duke of Calabria, with a salary of 432 nomismata, and in having its turmarch paid 216 nomismata.

[k] Except for the centarch of the spatharii, the count of the hetaeria, and the centarchs of the ships, already listed above.

[l] These draconarii were officers corresponding to the centarchs in the themes.

[m] These draconarii were standard bearers.

[n] The Tagma of the Hicanati had the same payroll as the Tagma of the Watch, with these differences in titles: domestic instead of drungary, protomandator instead of acoluthus, and semiophori instead of laburesii.

[o] The Tagma of the Walls had the same payroll as the Tagma of the Numera, except that its commander had the title of count.

TABLE 10
Payroll of the Army in 842

Units	Salary of head (lbs.)	Soldiers	Total men	Payroll (nom.)
THEMES AND CLEISURAE OF ASIA				
Anatolic	40	15,000	15,474	153,378
Armeniac	40	9,000	9,288	93,654
Thracesian	40	10,000	10,318	103,392
Opsician	36	6,000	6,193	63,072
Bucellarian	36	8,000	8,256	83,196
Cappadocia	24	4,000	4,131	42,300
Paphlagonia	24	5,000	5,162	52,254
Chaldia	12 [a]	4,000	4,131	41,436
Charsianum [b]	6	4,000	4,131	41,004
Seleucia [b]	6	5,000	5,162	50,958
TOTAL ASIA	264	70,000	72,246	724,644
THEMES OF EUROPE				
Thrace	24	5,000	5,162	52,254
Macedonia	36	5,000	5,162	53,118
TOTAL EUROPE	60	10,000	10,324	105,372
THEMES OF THE WESTERN CLASS				
Peloponnesus	0 [c]	2,000	2,069	20,592
Cibyrrhaeot	12	2,000	14,570	147,204
Hellas	0 [c]	2,000	4,399	43,452
Sicily	0 [c]	2,000	2,070	21,096
Cephalonia	0 [c]	2,000	2,069	20,592
Thessalonica	0 [c]	2,000	2,069	20,664
Dyrrhachium	0 [c]	2,000	2,069	20,664
Climata	0 [c]	2,000	2,069	20,664
TOTAL WEST	12	16,000	31,384	314,928
TAGMATA				
Scholae	40	4,000	4,125	59,328
Excubitors	12	4,000	4,125	50,112
Watch	12	4,000	4,125	48,240
Hicanati	12	4,000	4,125	48,240
Numera	12	2,000	2,064	24,048
Optimates	12	4,000	4,125	42,444
Walls	12	2,000	2,064	24,048
TOTAL TAGMATA	112	24,000	24,753	296,460
GRAND TOTAL	448	120,000	138,707	1,441,404

[a] The strategus collected additional pay of 12 lbs. from his theme's revenues.
[b] Cleisura.
[c] The strategus collected his pay of 12 lbs. from his theme's revenues.

then told his bureaucracy to draw up a pay scale to produce it. Like all good bureaucrats, they seem to have found a way to spend all the money appropriated, though unlike bureaucrats in a democracy they probably did not dare to exceed that sum by more than a trifling amount.

This payroll left out certain military departments that appear to have been paid along with the civilian bureaucracy or the palace staff. These were the offices of the Protostrator, the Logothete of the Herds, the Count of the Stable, the Protospatharius of the Basin, the Protospatharius of the Imperials, and the Drungary of the Fleet. The bodyguard under the Protospatharius of the Imperials had spatharii paid 144 nomismata apiece and candidati and imperial mandators paid 72 nomismata apiece; probably the spatharii were officers, the candidati regular bodyguards, and the imperial mandators messengers.[31] At this date the Drungary of the Fleet seems to have headed a department that simply arranged naval transport for other troops, and probably paid its part-time oarsmen by the campaign rather than by the year. They were in any case not part of the payroll recorded for 867. Basil I presumably provided regular pay for the oarsmen of the Imperial Fleet when he gave the fleet its own marines about 870, making it into the equivalent of a tagma.

PAY AFTER THEOPHILUS

Later emperors seem not to have made drastic changes in Theophilus's pay scale of 840. Constantine VII does, as we have seen, record Leo VI's salary list, which changed the salaries of strategi from 40, 36, 24, 12, and 6 pounds of gold to 40, 30, 20, 10, and 5 pounds. But Constantine refers to this scale as if it had passed out of use some time before. In 950 Liudprand of Cremona describes Constantine's grades of pay in descending order, beginning with a sack of gold so large that it had to be carried on the recipient's shoulders, a sum so large that it had to be dragged, then 24, 12, 7, 6, 5, 4, 3, 2, and 1 pounds of gold, with men receiving less than 1 pound being paid separately.[32]

Probably the first grade was 40 pounds. Liudprand says that it went to the Domestic of the Scholae, who earned 40 pounds in 840, and to the Drungary of the Fleet, who by acquiring permanent marines and oarsmen around 870 had become much more important than he was in 840, when he earned only 12 pounds. The grade of 36 pounds should have come next, though it may well have been paid only to strategi outside Constantinople, as it was in 840. Liudprand says that the grade of 24 pounds came next and went to 24 officials with the rank of magister; there were only one or two magistri in 840.[33] Liudprand notes that patricians came next and received 12 pounds, as they did in 840. He seems therefore to mention every grade mentioned by Jarmī down to 1 pound.

31. See Philotheus, 117.
32. Liudprand of Cremona, *Antapodosis*, VI.10, pp. 157–58.
33. Oikonomidès, *Listes*, 294.

Though Liudprand adds grades of 7, 5, and 4 pounds, these may possibly be mistakes on his part, as he anticipated the point where the difference between grades became 1 pound. His main interest in the ceremony was to find a chance to participate in it; in the end he wheedled a pound of gold for himself out of the courteous emperor. In any case, by Constantine's time the pay grades that had been 20 and 10 pounds under Leo VI were back at 24 and 12 pounds, as in Theophilus's day, and presumably the grades that had been 30 and 5 pounds were back at 36 and 6, as they had been under Theophilus.

Thus Leo's lowering of the top grades of the pay scale seems to have been a short-lived measure, already fading from memory by Constantine VII's time. If salaries had remained under Leo as they were in 842, the gradual increase in the numbers of themes would have raised the sum spent on salaries for strategi, not counting the western strategi who took their own pay from their revenues, from 448 pounds (32,256 nomismata) in 842 to 526 pounds (37,872 nomismata) by 910.[34] Leo's decreases more than compensated for this, bringing the salary bill for strategi down to 370 pounds, or 26,640 nomismata.[35]

Leo would also have raised the payroll slightly when he increased the command of centarchs from 40 men to 100 and created the pentecontarchs with commands of 50 men. These measures raised the number of regular officers in each 200-man bandum from six to seven:

	Number in rank	
	Before	After
Rank	ca. 902	ca. 902
count	1	1
centarchs	5	2
pentecontarchs	—	4

The total increase would have been 650 officers for the about 130,000 men in the army by the end of Leo's reign. If, as seems likely, Leo paid both centarchs and pentecontarchs 18 nomismata apiece, the addition of 11,700 nomismata would have been a fairly minor item.

Leo also increased the numbers of turmarchs and drungaries by an uncertain proportion, probably by about double. Turmarchs might thus have risen from 26 in 840 to around 50, and drungaries from 96 in 840 to around 200. If turmarchs were still paid 216 nomismata and drungaries 144, the increase would have been about 20,000 nomismata.[36] These sums

34. The payroll would have been increased by 12 pounds each for the strategi of Samos and the Aegean Sea and 6 pounds each for the cleisurarchs of Sebastea, Lycandus, and Leontocome, while the salary of the former cleisurarch of Charsianum would have risen from 6 pounds to 24.

35. See Constantine VII, *De Ceremoniis*, 696–97.

36. See above, pp. 105–6.

were a good deal less than the cost of 10,000 new soldiers by 911, which would have been 90,000 nomismata. None of these represented a really important increase.

The question also arises of how often these theoretically annual salaries were paid in practice. In 950 Liudprand saw Constantine VII distribute one year's pay, apparently according to long-established custom. In 867 Michael III's payment of 20,000 pounds was certainly for just one year, and since Michael was desperately short of money he would doubtless have delayed payment if he had had a precedent for it in recent memory. This brings us practically back to 840. On the other hand, the texts based on Jarmī's work include a statement that soldiers were ordinarily paid every three years, and sometimes as seldom as four, five, or six years.[37]

But Jarmī's direct experience of Byzantium ended when he was ransomed in 845, and almost all his knowledge seems to come from official Byzantine information prepared in 840. If Jarmī heard about late pay from the soldiers who guarded him between 837 and 845, they could easily have been referring to a practice that ended in 840. Perhaps more likely is that the preface of the official manual that Jarmī was using noted that in earlier times soldiers had often been paid three to six years late, but that now the munificent Emperor Theophilus was not only going to increase the army's pay but deliver it promptly every year. Such a commitment would have been difficult for Michael III to break 27 years later, even in a time of financial embarrassment.

This conclusion disagrees, however, with the established modern interpretation of another piece of evidence. Constantine VII writes in a military treatise that "in the old days" the themes were sent salaries "every four years," according to the following schedule:[38]

year 1: "the Anatolic, the Armeniac, the Thracesian";
year 2: "the Opsician, the Bucellarian, the Cappadocian";
year 3: "the Charsianian, the one of Colonia, the one of Paphlagonia";
year 4: "the one of Thrace, the one of Macedonia, the one of Chaldia."

Michael Hendy has suggested that in its original form this schedule went back to the creation of the themes in the mid-seventh century, and that the soldiers of the themes had been paid according to a similar cycle ever since then.[39]

In its present form, however, the salary schedule cannot be earlier than

37. Ibn Khurdādhbih, 84.
38. Constantine VII, *Three Treatises*, C.647–52, p. 134.
39. Hendy, *Studies*, 648–54.

863, when Charsianum was still a cleisura.[40] Even at that date, the schedule would still leave out the Cibyrrhaeots, the Aegean Sea, the Cleisura of Seleucia, and all the western themes. But the schedule's date could easily be a good deal later. The twelve themes in it are the same as the twelve strategi of the eastern themes listed by Philotheus in 899 and included in Leo VI's salary list in 910.

In fact, Hendy and others (once including myself) have failed to notice that the salary schedule refers not to the whole payrolls of the themes but only to the salaries of their strategi. All twelve of the titles in the schedule are in the masculine singular, though the Greek word "theme" (*thema*) is neuter. Earlier in the same treatise Constantine VII refers unmistakably to the Strategus of the Anatolics as "the Anatolic," the Strategus of the Armeniacs as "the Armeniac," the Count of the Opsician as "the Opsician," and so on.[41] He follows the same practice in this schedule. Perhaps after the abortive plot of Andronicus Ducas and several other leading generals in 905 Leo VI both lowered the salaries of his strategi and decided to pay them only every four years, which may have been their term of service.[42] In any case, other soldiers and officers should still have been paid annually, and by Constantine VII's time the strategi too had long been paid every year, so that Leo's arrangement belonged to "the old days."

In the first half of the tenth century the government began to ask some of its soldiers for money in place of military service. The state had already been willing to let holders of military land provide and equip someone else to serve in their place.[43] The next step was to take cash instead of a soldier. In 921 Romanus I asked the soldiers of the Theme of Peloponnesus to pay five nomismata apiece, or half that if they were very poor, rather than go on a campaign in Italy. In 949 Constantine VII asked for four nomismata apiece from some cavalry of the Thracesian Theme who were not joining his expedition against Crete. The proceeds were paid to soldiers of the Theme of Charpezicium who did go on the campaign.[44]

In the latter half of the tenth century, the number of strategi of tiny themes rose greatly, and the new rank of the dukes was created. If the pay scale remained more or less the same as in 950, when it was more or less the same as in 840, the *Escorial Tacticon* would indicate what officers' sala-

40. Theophanes Continuatus, 181 and 183.

41. Cf. Constantine VII, *Three Treatises*, C.84–92, p. 98. On p. 99 the translator, John Haldon, translates correctly the same names that he mistranslates on p. 135, where he even renders the Greek *Anatolikos* (masculine) as *Anatolikon* (neuter), the Greek *Armeniakos* as *Armeniakon*, and so on. Yet I misunderstood the passage too, in *Byzantine State Finances*, 14–15.

42. On Andronicus's plot, see Karlin-Hayter, "Revolt."

43. See Lemerle, *Agrarian History*, 124–25.

44. Constantine VII, *De Administrando Imperio*, 52, p. 256; id., *De Ceremoniis*, 666–67.

ries were about 972. The *Tacticon*'s seven dukes and catepans would appear to have earned 40 pounds of gold, since they are listed after the Strategus of the Anatolics and before the Strategus of the Armeniacs, both of whom had earned that much from 840 to 950.[45]

Then most or all of the new strategi would have earned 12 pounds of gold. All of them are listed after the lowest-ranking commander who had earned more, the Strategus of Chaldia. Nearly all of them are listed after the domestics of the Excubitors and the Strategus of the Cibyrrhaeots, who had earned 12 pounds in 840, and all of the new strategi are listed before the Drungary of the Watch, who had also earned 12 pounds. Since in the *Tacticon* the new Domestic of the Immortals follows the Domestic of the Hicanati and precedes the Domestic of the Numera, he should, like them, have earned 12 pounds.[46] The *Escorial Tacticon* extends to a point that corresponds to the end of the grade that I have assigned a salary of 3 pounds in the *Tacticon Uspensky* and Philotheus.[47]

By this time, however, the government would have been paying a great deal of money to a great many officers and soldiers, many of whom were becoming of marginal military value. The 800-man themes of battle-toughened Armenians on the frontier may actually have been more useful in wartime than the whole 9,600-man Thracesian Theme. The latter supplied barely 400 men for the expedition against Crete of 949, contributing money so that the rest could stay home and 700 men from the Theme of Charpezicium could campaign instead.[48] Yet neither the tiny new themes nor the flaccid old themes of the later tenth century had the military value of the large and battle-ready themes of 840, when Theophilus's pay scale came into effect. Lowering pay would nonetheless have been deeply unpopular.

This may well be the reason that Nicephorus II, about 964, issued the tetarteron, a nomisma that was one-twelfth lighter than the standard, and used it to pay many salaries.[49] By the reign of Nicephorus's successor John I, tetartera were a substantial proportion of the coins in circulation, perhaps as many as half. After being used less under Basil II and his immediate successors, tetartera seem again to have been about half the coins in use by the middle of the eleventh century.[50] The government had no

45. *Escorial Tacticon*, 263–65.
46. Ibid., 265–71.
47. Cf. ibid., 273.3–31, with *Tacticon Uspensky*, 57.21–61.6, and Philotheus, 151.19–155.9.
48. On the Thracesians in 949, see Treadgold, "Army," 125–28.
49. See Scylitzes, 275; the date is deduced from the order of events in the chronicle.
50. See Grierson, *Catalogue*, III.1, 28; and III.2, 582–85 (listing 5 tetartera at Dumbarton Oaks out of 27 nomismata of Nicephorus II, though the coin was only introduced midway in his reign); 592–96 (12 tetartera out of 26 nomismata of John I); 613–26 (15

reason to use tetartera to pay salaries denominated in pounds of gold, be-cause it would simply have needed to put more coins in the bags. As we shall see, the government's main expenditure was the military payroll. Therefore the tetartera probably went to some of the soldiers, decreasing the value of their pay by a twelfth. Which soldiers might these have been?

Many tetartera seem to have turned up in Constantinople, where mer-chants tried to refuse them, and they are mentioned in circulation in the Thracesian Theme. A number of specimens from the reign of Basil II have also been found in two hoards in the Dobrudja.[51] This scanty evidence is at least compatible with the obvious measure for the emperors to take: to pay the active soldiers of the tagmata and new frontier themes at the full rate in standard nomismata, but to pay the largely inactive soldiers of the older themes in tetartera, which were worth only eleven-twelfths as much.

The Thracesians would have been one of those less active themes. The Opsician and Bucellarians were others, from which tetartera would natu-rally have reached Constantinople. But tetartera would still have been the less common coins in the capital as long as the tagmata and bureaucracy were paid in standard nomismata, so that merchants could at least attempt to refuse tetartera. By Basil II's time Thrace and Macedonia would also have been largely inactive themes, and from them tetartera could have reached the Dobrudja.

Basil seems to have limited or discontinued the use of tetartera at some point. He was generous to his soldiers, to whom he distributed the Bul-garian royal treasures at the time of his final victory in 1018, and late in his reign he had so much money that he could cancel two years' land and hearth taxes and still leave a record surplus in the treasury.[52] That surplus should have allowed him to pay all his soldiers in standard nomismata, and enabled his immediate successors to follow his example.

Though this is a hypothetical reconstruction, every explanation of the Byzantine coinage must be more or less hypothetical. The explanation finds an apt parallel in what occurred next. There cannot be much doubt that the disastrous debasement of the nomisma beginning in the reign of Constantine IX was intended to reduce the cost of the now largely useless

tetartera out of 71 nomismata of Basil II); 715–18 (2 tetartera out of 35 nomismata of Romanus III); 722 (apparently no tetartera of Michael IV, though there are problems of attribution); and 727–30 (no nomismata of Michael V known, but a pattern for tetartera as well as for full-weight nomismata).

51. Ibid., III.1, 38–39.

52. For Basil's distribution of the Bulgarian treasures, see Scylitzes, 358–59. For his reserve (200,000 pounds of gold or 14.4 million nomismata), see Psellus, I.31; and for the remissions of taxes, see Scylitzes, 373.

army. Constantine did the same thing more directly by collecting taxes from the Iberian or Armenian themes in lieu of military service. The same emperor also reintroduced the use of tetartera for something like half of his payments. Then he debased the tetartera as well.[53] Yet even he seems not to have changed the nominal amount of the army's pay. The main features of the pay scale of Theophilus appear to have been quite durable.

FROM THEOPHILUS BACK TO JUSTINIAN

During the first part of his reign Theophilus was practically wallowing in gold, a fact usually taken as a sign of the empire's economic and fiscal recovery in the early ninth century.[54] About 834 he used some of his treasure to redecorate his throne room. The decorations included a gold throne, life-sized gold lions, a large gold plane tree filled with gold birds, two gold organs with pipes studded with semiprecious stones, and a small gold building used to display more gold regalia and robes of gold thread.[55] Though Michael III melted down 20,000 pounds of these gold ornaments, this was such a small portion of the whole that the lions, tree, birds, and organs could later be put back in order, to be seen by Liudprand under Constantine VII.[56]

Theophilus also left a gold reserve of 97,000 pounds (6,984,000 nomismata) when he died in 842. But over the next fourteen years, despite very moderate expenditures by Theophilus's widow Theodora, the reserve rose only to 109,000 pounds (7,848,000 nomismata).[57] This comparison alone suggests that Theodora's regular expenses were considerably higher than those of Theophilus. The empire's biggest regular expense appears always to have been the military payroll.

Confirmation that pay was lower before Theophilus comes from the chronicle of Theophanes, which records that in 811, when Arab raiders stole the pay chest of the Armeniac Theme on the first Saturday of Lent, the amount lost was 1,300 pounds of gold, or 93,600 nomismata.[58] At that date the Armeniac Theme had 14,000 men, as appears in Table 2. But if the Armeniacs had then been organized and paid as they were in 840, their

53. See above, pp. 40 and 80 with n. 85.
54. On the recovery, see Treadgold, *Byzantine Revival*, 358–67.
55. See ibid., 283–85.
56. Liudprand of Cremona, *Antapodosis*, VI.5, pp. 154–55; cf. Constantine VII, *De Ceremoniis*, 568–69.
57. Theophanes Continuatus, 253, records the figure for 842 and says that Theodora raised it to 100,000 pounds (probably at a date before 856); the same chronicle, p. 172, and Genesius, 64, record the somewhat higher figure for 856 and emphasize Theodora's thriftiness.
58. Theophanes, 489. This was soon before the regular payday; cf. above, p. 120.

payroll would have been 144,072 nomismata, about 54 percent more than it actually was.[59] Since at the rates of 840 the money for the soldiers alone would have been 126,000 nomismata, well over the full amount in 811, the soldiers' pay must have been less in 811.

In 840, when the Armeniac payroll averaged about 10.41 nomismata for each soldier, soldiers were paid an average of around 9 nomismata each. In 811, when the Armeniac payroll averaged about 6.69 nomismata for each soldier, soldiers were presumably paid an average of around 5 nomismata apiece. I once tentatively suggested that in 811 soldiers might have been paid 1 nomisma the first year, 2 the second, and so on as in 840, except that at the earlier date the annual increases would have stopped with 6 nomismata in the sixth and all later years.[60]

As has been noted above, however, computing pay by years of service was so inconvenient that the government seems to have abandoned it later in the ninth century, perhaps just a few years after its introduction in 840. That anything of the sort had been in use earlier seems extremely doubtful. If it was not, 5 nomismata, like 9 nomismata in the tenth century, should have been not an average but the standard pay of a regular soldier. Strikingly, 5 nomismata was precisely the amount of an annona, the unit of account used for paying soldiers and junior officers in the sixth century.

What is often dubiously assumed for the sixth century therefore appears to hold good at least for the early ninth: that each regular soldier was paid one annona. The exact pay scale for officers in 811 can only be guessed,

59. The calculations are as follows, assuming that in 811 the Armeniacs had turmarchs of Paphlagonia, Chaldia, and Charsianum in addition to the three turmarchs they had in 840:

Rank	Number	Rate	Total
strategus	1	2,880 nom.	2,880 nom.
turmarchs	6	216	1,296
count of the tent	1	144	144
chartulary	1	144	144
domestic	1	144	144
drungaries	14	144	2,016
counts	70	72	5,040
centarch of the spatharii	1	36	36
count of the hetaeria	1	36	36
protocancellarius	1	36	36
protomandator	1	36	36
centarchs (except for centarch of spatharii and count of hetaeria)	348	18	6,264
soldiers with decarchs	14,000	9	126,000
TOTAL	14,446 men		144,072 nom.

60. Treadgold, *Byzantine State Finances*, 74.

especially because the command structure was different at that time from what it became in 840. But there can be little doubt that almost all of the pay increase of 840 went to the common soldiers, while on average the pay of the officers stayed about the same.[61]

If the basic pay of regular soldiers was 5 nomismata apiece in 811, the amount of the Armeniac payroll indicates that the total payrolls of themes, including the officers, were then about a third higher than this basic pay alone. That is, given that the basic pay of the 14,000 Armeniac soldiers was 70,000 nomismata (5 × 14,000), the additional pay of 23,600 nomismata for officers was 33.7 percent of the basic pay. The comparable proportion for the payroll in 842 was about 19.8 percent, or roughly a fifth, since the officers' pay had failed to rise along with the soldiers'. We may therefore estimate the total army payroll in 811, omitting oarsmen and ships' officers, at some 600,000 nomismata (90,000 soldiers × 5 nomismata × ⅓).

For oarsmen and naval officers the proportion would have been different from this, and different from the 12.7 percent, or about an eighth, that it was in 842. Assuming that the pay of naval officers, like that of other officers, remained essentially unchanged by the pay reform of 840, the

61. Perhaps the simplest means of guessing the pay scale—though what happened need not have been simple—is to assume that the salaries of higher officers did not change at all between 811 and 840. Even in the sixth century, pounds of gold had generally been used for the higher salary grades, though lower grades were expressed in 5-nomisma annonae (and for cavalry in 4-nomisma capitus); cf. *Justinian Code*, I.27(1).21–42 and I.27(2).19–34. The results for the Armeniacs in 811 might then have been roughly as follows:

Rank	Salary in 840	Salary in 811(?)	Number	Total pay in 811(?)
strategus	2,880 nom.	2,880 nom.	1	2,880 nom.
turmarchs	216	216	6	1,296
count of the tent	144	144	1	144
chartulary	144	144	1	144
domestic	144	144	1	144
drungaries	144	144	14	2,016
counts	72	—	—	—
centarch of the spatharii	36	40	1	40
protocancellarius	36	40	1	40
protomandator	36	40	1	40
centarchs for 100 men	—	30	139	4,170
pentecontarchs	—	20	280	5,600
centarchs for 40 men	18	—	—	—
decarchs	[9]	10	1,400	14,000
common soldiers	[9]	5	12,600	63,000
TOTAL			14,446 men	93,514 nom.

I emphasize that other reconstructions are also possible.

payroll of the ships' officers and oarsmen of the Cibyrrhaeots for 842 (shown in Table 9) would have been as follows for 811:

Rank	Number	Rate	Total
centarchs of ships	67	72 nom.	4,824 nom.
protocarabi	134	72 nom.	9,648
oarsmen	12,300	5 nom.	61,500
TOTAL	12,501 men		75,972 nom.

The total officers' pay of 14, 472 nomismata was thus about 23.5 percent of the 61,500 nomismata paid to the oarsmen; for most purposes, adding a quarter should bring us close enough. Thus in 811 these oarsmen with their ships' officers should have earned about 75,000 nomismata (12,300 oarsmen $\times$ 5 nomismata $\times$ $\frac{3}{4}$ = 76,875 nomismata). This would make the total payroll of the themes and tagmata in 811 about 675,000 nomismata, less than half the 1,440,000 nomismata of 842.

We have seen that the basic organization of the themes seems to have undergone no change between the late seventh and early ninth centuries.[62] The soldiers' pay seems unlikely to have changed either. Basic pay can hardly have fallen below one annona, which was already low; the empire could scarcely have afforded two annonae, or 10 nomismata, since even after a major economic and financial recovery Theophilus did not quite reach that figure. Though minor changes might have been made in the pay of the officers, we have no particular reason to think that they were. As a working hypothesis, therefore, we might assume that a common soldier's annual pay had been 5 nomismata, or one annona, ever since Constans II introduced the military lands between 659 and 662.

Before the military lands were introduced, pay should have been considerably higher, but still expressed in a whole number of annonae, as it was before and afterward. If so, pay before 659 cannot have been less than 10 nomismata, or two annonae. Before Heraclius halved military pay in 616 it was twice as much as whatever the later sum between 616 and 659 was, making the original pay no less than 20 nomismata, or four annonae. In fact, the pay seems unlikely to have been more, since the next higher figure for pay between 616 and 659 in a whole number of annonae would have been three annonae or 15 nomismata, which would imply pay before 616 of 30 nomismata. This seems rather high for a common soldier. Moreover, it would mean that Maurice's abortive pay reform of 588, which was to reduce basic pay by a quarter, would have reduced it to 22½ nomismata, a fractional number of both annonae and nomismata; on the other hand, three-quarters of the lower figure of 20 nomismata would be

62. See above, pp. 98–104.

15 nomismata, or three annonae, which is quite satisfactory. If pay between 616 and 659 had been four annonae, or 20 nomismata, before 616
it would have been 40 nomismata, which Maurice would have tried to
reduce to 30; but both figures seem improbably high for basic pay. The
best guess would therefore be that basic pay was 10 nomismata before 659
and 20 nomismata before 616.

This conjecture naturally needs to be checked against the earlier evidence. As we look back, our first piece of hard evidence for military pay
applies to 641. In that year, according to the *Brief History* of the patriarch
Nicephorus, Constantine III made a payment to the army of 2,016,000
nomismata.[63] Constantine succeeded his father Heraclius on January 11
and died on April 23.[64] Since Easter fell on April 8 of that year, and we
have already seen that the army received its regular pay during Lent, this
sum surely included the regular payroll. But emperors also gave a donative
to the troops on their accession. In this case, when an accession and a
regular payday fell so close to each other, the two sums would naturally
have been paid together, both to save trouble in distributing them and to
impress the soldiers with the size of the payments.

Thus the figure recorded by Nicephorus should represent the number
of men in the army in 641 multiplied by the sum of the rate of their annual
pay and the rate of their accessional donative. All three variables are uncertain. But we know enough about all three of them that we are not
utterly helpless in trying to solve the equation. As for the regular payroll,
if it was the same in 641 as in 811 we already have the elements to estimate
it, by taking 5 nomismata times the number of regular soldiers plus one-
third for the officers. Actual pay in 641 was almost certainly more, to make
up for the fact that before 659 soldiers had no military lands. Yet basic pay
should still have been expressed in annonae of 5 nomismata, as it was before and afterward. The numbers to test are therefore 5, 10, 15, and
20 nomismata apiece, 10 being much the most likely.

Officers and ordinary soldiers seem to have received the same accessional donative.[65] This donative had long been set at 5 nomismata and a
pound of silver per man. The sum recorded by Nicephorus is however
given only in gold. In 578 Tiberius II had distributed an accessional donative of 9 nomismata per soldier, which was the rough equivalent of the
whole traditional sum. But by the time of Constantine III the empire was
in dire financial straits. Later in 641, unusually soon after Constantine III's

63. Nicephorus the Patriarch, *Short History*, 29.
64. See Treadgold, "Note on Byzantium's Year of the Four Emperors."
65. See Duncan-Jones, "Pay and Numbers," 544–45; and Haldon, *Byzantine Praetorians*, 121 and n. 155, who notes that the Scholae, though largely composed of officers,
received the same donative as ordinary soldiers.

donative, his half-brother and successor Heraclonas seems only to have been able to manage an accessional donative of 3 nomismata per soldier.[66]

Constantine should have been able to do better. For the purpose of our calculations, the consequences would be the same whether Nicephorus simply failed to mention the part of the donative that was paid in silver, or, as is perhaps more likely, Constantine economized by paying only the gold part of the usual donative. In either case, Nicephorus's figure would represent 5 nomismata per soldier. If Constantine, like Tiberius, paid the whole sum in gold, Nicephorus's figure would represent 9 nomismata per soldier. To account for the officers' share of the donative, we should add only their number, which was about a thirtieth in 840 and should have been about the same earlier.[67] Oarsmen, naval officers, and bodyguards can be ignored, because none were attached to the regular army in 641, and even in 840 and 867 the Imperial Fleet and Imperial Guard were paid separately.

As for the number of soldiers, we are not altogether in the dark. The total must have been a good deal smaller than the 150,000 men of 559 and a good deal larger than the 80,000 of 773. By 641 the empire had already suffered the great bulk of its territorial losses between those two dates. The major exceptions were Africa, of which scarcely anything had been lost, and Italy, of which about half the land had been lost, though quite possibly less of the army. As appears in Table 3, Africa had probably had 15,000 soldiers in 559 and Italy 18,000—besides the 2,000 who were still in Sicily in 773.

So in 641 the army cannot have had many fewer than 100,000 men, the figure that would be reached by adding some three-quarters of the original Army of Africa and half the original Army of Italy to the total for 773, while assuming no further losses in the eastern armies between 641 and 773. Nor can the army of 641 have had many more than 117,000 men, which would mean adding the whole original strength of the armies of Africa and Italy and assuming that the eastern armies still had an average of about 5 percent more men in 641 than in 773.

The equation should not tax the algebra even of an historian. If x is the number of soldiers in 641 and we assume basic pay of 5 nomismata per soldier and a donative of 5 nomismata per man:

$$5\left(x + \frac{x}{3}\right) + 5\left(x + \frac{x}{30}\right) = 2,016,000;$$
$$x = 170,366.$$

---

66. On all these accessional donatives, see Hendy, *Studies*, 177, 481, and 625–26.

67. In 840, the number of soldiers and officers (less the 14,831 ships' officers and oarsmen in the Cibyrrhaeots and Hellas) was 123,876, so that the 3,876 officers represented 3.23% of the 120,000 soldiers.

About 170,000 soldiers is obviously far too high, since it exceeds even the army of 559. Let us try basic pay of two annonae, or 10 nomismata:

$$10\left(x + \frac{x}{3}\right) + 5\left(x + \frac{x}{30}\right) = 2,016,000;$$
$$x = 108,973.$$

About 109,000 soldiers is an extremely plausible number for 641. If we assume a donative of 9 nomismata per man and pay of 10 nomismata per soldier, we get about 89,000 soldiers, which definitely seems too low. If we assume a donative of 9 nomismata per man and pay of 5 nomismata per soldier, we get about 126,000 soldiers, which definitely seems too high.[68]

The conclusion seems difficult to escape that in 641 the empire had about 109,000 soldiers, with basic pay of 10 nomismata a man, or two annonae. Thus when Constans II distributed military lands he seems to have cut pay in half again, as his grandfather Heraclius had done before him. The simplest means of accounting for the number of soldiers in 641 is to suppose that then the Army of Italy (with Sicily) had 16,000 soldiers, the Army of Africa still had 15,000, and the other armies had the same strength as in 773. But a somewhat different distribution is also quite possible, involving more losses in Italy and perhaps even Africa before 641, with corresponding losses in the eastern armies between 641 and 773.

Though 10 nomismata a year was not a princely sum, it should have been enough to keep a soldier and his family from destitution. It was probably not enough to keep the soldier properly equipped as well; but arms and uniforms could have been supplied in kind, as Maurice tried to do in the late sixth century while cutting cash pay. This basic pay of 10 nomismata would then have been the result of Heraclius's reduction of government salaries by half for the payday of 616.[69] Like Maurice, Heraclius would probably have had to give the soldiers something to compensate for so drastic a reduction in pay. Before 616 basic military pay was presumably twice the amount in 641. It follows that the earlier figure was 20 nomismata, or four annonae.

That was evidently the sum that Maurice had so much trouble paying. For the payday of 594 Maurice tried to substitute a free issue of uniforms, a free issue of arms, and a residual payment in gold. Apparently Maurice was replacing earlier arms and uniform allowances with these issues in

68. For the sake of argument, if we assume a donative of 3 nomismata per man (that given by Heraclonas) and pay of 10 nomismata per soldier, we get about 123,000 soldiers, which still seems too high.

69. *Paschal Chronicle*, 706. This entry also notes that payments were made in the new silver coin known as the hexagram; but that change, which was temporary, seems not to have involved any further reduction in the value of the payments. See Hendy, *Studies*, 494–95.

kind. But that arrangement was so disadvantageous to the recipients that Maurice tried to mollify them by two concessions. He provided that soldiers disabled in battle would continue to receive pay, and that the sons of soldiers killed in battle would be enrolled in their fathers' places. Even with these new benefits, the new provisions for pay were so unpopular that Maurice's general Priscus had to rescind them to avoid a mutiny.[70]

For the payday of 588, the historian Theophylact says that Maurice ordered the soldiers' pay to be reduced by a quarter, while the church historian Evagrius says somewhat vaguely that Maurice's order concerned "the soldiers' steadfastness in battle, their exact allotment of arms, and what they received from the treasury." When the order was promulgated the Army of the East rose in a mutiny that lasted until Maurice distributed the usual pay the following year.[71] Evidently Maurice had tried to replace an arms allowance that made up a quarter of the soldiers' pay with a free issue of arms, perhaps compensating the soldiers by offering bonuses for bravery in battle.

Since basic pay at the time was 20 nomismata, or four annonae, the arms allowance must have been 5 nomismata, or one annona. The uniform allowance seems also to have been 5 nomismata, so that what Heraclius did in 616 was to end both allowances, probably replacing them with issues of arms and uniforms as Maurice had planned in 594. Obviously both allowances were much inflated, or the government would not have been so eager to substitute the arms and uniforms themselves and the soldiers would not have been so determined to resist the substitution.

In fact, a law of 375 assigned recruits an initial allowance of 6 nomismata for all their gear, most of which would not have needed to be replaced every year.[72] A soldier's uniform seems to have consisted of a cloak (*pallium*), a mantle (*chlamys*), a shirt (*sticharium*), a belt, and boots.[73] A law of 396 raised the soldiers' allowance for a mantle from two-thirds of a nomisma to 1 nomisma.[74] Casual references show cloaks that cost a quarter of a nomisma and shirts around a twentieth of a nomisma.[75] Diocletian's edict on prices of 301 allows the equivalent of about a tenth of a nomisma for a pair of military boots and about the same price for a military belt.[76]

Allowing for two shirts, a full uniform would therefore have cost something like 2½ nomismata and should have lasted at least a year. Arms would

70. Theophylact, VII.1.1 – 9.
71. Ibid., III.1.1 – 4.6; Evagrius, VI.4 – 6 and 9 – 13.
72. *Theodosian Code*, VII.13.7.2.
73. Jones, *Later Roman Empire*, 624 – 25.
74. *Theodosian Code*, VII.6.4.
75. Irmscher, "Einiges über Preise," 28.
76. Diocletian, *Edict*, 9.6 and 9.11 (100 and 70 denarii for military boots), 10.8a – 10.12 (100, 200, 100, 60, and 75 denarii for military belts), and 28.1 (1 pound of gold equals 72,000 denarii, so that the later nomisma, at 72 to the pound of gold, was worth 1,000 of the denarii of the year 301).

have cost somewhat more, accounting for the roughly 3½ nomismata left over from the recruit's initial allowance. But only a very careless, cowardly, or audacious soldier would have needed a new sword, helmet, and shield every year. Given that arms should have needed replacement less often, the government had some reason to equate the uniform allowance with the arms allowance. At 10 nomismata, the combined allowances were about twice as much as soldiers actually needed for uniforms and arms annually.

The remaining 5 or so nomismata were in effect a supplement to the soldiers' basic pay. The official amount of this was 10 nomismata, or 2 annonae, the sum to which Heraclius reduced the soldiers' wages in 616. The second annona of basic pay may have been considered as an allowance for the soldier's family, a bonus awarded regular soldiers when they were promoted from recruits, a bonus for field soldiers as opposed to frontier soldiers, or simply a raise in pay introduced at some point. As with the generous allowances for uniforms and arms, the official explanation was less important than the practical result that soldiers were better paid.

FROM JUSTINIAN BACK TO DIOCLETIAN

The conclusion that full pay in the sixth century was four annonae, however, differs from the conclusions drawn by modern scholars from a pay scale promulgated by Justinian. This scale, included in an edict addressed to Belisarius in 534, applies to the clerks of the five new ducates of Africa, which Justinian was creating at the time, after Belisarius's reconquest. The emperor gives these clerks military ranks. He assigns them pay expressed in 5-nomisma annonae, which in theory represented a soldier's annual rations, and in 4-nomisma capitus, which similarly represented a year's fodder for a cavalryman's horse.

The scale runs as follows:[77]

Rank	Annonae	Capitus	Nomismata
assessor	8	4	56
primicerius	5	2	33
numerarius	4	2	28
ducenarius	3½	1½	23½
centenarius	2½	1	16½
biarchus	2	1	14
circitor	2	1	14
semissalis	1½	1	11½

All of these are military ranks except for the assessor and numerarius, who to judge from their positions in the hierarchy should have ranked as a tribune and a senator respectively. The ranks of common soldier and

77. *Justinian Code,* I.27(2).19–36.

recruit are omitted, doubtless because no clerk ranked so low. But since the title of the semissalis shows that he received pay and a half, the pay of a soldier can be assumed to be one annona and one capitus, making 9 nomismata. (The recruit perhaps received half an annona and one capitus, making 6½ nomismata.) Infantry soldiers and officers presumably received the annonae in the pay scale but not the capitus. Since these clerks had military ranks and would have accompanied the dukes on campaigns, they evidently received the same amounts as actual officers and soldiers.[78]

Though all these conclusions seem justified, they specifically apply only to the frontier troops enrolled in the ducates, who by 534 had declined so far in status that their pay was already suspended in the East and was to be canceled altogether in 545. What appears unwarranted is to assume that the same pay was given to field troops. They alone were the subjects of Maurice's abortive reforms, Heraclius's halving of salaries, and Constantine III's payment, and only they survived to become the themes who were paid in 811. The field soldiers were those who evidently received basic pay of 20 nomismata, including 10 nomismata in uniform and arms allowances.

Justinian's pay scale for the African ducates can be combined with the explanations of these military ranks given in Chapter 3 to compute the payroll of a frontier regiment at the time. Justinian assigns 2 annonae to both biarchi and circitors, the two ranks appropriate for decurions, so that this would have been the pay of both sorts of decurion. Justinian then assigns ducenarii and centenarii, the ranks appropriate for centurions, respectively 3½ annonae and 1½ capitus and 2½ annonae and 1 capitus. Thus for all centurions 3 annonae and 1¼ capitus should do as a rough average. The soldiers' pay should have averaged out at roughly the 1 annona and 1 capitus assigned a regular soldier, with the semissales and recruits counterbalancing each other.

We can therefore compute the payrolls of frontier regiments in 534 approximately as follows:

Number in rank	Infantry		Cavalry	
	Salary	Total	Salary	Total
1 tribune	40	40	56	56
1 vicarius	25	25	33	33
1 primicerius	25	25	33	33
1 adjutor	20	20	28	28
5 centurions	15	75	20	100
11 junior officers	10	110	14	154
100 decurions	10	1,000	14	1,400
400 soldiers	5	2,000	9	3,600
520 men total		3,295 nom.		5,404 nom.

78. Cf. the conclusions of Jones, *Later Roman Empire*, 634; and Haldon, *Byzantine Praetorians*, 122–23.

This then, was the pay that Justinian abolished in 545. Since 5 nomismata was not enough to support a family, the soldiers must already have found other means of supporting themselves, and in the sixth century we find them living as boatmen, basket weavers, and farmers.[79] But Justinian must have continued giving his frontier troops something to keep them serving even as a militia. Since the early fifth century they had been allowed to cultivate state lands attached to their forts, and this privilege naturally continued.[80] A papyrus shows that Egyptian frontier troops still received some rations in the mid-sixth century, perhaps when they were on guard duty or being drilled.[81] Probably Justinian also continued the frontier cavalry's capitus, which were for fodder rather than formal pay, and continued to issue horses, arms, and uniforms in kind to the frontier regiments.

The arms and uniforms would have been worth about 5 nomismata a year and the fodder 4 nomismata a year, while the horses might have averaged out to about 1 nomisma a year.[82] Since at least the horse and uniform were also useful for civilian purposes, these issues were payment enough for what had by this time become a part-time job. For the oarsmen of the fleets the only compensation would have been campaign pay when they served, but that could have been often. Oarsmen of the central navy apparently received no more regular pay until Basil I made the Imperial Fleet a fully professional force around 870. Oarsmen can hardly have been included in the payrolls for either 641 or 867.

In Justinian's payroll for frontier infantry, as in the Armeniac payroll for 811, the additional pay for officers amounts to about a third of the basic pay. That is, under Justinian basic pay of 5 nomismata apiece for 500 men would be 2,500 nomismata, while the full total of 3,295 nomismata is 31.8 percent higher than this. The slightly lower percentage under Justinian in comparison with 811 can be explained by the Armeniacs' having some officers at the higher levels of drungus, turma, and theme. The African dukes' clerks were really bureaucrats rather than soldiers; but if Justinian's salary for a duke of 1,582 nomismata is included in the total, an average ducate of perhaps 11,500 men or 23 regiments would have had total pay that was 34.6 percent more than its basic pay.[83] In either case, the proportion of additional pay for officers was near enough to a third.

79. Jones, *Later Roman Empire*, 662–63.
80. Ibid., 653–54.
81. Ibid., 672–73.
82. The official allowances for horses ranged from 15 to 23 nomismata a horse (ibid., 625–26), while the useful life of a horse was about 20 years (*Paulys Realencyclopädie*, XIX, cols. 1434–35, s.v. *Pferd*).
83. For the salary of a duke (and his clerks, who earned a total of 674½ nomismata), see *Justinian Code*, I.27(2).20–21. Assuming that the frontier troops had been reduced by about the same proportion as the field troops (see above, p. 63), I take about 91% of the

Since these frontier troops disappeared before the themes were created, their pay scale with its proportion of about a third of additional pay for officers could not have developed directly into the pay scale of the themes in 811. The ancestors of the themes were the field troops. But if their pay scale was simply that of the frontier troops multiplied by four, the percentage of their pay that went to officers would also have been around a third. When the field army's salaries were cut in half twice, this approximate percentage would still have been maintained, despite some minor changes in the command structure. This is evidently what occurred, so that the pay scale of Justinian's field troops was in fact that of his frontier troops multiplied by four.

Because in the field armies the men rather than the horses were the ones with higher status, the capitus for the cavalry were probably the same for field troops as for frontier troops. The payrolls of field regiments would then have been as follows:

Number in rank	Infantry		Cavalry	
	Salary	Total	Salary	Total
1 tribune	160	160	176	176
1 vicarius	100	100	108	108
1 primicerius	100	100	108	108
1 adjutor	80	80	88	88
5 centurions	60	300	65	325
11 junior officers	40	440	44	484
100 decurions	40	4,000	44	4,400
400 soldiers	20	8,000	24	9,600
520 men total		13,180 nom.		15,289 nom.

For the higher officers of the field armies we have no sixth-century figures. But in 840 the strategi of the Anatolics, Armeniacs, and Thracesians, and the Domestic of the Scholae, all received 40 pounds of gold apiece. Their salaries in 811 were little different, and may well have been the same as in 840. These strategi were the successors of the masters of soldiers of the armies of the East, Armenia, Thrace, and in the Emperor's Presence, who should therefore have received approximately four times as much in the sixth century, or 160 pounds (11,520 nomismata). The highest salary we know for the sixth century was that of the Praetorian Prefect of Africa, which was 100 pounds of gold (7,200 nomismata).[84] Since the

---

average strength of a ducate in 395 (some 12,500 men), and calculate as follows: salary of duke, 1,582 nom. + pay for 23 regiments (23 × 3,295 nom.), 75,785 = 77,367 nom. total; total for 11,500 men × 5 nom. = 57,500 nom.; pay for officers in addition to this, 19,867 nom. (34.6%).

84. *Justinian Code*, I.27(1).21.

Prefect of Africa was less important than the eastern masters of soldiers, the proportion appears reasonable.

In the sixth century the field forces were evidently well paid, and their pay scales seem to have gone back to Anastasius I. In the fifth century an annona had been reckoned at just 4 nomismata, but soldiers had been paid a donative of 5 nomismata every five years beginning with the reigning emperor's accession. By Justinian's reign annonae were reckoned at 5 nomismata, and according to Procopius the quinquennial donative was never paid after 518. A. H. M. Jones suggested that "Justinian rationalized the pay system by converting the quinquennial donative into an annual payment of one solidus [nomisma] a year and amalgamating it with the commutation for annona." [85]

Jones's basic explanation seems likely; his date, less so. Since the last quinquennial donative recorded is that of 511, on the twentieth anniversary of Anastasius's accession, the twenty-fifth anniversary of Anastasius's accession in 516 is also a possible date when the donative might have been commuted.[86] The expense of the quinquennial donative had traditionally been defrayed by a quinquennial tax known as the *collatio lustralis*, which was abolished by Anastasius in 498. The same emperor might well have ended both tax and donative, especially because Anastasius was famous for his financial reforms.[87]

The change would have been a very generous one, because increasing each of a field soldier's four annonae would have meant paying him 20 nomismata instead of 5 during the course of five years. Anastasius was known for his immense reserve of gold and for his generosity, while Procopius complains of Justinian's stinginess. Finally, Anastasius had a good reason for generosity to the army in 516, when he had just put down the serious military revolt of Vitalian.[88] The probability is therefore that Anastasius, not Justinian, abolished the quinquennial donative and raised the annona from 4 to 5 nomismata.

Anastasius, who made a general practice of converting payments to the army in kind into payments in cash, was probably also the emperor who set the uniform and arms allowances at an annona each.[89] The resulting pay, beginning with 20 nomismata for a common soldier—or perhaps rather with 15 nomismata for a recruit—was large enough to make military service popular, so popular that for Maurice to guarantee sons their

85. Jones, *Later Roman Empire*, 670; referring to Procopius, *Secret History*, 24.27–29.
86. On the donative of 511, see Hendy, *Studies*, 189–90.
87. On Anastasius's abolition of the *collatio lustralis* in 498, see Stein, *Histoire*, II, 203–4. For the connection with the donative, see King, "Sacrae Largitiones," 146.
88. On Vitalian's revolt, see Stein, *Histoire*, II, 177–85.
89. See ibid., 199–203; referring to John Malalas, 394; and Evagrius, III.42.

fathers' places in the army was later an important benefit. Significantly, in 512 Anastasius banned the branding or tattooing of free men, though recruits had routinely been branded since the time of Diocletian to prevent them from deserting.[90] Such a precaution had therefore become unnecessary by the latter part of Anastasius's reign.

Earlier, however, recruits had not only been branded but sometimes locked up. Potential recruits tried hard to get exemptions from service, and some even cut off their thumbs.[91] Before Anastasius the troops evidently received either arms and uniforms in kind or adequate but not generous allowances to pay for them, say 5 nomismata a year. Without these allowances, field troops would have received just 2 annonae, which moreover would have been worth only 4 nomismata apiece. The quinquennial donative would have represented the equivalent of another nomisma a year.

Thus instead of 20 nomismata, or some 15 nomismata plus arms and uniforms, field soldiers' pay would have been only about 14 nomismata, or some 9 nomismata plus arms and uniforms. Anastasius consequently increased field soldiers' discretionary pay by about two-thirds, which must have caused a very great improvement in their standard of living. Frontier soldiers would on average have earned 5 nomismata more than the cost of their equipment both before and after Anastasius's reforms; Anastasius seems not to have regarded them very highly.

As for the Scholae, since even their troopers seem to have held the rank of circitor, they should have received twice the 2 annonae of ordinary field troops.[92] This made 4 annonae or 16 nomismata, plus donatives, uniforms, arms, horses, and fodder.[93] After Anastasius's reforms, the Scholae and Excubitors presumably received 40 nomismata. Yet by then the amounts that the Scholae paid for their commissions in the first place would have been at least as much as their later salaries, so that on average they gained nothing and the government paid nothing.

Under Diocletian, before the distinction between frontier and field armies was made, papyri indicate that ordinary soldiers received pay and donatives of 12,000 denarii a year, about the equivalent of 10 aurei of that date or 12 later nomismata. Most of this came in donatives, because after the inflation of the third century the official soldier's pay of 1,800 denarii was worth less than 2 later nomismata. Because the men's arms and uniforms were also supplied in kind, the comparable figures would be 9 nom-

---

90. John Malalas, 401. On earlier branding, see Jones, *Later Roman Empire*, 616–17.
91. Ibid., 616–19.
92. On troopers' holding the rank of circitor in the Scholae, see Frank, *Scholae Palatinae*, 56–57.
93. Note that this conclusion agrees with that of Haldon, *Byzantine Praetorians*, 121–22, that Scholarians received four times the pay of ordinary (frontier) soldiers.

ismata for field soldiers before Anastasius' reforms (3 less than under Diocletian) and about 15 nomismata afterward (3 more than under Diocletian). Under Diocletian the commander of a cavalry regiment received 64,000 denarii, the equivalent of 64 later nomismata. This was a bit more than the 56 nomismata for a cavalry tribune in the frontier forces under Anastasius, but barely more than a third of the 176 nomismata for a cavalry tribune in Anastasius's field armies. Yet Diocletian's men may not have been even as well off as these figures suggest. The inflation of the coinage reduced the value of every payment before long, and difficulties in converting denarii into gold make all comparisons with later dates somewhat hazardous.[94] In 301 Diocletian had evidently tried to raise the value of military pay by retariffing the denarius and controlling prices, but his measures soon failed.[95]

Tracing with any accuracy the level of military pay during the continuing bronze inflation of the fourth and fifth centuries and through various changes in donatives and commutations seems not only impossible but pointless. Although the small residue of official pay under Diocletian disappeared entirely in the inflation, donatives, along with various allowances that came to be regarded as pay, insured at least the field troops of a living wage.[96] Nonetheless, during the later fourth and earlier fifth centuries soldiers seem to have become increasingly undisciplined and liable to extort food and other goods from civilians.[97] A law of 438 admits that by then frontier troops were able to survive on their pay only with the greatest difficulty, and other laws show that the government was already granting them land to cultivate to support themselves.[98]

We may thus distinguish several changes in pay between the third and eleventh centuries. Under Diocletian a soldier's pay was at least nominally equivalent to 12 later nomismata, excluding arms, uniforms, horses, and fodder. By the late fifth century basic pay had fallen to about 9 nomismata for field soldiers and 5 nomismata for garrison soldiers. By inflating arms and uniform allowances to 10 nomismata, about twice what arms and uniforms actually cost, and converting donatives into pay increases, Anastasius raised real pay to some 15 nomismata for field soldiers, while he left the pay of garrison soldiers approximately as it had been. Justinian eliminated the regular pay of garrison soldiers, but kept that of field soldiers the

94. For pay under Diocletian, see Duncan-Jones, "Pay and Numbers," 549–51. Since these figures relate to the year 300, I have converted them into gold on the basis of Diocletian, *Edict*, 28.1, which sets the price of a pound of gold (72 later nomismata) at 72,000 denarii in 301. But all the prices in the edict, though intended to be maximums, soon proved to be too low.

95. See Hendy, *Studies*, 448–62, esp. 458–61.

96. Cf. Jones, *Later Roman Empire*, 623–30.

97. Ibid., 648–49 and 631–32.

98. See ibid., 653–54 and n. 109, citing *Theodosian Code* II, *Novels*, IV.1.

same. Heraclius cut the real pay of field soldiers to 10 nomismata, apparently by returning to free issues of arms and uniforms.

When Constans II distributed military lands, he cut nominal pay to 5 nomismata. Since he made the soldiers responsible for their own arms, uniforms, horses, and fodder, the military expenses of infantry would have amounted to roughly the amount of their pay, while the expenses of cavalry would have been about twice as much. In fact the military lands, which were evidently larger for cavalry than for infantry, provided most of the real income for both kinds of soldier. Later, by providing the tagmata with arms, uniforms, horses, fodder, and rations besides, Constantine V left their soldiers with the full use of their 5 nomismata of pay and with another 5 nomismata's worth of rations, over and above the income of their military lands.

Under Theophilus basic pay rose to an average of 9 nomismata, which roughly covered the military expenses of thematic cavalry, gave thematic infantry about 5 nomismata over their expenses, and left the whole 9 nomismata clear for tagmatic soldiers, whose expenses were covered separately. This pay seems not to have changed significantly until the later tenth century, when Nicephorus II may have reduced its value for the older themes by a twelfth by paying it in tetartera. In the eleventh century debasement of the nomisma eventually reduced the real pay of all regular soldiers by more than half. When Constantine IX demobilized the Armenian themes, he deprived them of pay worth about 7 old nomismata and relieved them of military expenses averaging roughly that much. He apparently let them keep their military lands in return for a tax of an unknown amount, but one that they seem not to have found unduly burdensome.

All this seems to indicate that in the early Byzantine period 15 nomismata a year was a satisfactory family income, sufficient to attract eager recruits to the army. Twelve nomismata was adequate but not very attractive, while 9 or 10 nomismata was near the minimum for a family. Though 4 or 5 nomismata made a welcome supplement to one's income, it was too little to support a family without other resources. To understand exactly how well the soldiers of the themes and tagmata were supported will take us beyond the matter of pay to the subject of the military lands. Yet if a family could live badly on 9 nomismata alone, it could presumably live far better on 9 nomismata plus the income of a farm.

What already seems clear is that the two major military pay increases, those of Anastasius I and Theophilus, began major improvements in the performance of the army. After Anastasius's pay reforms, probably in 498 and 516, the army not only made the Balkans more secure than they had been since the second century but won conquests under Justinian that were unparalleled in Roman history. We shall see that the sixth-century mutinies occurred only when the soldiers' new standard of living was threatened, usually when their pay was overdue.[99] Theophilus's pay increase in 840 brought the period of serious military unrest in Byzantium to an end.[100] After this increase, the army started to make the second great wave of conquests in Byzantine history. Although these conquests were somewhat smaller and more gradual than those made under Justinian, they were won from a much smaller base and against fiercer opposition. The not at all remarkable conclusion is that the soldiers fought better and more loyally when they were well paid. This has, however, never been noticed before, because no one has had a clear idea of what the pay was.

99. See below, pp. 203–6.

100. Kaegi, *Byzantine Military Unrest,* 270–92, notes that the emperors had better control of the army after 843, but comes to no clear conclusion about the reasons. On pp. 302–3, he remarks that "the role of economics in military unrest between the fifth and mid-ninth centuries was not always clear. . . . One may draw hypotheses and inferences, but nothing more."

CHAPTER FIVE

The Army and Society

Until the late eleventh century, the armed forces must always have been the largest employer in the empire. In the fourth century, when they counted some 645,000 soldiers and sailors in both East and West, the whole government bureaucracy had only 30,000 or so officials.[1] The biggest private estates may sometimes have employed more men than the bureaucracy, but not nearly as many as the army.[2] The Church probably came second to the army in its number of employees, but they were largely celibate and had few dependents. Since the great majority of soldiers had wives and children, and some supported other relatives and servants as well, military households must have included four to six times as many people as the soldiers themselves. This mass of people naturally had a major impact on the economy, and on society in general.

In an economy that consisted chiefly of subsistence farming, an army of any real size put a noticeable burden on taxpayers. With substantial pay in cash, and duties that originally did not include farming or manufacturing, soldiers also offered a large market to those who sold food, clothing, horses, and other goods; this was especially true in the countryside, where most others had little money and produced most of what they needed for themselves. The military payroll was evidently the Byzantine government's main means of distributing currency to its subjects. When the soldiers received military lands in the seventh century, the social and economic consequences must also have been significant. Since social and

1. Jones, *Later Roman Empire*, 1057.
2. On private wealth in the empire, see Hendy, *Studies*, 201–20. The largest incomes he cites, 40 centenaria or 288,000 nomismata in the West in the early fifth century, were enough to support 32,000 families on 9 nomismata apiece. Though the wealthiest easterners were less affluent, Belisarius once maintained a private retinue of 7,000 men (Procopius, *Wars*, VII.1.20).

economic conditions were the sort of thing that contemporary sources took for granted, they are extremely difficult to trace. Yet the available evidence suggests some conclusions about the army's impact on society that range from plausible to highly probable.

MANPOWER

Even in Byzantine times, farmers produced some surplus, so that not everyone needed to work the land. Up to a certain size, the army would not have taxed the empire's agricultural production and manpower to any appreciable extent. Above that size, the army would have caused something of an economic and demographic drain, impoverishing some remaining farmers and leaving too little surplus to feed part of the population in times of scarcity. Above some larger size, the army would have placed a crushing and ultimately unsustainable burden on the population, ruining taxpayers and causing famines and economic collapse. Knowing where the Byzantine army belonged on this scale would be of obvious historical interest to us.

But the question is a complicated one. For one thing, it can easily be confused with the related but different question of the state's ability to pay the army. If the system of taxation and distribution was inefficient and corrupt, the state might have had difficulty paying an army that the population could otherwise have sustained easily. Conversely, a ruthlessly efficient system or very low pay might have enabled the state to finance an army that would have been too big for the economy to support at an adequate level without great hardship to taxpayers.

Moreover, even if widespread poverty and hunger could be proved, the size of the army need not have been the main reason for these, or even one of the reasons. The only means of seriously examining whether the army constituted a serious burden on the empire's manpower is to relate the size of the army to the size of the population at different dates. If the highest proportions came at times of acute economic distress, the size of the army might well have been an important reason for that distress—although even this conclusion would only be a reasonable deduction rather than something approaching proof.

Some scholars maintain that nothing useful can be said about the total population in Byzantine times.[3] If pressed, they would probably admit that the eastern empire in the fourth century could hardly have had fewer than ten million people or more than a hundred million, and that saying even this would be of some use to someone who did not know it already. What they really mean is that the surviving scraps of evidence, mostly

3. E.g., MacMullen, "How Big?" 459; and Hendy, *Studies*, 8.

scattered figures for the size of cities, form a hopelessly inadequate basis for estimating the total population of the empire. This is perfectly true. In contrast to the army, we have no overall totals or individual figures from which totals could be calculated. Though the Byzantine government occasionally took censuses from which such calculations could have been made, nothing survives from them today that can reasonably be used for that purpose.

There is, however, another way to estimate the population—not a very precise or reliable method, but much better than mere guesswork. This is to extrapolate backward from modern demographic evidence, which becomes dramatically better soon after the Ottoman conquest, and to extrapolate forward from ancient demographic evidence, which is at least better than that for Byzantine times. The ancient evidence includes, notably, the text of an inscription of Pompey the Great saying that in the first century B.C. he conquered 12,183,000 people in Anatolia and Syria.[4] Extrapolations from such ancient and modern evidence have been made on a worldwide basis by Colin McEvedy and Richard Jones, aided by common sense and a good grasp of the problem.[5] Some of their conclusions can be checked against estimates for Byzantine tax revenues, with encouraging results.[6]

The worst problem with extrapolating trends in the absence of specific evidence for the time in between is that, though the trend over the long term should be correct, it could easily have reversed itself in the shorter term. In one place McEvedy and Jones seem to have fallen into this trap, by almost ignoring the mortality caused by the bubonic plague under Justinian and consequently missing a preceding demographic recovery that the plague cut short. They calculate that the bubonic plague killed between a quarter and a third of the European population in 1347–53.[7] Procopius estimated in 550 that the plague had killed about half the empire's population since its first appearance in 541, while a recent modern estimate is about a third.[8]

As we shall see, the figures already established for the army's size and pay indicate that the empire's revenue about 565 was approximately the same as in 518, though taxes had risen slightly and a vast area of North Africa, Italy, and Spain had been conquered in the meantime. In 565, revenue seems to have been about a quarter lower than it had been in 540,

4. Pliny, *Natural History*, VII.97. Pompey included people that he killed, but they cannot have been a very large percentage.

5. McEvedy and Jones, *Atlas*, citing Pompey's inscription on p. 136.

6. Cf. Treadgold, *Byzantine Revival*, 456 n. 482.

7. McEvedy and Jones, *Atlas*, 24–25. Otherwise on the bubonic plague in history, see Biraben, *Hommes et la peste*, I, esp. 22–48; and McNeill, *Plagues and Peoples*.

8. Procopius, *Secret History*, 18.44. Cf. Allen, "'Justinianic' Plague," 11–12.

just before the plague. This difference seems to represent the death of about a quarter of the taxpayers between 540 and 565. Yet revenue in 518 was about a sixth higher than in 457, though no territory had been gained since then. The obvious explanation is an increase in the number of tax-payers between 457 and 518, presumably continuing until the plague be-gan in 541.[9]

McEvedy and Jones assume a steady decline in population all around the Mediterranean from about 200 to 600. Their estimates seem reason-able for the period after 565, when the plague became less virulent, though epidemics continued to recur during the next two hundred years. Their estimates seem less reasonable for the period from 300 to 400. Dur-ing this period the empire was still suffering from the effects of two deadly epidemics in 165–80 and 251–66, which may have marked the first ap-pearances of smallpox and measles in the Mediterranean.[10] Yet most of the losses should have occurred during those epidemics, not in the fourth century. Therefore, the estimates of McEvedy and Jones should probably be adjusted by assuming that the population of the empire in 300 was only a little higher than in 395, that in 518 the population was roughly equal to that of the much larger empire of 565, and that in 565 it was about three-quarters of what it had been in 540. The resulting estimates appear in Table 11, where they are compared with the size of the army at different dates.

There a distinction is also drawn between full-time soldiers, who had no other profession, and part-time soldiers, who had other professions as well and were mostly self-supporting. The difference was obviously an important one for the soldiers' social and economic role, though this would have varied according to the exact composition and nature of their income. In military terms the distinction can be misleading, because part-time soldiers were not necessarily worse than others. Most of the poorly paid frontier soldiers of the later fourth century lacked other means of support and so must be counted as full-time soldiers, but they were second-rate troops. Though the thematic troops of the late ninth and early tenth centuries drew most of their income from military lands, they were ready for service on short notice and generally fought well.

The part-time soldiers included the frontier troops and fleets after their pay fell below a living wage sometime in the fifth century. The Scholae also counted as part-time soldiers by the early sixth century, when they were independently wealthy men who had bought their commissions for the sake of prestige. By the mid-seventh century, the frontier troops apart from the fleets had been entirely lost along with the frontiers, and the

9. See below, pp. 188–98 and Table 12.
10. On these quite obscure epidemics, see McNeill, *Plagues and Peoples*, 103–9.

TABLE II
Estimated Population and Army Size from 284 to 1025

Year	Estimated population (millions)	Full-time soldiers	Part-time soldiers	All soldiers
284	19 [a]	253,000 (1.3%)	—	253,000 (1.3%)
305	19 [a]	311,000 (1.6%)	—	311,000 (1.6%)
395	16.5	335,000 (2.0%)	—	335,000 (2.0%)
518	19.5 [b]	95,300 [c] (0.5%)	206,000 [d] (1.1%)	301,300 (1.6%)
540	26 [e]	145,300 [c] (0.6%)	229,000 [d] (0.9%)	374,300 (1.4%)
565	19.5	150,300 [c] (0.8%)	229,000 [d] (1.2%)	379,300 (2.0%)
641	10.5	109,000 (1.0%)	20,000 [f] (0.2%)	129,000 (1.2%)
775	7	18,400 [g] (0.3%)	100,100 [h] (1.4%)	118,500 (1.7%)
842	8	24,400 [g] (0.3%)	130,200 [h] (1.6%)	154,600 (1.9%)
959	9	29,200 [i] (0.3%)	150,200 [h] (1.7%)	179,400 (2.0%)
1025	12	43,200 [i] (0.4%)	240,000 [h] (2.0%)	283,200 (2.4%)

NOTE: All population estimates are adapted from McEvedy and Jones, *Atlas*, and rounded to the nearest half million. Figures do not include the Western Roman Empire. Army figures, some of which are less precise than they may appear, include both soldiers and oarsmen.

[a] Revised from McEvedy and Jones, whose estimate would be 21M.
[b] Revised from McEvedy and Jones, whose estimate would be 14.5M.
[c] Field soldiers and Excubitors.
[d] Frontier soldiers, Scholae, and oarsmen.
[e] Revised from McEvedy and Jones, whose estimate would be 20M.
[f] Oarsmen.
[g] Tagmata and bodyguards.
[h] Themes and oarsmen.
[i] Tagmata, marines of Imperial Fleet, and bodyguards.

Scholae and Excubitors were, if anything at all, officials of the bureaucracy. At least by the eighth century, the soldiers of the themes cannot be considered full-time troops in social and economic terms. The soldiers of the tagmata, however, may well have drawn more than half their income from the state, as bodyguards certainly did. In any case, the tagmata were always ready for service, and cannot have had time to contribute much to the civilian economy, as thematic troops seem to have done.

All the figures for army size are based on relatively good evidence. For 285 we have the total of John the Lydian, and the known positions of legions earlier in the third century show about how many of these soldiers would have been in the East when Diocletian divided the empire in 285. For 312 we have the figures of Zosimus; but since at that date about 16,000 eastern troops seem to have been temporarily in the West, they can be added to the eastern total to give a more typical figure for 305. For 395 we have the catalogue of units in the *Notitia Dignitatum*, which when multiplied by their official strength yield figures that agree well with other evidence, including Zosimus.

For the sixth century we have Agathias's total for the field forces in 559. This should have been about the same in 565, the same less Spain in 540, and the same less Armenia, Africa, Italy, and Spain in 518. Procopius's figure for the fleet in 534 is probably more or less the total. The frontier troops can be estimated by assuming that they had decreased by about the same proportion as the mobile army since the fourth century, roughly a tenth, then making some allowance for Justinian's new frontier troops in Africa. For 641 we have the total that follows from the combined payroll and donative recorded by the patriarch Nicephorus, to which we should add a figure for the oarsmen of the central fleet; this should have been roughly equal to the number of Mardaïtes who later in the century apparently took over those oarsmen's duties of rowing the marines of the Carabisian Theme.

For 773 we have Theophanes' total and for 840 Jarmī's total. Both are almost certainly derived from official figures, and should also be applicable to 775 and 842, dates that come conveniently at the ends of the reigns of Constantine V and Theophilus. Jarmī's distribution of soldiers among the themes and tagmata allows us to reconstruct the earlier pattern with some confidence. The numbers of oarsmen at both dates can be closely calculated from the official figures at the time of the expedition against Crete in 911. Then the earlier figures can be adapted for 959 with a fairly small margin for error, and for 1025 with a margin that is larger but probably under 10 percent.

Despite the general reliability of the numbers for the army, minor differences in the percentages of men under arms in Table 11 should not be taken very seriously, because the population estimates are extremely rough. If those estimates lead to unlikely conclusions, we should be ready to conclude that the estimates are wrong rather than that the implausible conclusions are right. But by and large the estimates lead to plausible conclusions.

They suggest that the numbers of men who served full- or part-time in the Byzantine army and navy fluctuated between a high of about 2.4 percent of the population in 1025 and a low of about 1.2 percent in 641. The highest percentage, for 1025, implies that military families formed about a tenth of the population; the lowest percentage, for 641, implies that they were about a twentieth. The highest absolute number for full-time soldiers comes in 395. At that date, all the soldiers can be considered full-time, and they accounted for some 2 percent of the population.

The eastern army of about 253,000 that Diocletian took over at his accession in 284 seems not to have greatly strained the empire's manpower, but it also failed to keep out the empire's enemies. Regardless of what was happening in the West, where the army grew much more, Diocletian was fairly moderate in his new recruitment in the East, where he was familiar with defensive needs and managed the army himself. He increased its strength by almost a quarter, to 311,000.[11] This was enough to defeat the Persians and Goths. The main reason that Diocletian had trouble attracting recruits was probably that he paid them rather badly, not that able-bodied men were scarce. Among a population that seems to have been decreasing, 58,000 or so recruits would still have been missed on the farms and elsewhere. Nevertheless, Diocletian seems to have struck a reasonable balance between the eastern empire's military and economic needs.

By 395, when full-time soldiers appear to have formed a larger proportion of the empire's population than at any other date, the balance was less reasonable. The population had apparently fallen a bit, while the army had grown somewhat. The increase in the size of the army since 305 that appears in Table 11 is reduced by the administrative transfer of western Illyricum with some 63,000 soldiers to the western empire. If we include those western troops, the East would have had 365,500 soldiers, some 54,500 more than in 305. Meanwhile the army had come to fight less well and to include many more barbarians than before.

The fourth and early fifth centuries were the time when the army must have put the greatest strain on the empire's manpower. Most of the evidence for serious poverty, famines, and abandonment of land belongs to this period, especially to the later fourth century.[12] During the fourth century a demographic recovery might perhaps have been expected, as the population built up some resistance to the diseases that had arrived in the second and third centuries. But if such a recovery occurred at all, it was too weak to leave clear traces in our admittedly scanty sources of information. Only in the fifth century do archeological remains and literary evidence begin to show a definite rise in prosperity, which enabled Anastasius I to cut taxes and run a large surplus. By this time, the largest part of the army, the frontier troops, had returned to the agricultural work force. The size of the army seems likely to have been one cause of the empire's earlier troubles.

Yet other factors were surely present as well, and the importance of the army's size can be exaggerated. In the western empire as it was in 305, Zosimus's figures point to an army of some 270,000 men, compared with a population estimated by McEvedy and Jones at about 23.5 million. This

11. Here I add the about 16,000 men who apparently deserted from Galerius to Maxentius in 307; see above, p. 55.

12. See Jones, *Later Roman Empire*, 808–23 and 1040–48.

is a little over 1.1 percent, and the proportion seems to have been much the same in 395, though estimating the army's size from the later evidence of the *Notitia* requires some guesswork.[13] If this number of men under arms contributed substantially to the fall of the West, then the East should have fallen first, because in proportion it had about twice as many men under arms and was surely less than twice as rich. In the early fifth century, the barbarians must have helped reduce the burden of the army on the western empire by reducing the army; yet the West failed to benefit. Manpower was clearly not the main factor.[14]

By 518, presumably assisted by the demographic recovery, Anastasius left a mobile army that was well paid, relatively efficient, and once again overwhelmingly native. Though the frontier troops were much inferior to the field forces, they also cost much less and made some contribution to the civilian economy. Justinian was able not merely to dream of reconquering the West, but to succeed in retaking North Africa and Italy with surprisingly little trouble by 540. In doing so, he increased the army, but probably by a smaller proportion than the conquests increased the empire's population.

Then the plague wiped out about as many people as Justinian had regained through his conquests, leaving the army overextended. Pay remained good enough to maintain the strength of the mobile army without resorting to conscription; but that meant that a considerably smaller civilian population was left to support an army of equal size. Without regular pay, the frontier forces deteriorated still further, but at least they cost less and were feeding themselves as farmers. Toward the end of the sixth century Maurice found the army difficult to pay, though even while failing to cut its cost he managed to avoid bankruptcy. The plague would surely have caused grave economic and fiscal troubles even if the army had been smaller.

By 641, enemy conquests had eliminated the frontier troops, except for the oarsmen of the fleet, leaving the empire with what was probably its smallest percentage of soldiers throughout the whole period from 284 to 1081. Since civilians had been lost more rapidly than field troops, however, the percentage of the population who were full-time soldiers increased, to about 1 percent instead of the 0.6 percent of 540 or the 0.8 percent of 565. These troops were harder to pay than to feed. Although the government had to cut pay in half, not even all the foreign invasions seem to have led to persistent famines. The reason for giving the soldiers military lands was of course to provide them with a means of sup-

13. I would suggest a figure of around 225,000 men for the army of the western empire in 395, when its area was larger than in 305 and the estimates of McEvedy and Jones would put its population at about 21.5 million.

14. Ferrill, *Fall*, rightly stresses the military causes of the fall of the western empire.

port, not to increase the agricultural population. The military lands nonetheless had that effect. We shall see that though cavalrymen in particular may not have needed to work their lands, soldiers did do farmwork and must have spent more than half their time on managing their farms.[15]

Between 641 and 775, Byzantium lost still more of its population, principally in Italy and North Africa. Since it lost fewer soldiers, however, their percentage returned to the range of about 1.5 to 2 percent of the population that was typical of the earlier period. Though the troops of the tagmata apparently continued to have military lands, their duties became heavier than those of thematic troops, and unlike thematic troops they were supplied with uniforms, arms, rations, mounts, and fodder. Since tagmatic troops could be transferred for long periods far from their permanent homes in Thrace and northwestern Anatolia, they were essentially full-time soldiers.

Yet the tagmata had many fewer men than the themes. Between 775 and 1025, the tagmata grew at about the same rate as the population at large. The themes grew faster, probably raising the percentage of the empire's subjects in the army to an all-time high. The latter increase is largely illusory, however, because while new themes were added the older ones began to deteriorate. However ineffective the thematic troops may have been, they remained on the payroll; but at least they were still farmers or landlords rather than mere parasites.

The general conclusion that can be drawn is that the army never took any crippling proportion of the empire's manpower away from more productive pursuits. The one period in which the army may have burdened the economy significantly was from about 300 to 450, when a shortage of manpower does seem to have been a problem. This was also the time when the army relied most on recruiting barbarians. One reason for relying on barbarian soldiers does seem to have been that Byzantines could not easily be spared from agriculture, while barbarians would not otherwise have been contributing anything to the empire's economy. Nonetheless, in the earlier fourth century the empire had supported nearly 2 percent of its population as full-time soldiers without extensive barbarian recruitment. This burden may have caused some hardship, but it was bearable. An overlarge army never became a major liability for Byzantium.

MONEY AND TRADE

The Byzantine state coined money primarily to finance its own needs, and the most vital and expensive of those needs was its defense. Military expenses must always have represented well over half the state budget, and

15. See below, pp. 173–79.

the army payroll must have been much the largest single item. Of course, once the coinage came into circulation through government payments, it provided the people with a more or less abundant medium of exchange; it helped everyone to pay taxes, and fostered trade and urban life. But the government seems scarcely to have been aware of these advantages; and in any case its attitude toward trade and private profits in general was ambivalent. The economic consequences of the military payroll were therefore large, but largely unplanned.

Diocletian, who made much use of issues in kind to the army, paid both its donatives and its wages in bronze coins.[16] Constantine apparently began paying the army's quinquennial donative in gold coins, and his successors paid their accessional donatives in gold and silver.[17] The army continued to receive its wages and annual donatives in bronze until bronze inflation made them so inconsequential that they were dropped, probably toward the end of the fourth century.[18] By the later fourth century, however, soldiers often received allowances in gold instead of uniforms and horses.[19] During the first half of the fifth century, the government began to convert issues of rations and fodder into four-nomisma annonae and capitus, which soon became the soldiers' real wages.[20]

Since the dates and amounts of the commutation of issues in kind during the fourth and fifth centuries are impossible to determine with any precision, their effects on the availability of the coinage are hard to trace. But without question the gold coinage was relatively insignificant under Diocletian, as we would expect if the army was paid not in gold but in bronze. Under Diocletian the bronze coinage was still subject to considerable inflation, which was also to be expected as long as Diocletian paid out such enormous sums in coins with little intrinsic value.

By confiscating the treasures of pagan temples and minting the first nomismata at 72 to the pound of gold, Constantine was the first emperor to furnish the empire a gold coinage of substantial volume. This he would largely have distributed through his quinquennial donatives. Since natu-

16. Duncan-Jones, "Pay and Numbers," 542–45 and 549–51.

17. The anonymous *De Rebus Bellicis*, I–II, says that under Constantine gold taken from pagan temples was substituted for bronze in small payments, among which the treatise has just included military donatives. Since Constantine confiscated no temple treasures until 324, this could not apply to his accessional donative in 306, but only to his quinquennial donatives, probably beginning with that of 326. Cf. Libanius, *Orations*, 30.6 and 30.37, who reports that Constantine used the confiscated temple treasures to build Constantinople between 324 and 330. The first recorded accessional donative paid in gold was Julian's in 360; see Hendy, *Studies*, 177. Hendy suggests that the donative of 5 nomismata and a pound of silver went back to Diocletian; but since the nomisma struck at 72 to the pound of gold was created by Constantine (Diocletian's aureus being struck at 60 to the pound), this seems unlikely.

18. Jones, *Later Roman Empire*, 623–24.

19. Ibid., 624–26.

20. Ibid., 630 and 670.

rally people preferred the gold coinage to the bronze, or to the billon coins of bronze with a small silver content that Constantine issued in large numbers, the bronze and billon still suffered from inflation. The inflation seems however to have slowed somewhat since Diocletian's day, perhaps because the overabundance of the base-metal coins decreased as they came to be used less for payments to the army.[21]

Anastasius I finally supplied a fairly stable base-metal coinage when he minted the bronze follis. By increasing the pay of the army in gold, and perhaps by entirely ending payments to the army in base metal, Anastasius appears to have brought supplies of the two sorts of coinage into some sort of balance. This balance was more or less maintained until the debasement of the gold coinage in the eleventh century. Though the nomisma was the main store of value, it was so valuable that it could only circulate properly along with folles to make change for it. The government could provide folles in return for nomismata at a substantial profit, because it was exchanging an amount of bronze for an amount of gold with a much greater intrinsic value.[22]

Obviously the government did not station soldiers where it did in order to distribute its coinage evenly over the empire for the convenience of taxpayers and traders. Yet the evidence of the *Notitia Dignitatum* shows that the troops happened to be quite widely distributed through the eastern empire about 395, as appears in Map 6. As appears in Map 7, a similarly wide distribution continued into the sixth century, when even the frontier troops were still receiving some money for supplies.

The frontier troops covered the frontiers in the widest sense, including all of Egypt and Palestine and almost all of Syria. They also covered a broad border zone along the Danube in the Balkans. The mobile armies of Thrace and Illyricum had stations in parts of the Balkans to the south of the border zone. The armies in the Emperor's Presence and the Scholae would have occupied additional areas around the capital in southern Thrace and northwestern Anatolia.

Although few soldiers were to be found in the islands and coastal areas of Greece and Anatolia away from Constantinople, these were the places with the best communications, since by far the cheapest transport was by sea. Once soldiers bought goods or goods were bought for them, the coins would be likely to find their way to the coasts in other transactions. Some of the oarsmen of the fleets would also have been based on the coasts and islands, and even those who were not would have visited these areas while on campaign and spent some of their pay there.

21. For the development of the coinage during the fourth and fifth centuries, see Hendy, *Studies*, 284–96 and 448–75.
22. See ibid., 475–78 and 285–89.

The other region where few troops were to be found was the interior of Anatolia. There, however, the government spent money on the stations, couriers, wagons, horses, and mules of the public post, which largely served to send supplies collected by taxation in kind to the armies on the eastern frontier. Not long after Anastasius converted most of these taxes in kind and issues to the army into gold, Justinian greatly reduced the size of the post. Then contemporaries complained that landowners could no longer sell their crops to the post, so that they lacked the money to pay their taxes.[23] But this was a problem limited to a particular time and place. Otherwise the system worked rather well.

Heraclius's halving of military pay would have reduced the number of coins in circulation to some extent, but not by as much as half. Heraclius seems to have replaced part of the lost pay by buying arms and uniforms for the troops with bronze coins.[24] In his time soldiers became even more concentrated in what remained of the empire in Anatolia, since they had been driven out of the Balkans, Syria, and Egypt. As a result, in parts of the interior of Anatolia the availability of coins may even have increased.

The real change came with Constans II's introduction of the military lands to replace not only half the soldiers' remaining pay but the money, much of it bronze, that had been spent on their arms, uniforms, horses, and fodder. In the ninth century, and presumably from the beginning of the theme system, thematic soldiers were responsible for providing even their own rations on campaigns.[25] Coming at a time when the army was already concentrated in Anatolia, this change would have reduced the empire's money supply by much more than half. The greatest reduction would have come in the bronze coinage, since almost all that remained of military spending was the soldiers' reduced salaries in gold.

As has long been noticed, every Byzantine archeological site shows a dramatic decrease in coin finds between the middle of the seventh century and the middle of the ninth. This is primarily a decrease in bronze coins, since they form the great majority of those found for all periods; for the period of scarcity the falling-off in the few gold coins found is somewhat less dramatic than for the bronze, while Byzantine silver coins had never been very common. In some places, particularly in Anatolia, no coins at all, whether bronze, silver, or gold, are found from this period of around two hundred years. Hendy has recently pointed out that the decrease begins suddenly in the reign of Constans II, when coins of the type minted between 641 and 658 are proportionally far more common than those of the type minted between 658 and 668. Hendy connects the de-

---

23. See the discussion ibid., 294–96 and 602–7.
24. On Heraclius's use of bronze to pay for supplies, see ibid., 643.
25. Ibn Khurdādhbih, 85.

crease with the beginning of the military lands. He also notes the increase in both gold and bronze coins that dates from the reign of Theophilus (829–42), and connects this increase with the preceding financial reforms of Nicephorus I (802–11).[26]

Nicephorus certainly did conduct a new census and improve the efficiency of taxation, causing a great improvement in the government's finances.[27] But the amount of the Armeniacs' payroll for 811 indicates that he did not increase the pay of the army, though his increase in the size of the army by some 6,000 men would have raised the amount of the military payroll somewhat in Greece and around Constantinople.[28] By themselves, Nicephorus's financial reforms would merely have increased the amount of gold in the treasury, not the gold coinage in circulation. Nicephorus in fact accumulated a large reserve. Although much of it was spent on largess by his extravagant son-in-law Michael I, the effects of more efficient taxation evidently continued to fill the treasury, without greatly expanding the money supply, until the reign of Theophilus.[29]

Coinage became much more common only under Theophilus, and specifically with the types of gold nomisma and bronze follis that he minted from about 835 to about 840.[30] This is the period of Theophilus's increase in military salaries, which would first have been paid in Lent of 840 but would have required a good deal of preparatory minting. Besides almost doubling his ordinary soldiers' pay, Theophilus expanded the payroll by enrolling the 30,000 Khurramite refugees from the caliphate, who represented an increase of fully a third in the army's strength.

These new nomismata would have been paid directly to the soldiers. Some of the new folles may have been spent on supplies for the tagmata. But Theophilus, who was known for his weekly visits to inspect the markets of Constantinople, may also have come to realize that buyers and sellers needed more small coinage, and that the soldiers in particular needed it if they were to spend their new earnings on buying better equipment. More folles could have been distributed easily enough by giving more of them in change when taxes were collected—or perhaps when arms or uniforms were sold to the soldiers of the themes. Although such a measure would have shown a quite unusual amount of attention to the

---

26. Hendy, *Studies*, 640–45.

27. See Treadgold, *Byzantine Revival*, 146–70 and 190–92.

28. Nicephorus's recruits were in his new Tagma of the Hicanati and Theme of Thessalonica. Though he also converted 4,000 Mardaïtes of the West from oarsmen in Hellas to soldiers in Peloponnesus and Cephalonia, this would have had no effect on the payroll apart from adding a little more pay for their officers and changing some of the places where the money was spent. See above, pp. 69 and 72.

29. On Michael I's expenditures, see Treadgold, *Byzantine Revival*, 177, 181, and 185–86.

30. For the dates of these types, see Treadgold, "Problem."

needs of ordinary subjects, the sources repeatedly attribute such attentiveness to Theophilus.[31]

After the settling of soldiers on military lands, their distribution over the empire was quite even, much more so than in earlier times. As Map 8 shows, soldiers were settled all over the empire in 840, as they had been in 775 and doubtless since the introduction of the military lands. The addition of the Mardaïte oarsmen in the Cibyrrhaeots and Hellas in the late seventh century meant that the number of men in the coastlands and islands who drew military pay was larger than in the early Byzantine period.

After 840 the empire once again had a fairly substantial coinage in both gold and bronze. Though no further increase occurred in the rate of pay, the payroll continued to grow along with the number of soldiers. As the empire expanded its frontiers during the tenth and early eleventh centuries, the newly conquered areas received their share of troops and military pay. The infusion of cash must have made a noticeable difference in the Balkans north of Greece, where the economy was so primitive that Basil II had to let the conquered Bulgarians pay their taxes in kind, and in Cilicia and Syria, where the raids that preceded the Byzantine conquest had devastated and depopulated the land.[32]

The main stages in the development of the Byzantine monetary economy were therefore Constantine I's beginning to pay military donatives in nomismata, the commutation of military pay to nomismata that was completed by Anastasius I, Constans II's great reduction in military payments when he introduced military lands, and Theophilus's large increase in the military payroll. Although soldiers can hardly have been the richest men in an empire where most wealth was concentrated in land, a disproportionate amount of the empire's coinage passed through their hands. Since many Byzantine magnates were largely self-sufficient, soldiers must also have been comparatively heavy spenders, especially before they acquired their military lands, and again after Theophilus raised their pay.

LAND AND MILITARY LAND

At the beginning of the Byzantine period, as in earlier Roman times, few active soldiers owned land, and no regular soldier was supposed to engage in farming. In the fourth century, discharged veterans were still given farms from state land, but this practice seems to have lapsed by the early fifth century. At that time, frontier troops were allowed to cultivate

31. On Theophilus's care for his subjects, including his weekly visits to markets, see Treadgold, *Byzantine Revival*, 266–68, 271–72, 287–89, 322, and 326.
32. On the Bulgarians' taxes in kind, see Scylitzes, 412.

the lands attached to their forts; but this was part of the process by which they became only part-time soldiers, as their pay fell below a living wage.[33] Because the field troops were still quite mobile, as long as they were on active duty they would have had trouble even supervising land worked by others, let alone working it themselves. The few of them who held land cannot have held much of it.

Since by the mid-seventh century the lands of the frontier troops had been lost along with the troops and the frontiers, the military lands of the themes were an entirely new development. We shall soon see that they were of considerable value and extent. Where did they come from? Though the sources say nothing, the only sources to make explicit mention of military lands are laws, and for the seventh century practically no laws survive.

The possibilities that have been suggested for the origin of the military lands are purchase by the soldiers, confiscation from landholders, and allotment from the imperial estates. Though some soldiers doubtless did buy land later to add to their original grants, that the great mass of the impoverished soldiers of the seventh century could have bought enough land to support themselves at once seems impossible. Arbitrary confiscation by the government usually raised protests that appear in even the most meager of sources, but no such protests are recorded. For example, the sources bitterly denounce confiscations of property from a few magnates made by Justinian II at the end of the same century, which led to his overthrow in 695.[34] Wholesale confiscations between 659 and 662 would have presented an enormous risk for the embattled Constans II, who had made many enemies by his religious policies and was assassinated by military rebels a few years later.

Some land was always being confiscated legally, from owners who had abandoned their holdings, died without heirs, been convicted of rebellion, or defaulted on their taxes. No doubt the unsettled conditions of the seventh century would have led to more such confiscations than before. But such land had long passed directly to the imperial estates. If it went to the soldiers instead, it amounted to the third possibility for the origin of the military lands, redistribution from those estates.

In the sixth century, the imperial estates seem to have included something like a fifth of the empire's land, spread widely over the provinces. The estates contributed vast revenues under the supervision of one of the emperor's chief ministers, the Count of the Private Estate. They were manned by tenants or slaves, and were ordinarily leased to private managers who paid rent to the count's office. In the ninth century, when the

---

33. Jones, *Later Roman Empire*, 635–36 and 653–54.
34. Theophanes, 367–69; Nicephorus the Patriarch, *Short History*, 39–40.

imperial estates appear again in the sources, they consisted of a few scattered tracts under a low-ranking official, the Great Curator, who also supervised imperial palaces. On the other hand, the military lands, unknown in the sixth century, became highly important. Tenth-century legislation assumes that soldiers held them in return for military service, as if by doing the service they were paying rent for public land.

Although the evidence for concluding that the military lands were drawn from the imperial estates is circumstantial, the circumstantial case is so strong that it recently led both Hendy and myself to that conclusion independently.[35] Of course, if the imperial estates were not large enough in some areas to support the troops needed there, the state could have forced landowners to trade their holdings for imperial lands elsewhere. Nicephorus I later forced a number of people to buy or accept lands in this sort of way.[36]

A law of Constantine VII specifies that cavalrymen had to maintain lands worth at least four pounds of gold (288 nomismata), and notes that this was a long-established minimum. The same law says that marines of the themes of the Cibyrrhaeots, Samos, and the Aegean Sea were to keep lands worth the same amount, while marines of the Imperial Fleet and the other naval themes (apparently Hellas, Peloponnesus, Cephalonia, and Nicopolis, all of which had marines in the tenth century) had to maintain lands worth at least two pounds (144 nomismata).[37] Constantine writes elsewhere that cavalrymen should each have land worth five pounds (360 nomismata), "or at least four pounds," and that marines of the Imperial Fleet should have land worth three pounds (216 nomismata).[38] Five and three pounds thus seem to have been the standard valuations, though the legal minimums were a pound lower in each case.

While the only marines with full-sized allotments were those in the original territory of the Cibyrrhaeot Theme, the other naval themes had been affected by the resettlement of the Mardaïtes of the West in the early ninth century by Nicephorus I. Nicephorus therefore seems to have given his new marines somewhat smaller allotments than had been customary earlier. The lower values of land for marines of the Imperial Fleet may also reflect the fact that by the time they were recruited, about 870, land for them must have been fairly scarce around Constantinople, where they needed it; but such land could still be found, since about 840 Jarmī still mentioned some imperial estates around the capital.[39]

35. Cf. Hendy, *Studies*, 634–40, published in 1985, and Treadgold, "Military Lands," published in 1984.

36. See Treadgold, *Byzantine Revial*, 160–64.

37. Zepos and Zepos, *Jus Graecoromanum*, I, 222–23. On the marines of Hellas, Peloponnesus, Cephalonia, and Nicopolis, see Treadgold, "Army," 115–19.

38. Constantine VII, *De Ceremoniis*, 695.

39. Brooks, "Arabic Lists," 72–73.

Although later Nicephorus II specified that his new cavalry with heavy armor should be supported by land worth sixteen pounds of gold (1,152 nomismata), such heavy cavalry were few, possibly as few as 504 for the whole army.[40] Their allotments, with four times the minimum value of those of ordinary cavalrymen, could have been provided in two ways. The heavy cavalry might have been drawn from a handful of wealthy soldiers who happened to have acquired this much land already and were then instructed to register it as military land. But a more likely explanation is that three or four ordinary cavalrymen were instructed to contribute money to equip one of them as a heavy cavalryman, while the others stayed home during the campaign.

Apart from the heavy cavalry, who are known to have been created in the tenth century, the minimum and standard valuations of lands for the other cavalry and marines may go back all the way to the seventh century. If anything, allotments then could have been worth more. When Theophilus settled his 30,000 Khurramites all over the empire, increasing the army by a third, he required women from military families to marry some of them; along with their wives, the Khurramites probably acquired portions of existing military land, reducing the allotments of the rest and the average allotment for all.[41] If so, before the resettlement of the Khurramites the average value of a cavalryman's land might have been about a third more, perhaps seven pounds instead of five.

In any case, property worth even five pounds of gold was much larger than an ordinary peasant plot. At a typical price of about half a nomisma for a modius of plowland (0.08 hectare or 0.2 acre), five pounds would have been the value of a good-sized farm of some 720 modii (58 hectares or 144 acres).[42] At a later date in Macedonia, peasants with two oxen typically worked farms of about 50 modii, while poorer peasants with just one ox had farms of about 25 modii. Nearly all holdings that were worked by a single peasant family, in Macedonia or elsewhere, seem to have been smaller than 100 modii.[43] Each cavalryman thus had land that could have supported some 30 peasant families, and would have needed at least seven men to work all of it. The valuations of three pounds for the marines of the Imperial Fleet and other naval themes would have represented a farm of some 432 modii, which would have occupied no fewer than four farmers and could have supported 17 peasant families.

Approximate though these figures are, they should be enough to re-

40. Zepos and Zepos, *Jus Graecoromanum*, I, 255–56. For the number of heavy cavalry, see above, pp. 113–14.

41. See Treadgold, *Byzantine Revival*, 282–83.

42. See Cheynet et al., "Prix et salaires," 344–45.

43. Lefort, "Radolibos," 219–22.

solve the old debate over whether the soldiers of the themes were "farmer-soldiers."[44] A cavalryman who had seven or more tenants, slaves, hired hands, or relatives working for him was not needed constantly on his farm, and could be called up for service at any time. Leo VI's *Tactica* advise strategi to select for campaigns soldiers from their themes who are "rich, so that they, when engaged in their personal military service on an expedition, . . . have at their own homes others working their land and able to supply the full military equipment of a soldier."[45] In this sense, the cavalrymen could be considered rich; they did not absolutely need to work for a living.

On the other hand, they were not exactly grandees either, so opulent that farm work was beneath them. When they were not campaigning, cavalrymen with seven or even thirty men working for them probably did take an active part in farming, as Leo seems to assume that they would. An anonymous military treatise written in the late tenth century warns generals to drill their soldiers regularly, because otherwise, "selling their military equipment and their best horses, they will buy oxen and other things useful for farming."[46] This was in fact the manner in which the themes eventually fell into decay. The cavalrymen were not absentee landlords, and can be termed farmers, although prosperous ones. The term "farmer-soldier" is therefore a defensible one, though it may be misleading; it tends to minimize the soldiers' prosperity, and to overlook the fact that those who held military land could supply someone else to serve as a soldier.

The land legislation of the tenth century gives no minimum value for the lands of the infantry. A law of Romanus I appears to count them among the poor landholders, who must have had a good deal less land than cavalrymen.[47] We have seen that an infantryman's expenses were no more than half those of a cavalryman, who had to maintain and feed a horse and must often have kept a squire as well. The infantry needed only to supply their uniforms and arms, which even their pay of five nomismata before 840 should have covered, and their food, which they would also have eaten if they stayed home. Under these circumstances, as long as they remained free to work the land during the times of planting and harvesting, the infantrymen should have been able to support themselves on the 50 modii of land standard for a peasant with two oxen.

Since many of the infantry could and did fight even during the planting

---

44. On this debate, see Kaegi, "Some Reconsiderations," 39–43.
45. Leo VI, *Tactica*, IV.1, cols. 697D–700A.
46. *On Campaign Organization*, 28, p. 318.
47. See Treadgold, "Military Lands," 625; citing Zepos and Zepos, *Jus Graecoromanum*, I, 198–204, esp. 204.

and harvesting seasons, probably most of them had more land than this. Originally they are likely to have been allotted imperial land that was already worked by one or two tenants or slaves, and could support another family besides. Since the infantry were evidently in a less privileged category than the marines of the Imperial Fleet, most infantrymen would have had land worth less than the two pounds of gold prescribed as the minimum for those marines. Two pounds' worth of property was considered the dividing line between rich and poor by Leo III, whose *Ecloga* fined the seducer of a virgin a pound of gold if he was "rich," but half his fortune if he was poorer.[48] One might guess that at first the government had assigned infantrymen property worth about a pound of gold, perhaps 150 modii. With that much they could have been spared from their farms in an emergency, especially because they could have used their campaign pay to hire a farmhand, or to buy food to make up for their lost production.

As for the productivity of military lands, the not very abundant evidence suggests that Byzantine crop yields were between four and five modii of wheat from each modius of land.[49] The normal price of a modius of wheat averaged around a tenth of a nomisma.[50] A cavalryman who planted wheat might therefore have expected a crop worth around 324 nomismata a year, and an infantryman a crop worth perhaps 67 nomismata a year. These quite approximate figures are not particularly informative, because little of this crop would have been sold for cash, and the larger part of it would have been used or consumed by the soldier and his dependents. Yet there should still have been plenty left over to keep the soldiers properly armed, clothed, mounted, and fed, at an expense of about 10 nomismata a year for cavalry and 5 nomismata a year for infantry. For an ordinary cavalryman to have cash savings of three pounds of gold (216 nomismata) was not unusual in the early tenth century.[51] Since this sum would have taken twenty-four years to save from his pay, most of it probably came from selling what his land produced.

The soldiers of the tagmata are often assumed not to have had military lands. Yet Constantine VII's minimum values for military estates refer simply to the cavalry, not to the cavalry of the themes. When Constantine distinguishes between the two valuations of military lands for the marines, he clearly mentions the holdings of the marines of the Imperial

48. Leo III, *Ecloga*, 17.29. The law obviously assumes that no one with a fortune of less than two pounds would claim to be rich, since he would then have needed to pay a higher penalty.

49. Oikonomidès, "Terres," 335−36.

50. Cheynet et al., "Prix et salaires," 356−66, esp. 365. A modius is 13 kilograms.

51. See Pseudo-Symeon ("Symeon Magister"), 713−15.

Fleet, who were classed with the tagmata. Since the tagmata seem originally to have been soldiers of the Opsician Theme, they are not likely to
have been deprived of their lands when they were upgraded in status.[52]
Nor were their free rations, arms, uniforms, horses, and fodder, worth
some 15 nomismata a year, enough to give them a higher income than the
cavalry of the themes with their sizable lands, unless the tagmata kept
lands of their own.

Oarsmen, however, may well have lacked military lands. The oarsmen
of the Imperial Fleet seem always to have done without them. Justinian II
might have been hard put to find sufficient lands for almost 20,000 Mardaïtes in the fairly small and poor coastal areas where they were settled,
especially because large land grants had already been found there for the
marines of the Carabisians. When Nicephorus I converted the Mardaïtes
of the West from oarsmen in the Theme of Hellas to soldiers in the new
themes of Peloponnesus and Cephalonia, they would have received military lands in their new themes, but they did not necessarily leave such
lands behind in Hellas. Although usually one can assume from the agricultural nature of the empire's economy that any large number of men
would have had to draw their livelihood from the soil, there was one other
occupation that could support large numbers of people, and was especially
suitable for men who lived on seacoasts and islands and were familiar with
boats. That was of course fishing, which required no farmland.

Plainly the soldiers' lands covered a large part of the cultivated area of
the empire. In 840, for example, the empire seems to have had something
like eight million people, or about two million rural households. Since
Byzantine territory was by no means crowded at that time, these households probably farmed average holdings near the top of the range found
in later Macedonia, say 75 modii apiece for a total of some 150 million
modii.[53] This was about 62 percent of the area cultivated in Turkey in
1950, which had a presumably larger rural population of some two and
a half million households but about the same total area as the empire
in 840.[54]

The size of the military lands in 840 might thus be computed more or
less as follows:

52. See above, pp. 70–72.
53. Cf. Lefort, "Radolibos," 220–21.
54. Güriz, "Land Ownership," 74 table 2, recording a cultivated area of 194,519,400
dönüm (19,451,940 hectares = 243,149,250 modii) and 2,527,800 rural households. In 840
the extra land that Byzantium had in the west but Turkey does not was approximately
equal in area to the extra land that Turkey has in the east but Byzantium did not. Much
the largest part of the agricultural land of both states was in central and western Anatolia
and Thrace.

Landholders	Number	Holding	Total
cavalry of themes	16,000	720 mod.	11.52M mod.
cavalry of tagmata	16,000	720 mod.	11.52M mod.
Cibyrrhaeot marines	2,000	720 mod.	1.44M mod.
other marines	6,000	432 mod.	2.592M mod.
infantry of themes	64,000	150 mod.	9.6M mod.
infantry of tagmata	10,000	150 mod.	1.5M mod.
TOTAL			38.172M mod.

Though these estimates are very rough, they indicate that military lands might have accounted for around a quarter of the empire's cultivated area in 840.

The real proportion could have been as little as a fifth, if the average size of the lands of cavalrymen and marines had been closer to the prescribed minimums and the lands of the infantry had averaged about 75 modii. Admittedly the estimate of the total cultivated area is also conjectural, but it seems more likely to be too high than too low. In any case, the extent of the military lands was comparable to the extent of the imperial estates in the early Byzantine period. In the only regions for which approximate percentages can be calculated, imperial estates made up some 18.5 percent and 15 percent of the area of two of the provinces in Africa, some 16 percent of the region of Cyrrhus in Syria, and over half the province of First Cappadocia in central Anatolia.[55]

By the tenth century population pressure had begun to build up, and the emperors tried to prohibit rich and powerful purchasers from buying out smallholders, and particularly soldiers with military lands. Although anyone who held military land was supposed to be responsible for providing a soldier, influential landholders seem to have been able to evade their military responsibilities. In a brisk market for land, buyers would naturally have approached the soldiers, who had numerous and widely distributed holdings. Military lands were particularly dense in the region around the capital, where officials liked to acquire estates, and on the Anatolian plateau, where the great family estates of military officers were concentrated.[56]

Since not even the cavalry were truly wealthy and powerful men, they must have been tempted by attractive offers and vulnerable to threats, and particularly liable to sell off extra land that they did not need to live but did need to keep up their military obligations. The emperors tried to use their land legislation to prevent soldiers from selling any of their registered military land, or even unregistered land that they needed to meet their

55. Jones, *Later Roman Empire*, 415–16.
56. See Hendy, *Studies*, 85–90 and 100–108.

military expenses, especially when they had ceased to be called up for service at all frequently.

A related and probably more urgent concern of the emperors was to stop smallholders in general, especially in the fertile coastal regions, from selling out to magnates who had the power to evade taxation.[57] In this the government apparently had a good deal of success.[58] But it may have been less successful in protecting the main body of military lands on the Anatolian plateau. There the army of the themes was in a state of advanced decay by the mid-eleventh century. Originally the main cause for that decay was presumably that the army had become unaccustomed to military service. Yet if the soldiers merely got out of training, they could be retrained if they were needed later, as Romanus IV attempted to do in the late eleventh century. If, however, the soldiers sold the military lands they needed to support themselves properly and to provide their equipment, they would be much more difficult to call up and retrain in the future. This may well be one reason for Romanus's failure to restore the army well enough and quickly enough.

SUPPLIES AND WAREHOUSES

In the early Byzantine period, the state maintained a network of factories that supplied soldiers with uniforms and arms. As far as we can judge, these factories produced all the arms that were needed, but only some of the uniforms. Other uniforms were levied from taxpayers and supplied in kind to the soldiers, or purchased by the soldiers with their uniform allowances on the open market. The state also levied rations, horses, and fodder from taxpayers until these, like the uniforms, were gradually commuted to taxes in gold, a process that Anastasius I essentially completed.[59] The field troops seem to have received direct issues of rations on campaigns as late as the reign of Maurice, who was overthrown when he tried to economize by ordering his soldiers to live off the land north of the Danube.[60] By the sixth century, supplies for the frontier forces seem generally to have been commuted to gold.[61]

At first, especially before Constantine I, the empire had lacked a sufficiently abundant and stable coinage to allow the full commutation of sup-

57. The best study of the tenth-century land legislation remains Lemerle, *Agrarian History*, 85 – 156, though in his approach to the earlier military lands Lemerle seems to rely too much on an argument from silence at a time when the sources are silent about nearly all legal, economic, and agricultural matters.
58. Hendy, *Studies*, 131 – 38.
59. Jones, *Later Roman Empire*, 834 – 41.
60. Theophylact, VIII.6.10.
61. Jones, *Later Roman Empire*, 671 – 74.

plies to cash. Once Anastasius had established such a coinage, letting the troops supply and equip themselves had many advantages. They preferred it, since they could buy whatever supplies they liked and use whatever money was left over for their own purposes. In most cases they would equip themselves properly, because they would suffer the consequences if they bought food, clothing, or horses of poor quality, and they might even endanger their lives if they kept their weapons badly. Besides, they could be ordered at inspection to remedy any deficiencies in their equipment. Anastasius's allowances were generous enough to cover any regional differences in prices. The state made an effort to provide supplies to sell its soldiers when necessary, especially in the case of arms, which were needed in large quantities and had to conform to some uniform standards.

Otherwise supplying the army was mostly left to private enterprise. This saved the state the great expense of transporting bulky goods all over the empire and dealing with inevitable shortages and surpluses. The factories were located as near to the troops as possible; the *Notitia Dignitatum* lists fifteen arms factories of different kinds widely distributed over the East.[62] But the soldiers were even more widely distributed, and transportation costs, especially by land, were so high that goods were most cheaply produced where the regiments were actually stationed.[63] The result would have been a good market for people who produced food, clothing, fodder, and horses in rural areas, especially in the Balkans and along the eastern frontiers, where the population was sparse and the civilian economy often primitive.

When Heraclius cut pay in precious metal in half, and evidently reverted to supplying his troops with goods levied in kind or purchased with bronze coins, these changes by themselves would not have had a drastic effect on the overall market for military supplies. Most areas along the frontiers had already been lost to the empire. Other regions may actually have reaped some economic benefits from the arrival of troops withdrawn from lost provinces, who still needed to be supplied. Though Heraclius was not in a position to pay high prices, the bronze coinage did not inflate badly, and in this time of general crisis the civilian market must have been depressed. The soldiers lost income, but they were still furnished with whatever they really needed.

When Constans II cut pay in half once again, gave out military lands, and made soldiers responsible for supplying themselves, the market for military supplies would have changed radically. Soldiers were now dispersed more widely than ever over what remained of the empire. Though

---

62. *Notitia Dignitatum*, Or. XI.18–39.

63. The high cost of transport in ancient and medieval times is not in any serious dispute. See most recently Hendy, *Studies*, 554–61.

they could grow their own food and fodder on their military lands, and probably raise their own horses if they were cavalry, their remaining pay barely covered the cost of their arms and uniforms at average prices. In some areas prices would have been higher. Worse still, the decline in the military payroll would have reduced the money supply so sharply that the rural areas, where most troops were stationed, must have reverted to little more than a subsistence economy, with residual commerce that was overwhelmingly based on barter.

Under such circumstances, if soldiers had been left to provide for themselves without government help, many of them would have been unable to obtain proper equipment. In the eighth century arms were so valuable that Leo III assigned stern penalties for those who stole soldiers' arms and horses, and provided that the arms and horse a soldier inherited from his father should be set aside before reckoning the soldier's share of the estate.[64] A cavalryman's horse and arms seem in fact to have been the most valuable part of his movable property, and officers paid especially close attention to them at inspections.[65]

Such considerations led Hendy to propose that beginning in the mid-seventh century the soldiers bought their equipment from state warehouses run by officials called commerciarii.[66] These commerciarii and warehouses are attested by hundreds of lead seals originally attached to goods or documents, perhaps to bills of sale. Though a dozen of these seals date from the late sixth and early seventh centuries together, the great bulk of them date from the late seventh century through the early ninth.[67]

The seals' inscriptions at first recorded the name or names of the commerciarii with their rank, though later the names tend to be dropped. The seals usually give the locations of the warehouses, or rather of the jurisdictions within which the warehouses operated. Some of these are cities, but most of them are defined by the names of provinces of the early Byzantine period, or at a somewhat later date by the names of themes. For example, earlier we find seals with inscriptions like "Stephen, Patrician and General Commerciarius of the Warehouse of First and Second Cappadocia," while later we find them with inscriptions like "The Imperial Commercia of Hellas." The geographical distribution of these seals is wide. At least one seal has been found for practically every province and theme that the empire controlled at the time.[68]

64. Leo III, *Ecloga*, 16.2.1 and 17.10.
65. Cf. *Life of Philaretus*, 125–27, where for *harmata* ("chariots") we should certainly read *armata* ("arms," a Latin loan word).
66. Hendy, *Studies*, 626–34 and 654–62.
67. Zacos et al., *Byzantine Lead Seals*, I.1, 213–18.
68. See the maps in Oikonomidès, "Silk Trade," 45 and 47, though the omissions there are misleading. The first map, covering the years from 673/74 to 728/29, shows no seals

Most of these seals are easy to date, since they display portraits of the reigning emperors resembling those on coins, and are dated by years of the indiction, which began on September 1. Though indiction numbers repeated themselves every fifteen years, usually the imperial portrait and other indications reveal which year is meant. The earliest dated seal belongs to the indictional year 673/74, and the latest probably to 840/41.[69] Hendy has pointed out that before the indictional dating was introduced such seals had already begun to be common with the type datable to 654–59, under Constans II.[70]

This last observation, though correct, is somewhat misleading. Only one preserved seal is of the type of 654–59, while twelve seals are of the type of 659–68 and seven are of the type of 668–73.[71] This pattern suggests that the seals became common only at the very end of the period from 654 to 659, probably with the year 659 itself. In other words, the period of the abundance of these seals, from 659 to 840, is exactly that when coins were at their rarest, and when military pay seems to have been at its all-time low. Before 659 an ordinary soldier's pay would have been ten nomismata; and after 840 it would have been an average of nine nomismata; but from 659 to 840 it would have been a mere five.

Nicolas Oikonomidès has pointed out that commerciarii and their warehouses were connected with an office at Constantinople known as the Blattium, which to judge from its name sold purple-dyed silk, and with state factories that included the gold smelter.[72] In 694/95 commer-

---

for Galatia I, though seals of commerciarii of all Galatia and both Galatias exist for 654–59 and 659–68 (Zacos et al., *Byzantine Lead Seals*, no. 136 and 139n.). All the other provinces shown without seals on this map, except for those represented by seals of the cities of Constantinople, Thessalonica, and Mesembria, were either mostly or entirely outside Byzantine control at the time. The second map, covering the years from 730/31 to the early ninth century, shows no seals for the Armeniacs or Cibyrrhaeots, though two seals of commerciarii of the Armeniacs exist for 717/18, while the commercia of the Aegean Sea, a subdivision of the Cibyrrhaeots, have a seal probably dating to 734/35 (Zacos et al., nos. 222 and 249). Of the twelve other themes that Oikonomidès shows without seals, none existed in 730/31, ten still did not exist before 819, and eight did not exist before 840, when the seals Oikonomidès is cataloguing end. An eleventh theme, the Optimates, did not exist before 743, and the Optimates' theme is represented earlier by seals of the commerciarii of Bithynia in 731/32 and 733/34 and of Chalcedon and Thynia in 738/39 (Zacos et al., nos. 243, 248, and 252). The Bucellarians, founded about 766, were part of the Opsician Theme at the time of the seal of its commercia of 745/46 (Zacos et al., no. 263). I thus see no significant omissions of themes or provinces that the empire controlled, and no particular tendency for commercia to "'flee' the war zone," as Oikonomidès suggests on p. 45, though in the eighth century seals of commercia are more common in trading centers than elsewhere.

69. See Oikonomidès, "Silk Trade," 39 and 41–42.

70. Hendy, *Studies*, 626.

71. Zacos et al., *Byzantine Lead Seals*, 146 (table 2 n. 1) and 219–33, nos. 136–51 (omitting seals not of commerciarii but including the seal mentioned in the note on no. 139).

72. Oikonomidès, "Silk Trade," 50–51.

ciarii are also connected in inscriptions on seals with "the Slavic slaves." Hendy thought that these commerciarii were selling military equipment to the Slavic prisoners of war whom Justinian II had enrolled in the army, many of whom then deserted to the Arabs.[73] But since this desertion to the Arabs took place in 692, Oikonomidès is surely right to think that the commerciarii rather had charge of selling the remaining Slavs themselves. Justinian seems to have enslaved them as revenge for their countrymen's treachery, then sold them through the commerciarii to whoever would buy them.[74]

Yet Oikonomidès insists that the main if not exclusive function of commerciarii was to manage the production and sale of the imperial silk monopoly. On Oikonomidès's side are the seals' references to the Blattium, a clear literary reference to a commerciarius as a regulator of the silk trade in 630, and the fact that the sixth-century seals mention commerciarii at the silk-trading cities of Tyre and Antioch, one of whom also administered imperial estates near Antioch. Drawing on the work of John Nesbitt, Oikonomidès can also show that commerciarii were private businessmen who contracted with the state to perform commercial functions in certain regions during certain indictional—that is, fiscal—years.[75] The case seems conclusive that dealing in silk was one of the responsibilities of commerciarii from the sixth century to the ninth, and this probably was their main responsibility to begin with.

On the other hand, to believe that dealing in silk was the main occupation of a commerciarius throughout this period means assuming a great boom in silk trading and production. This boom would have extended to barren and cold regions of the Anatolian plateau where no one had money to buy silk and where silkworms could not be raised; and it would have ballooned precisely when the empire was at its poorest and most endangered, and its money supply at the lowest. This seems out of the question. What cannot be proved is that commerciarii did not deal in other state goods than silk. Oikonomidès's own evidence indicates that they also sold state-owned slaves and the products of public factories including the gold smelter, besides administering imperial estates.

Perhaps the most striking case of a commerciarius who had other duties was a certain Stephen the Patrician. Stephen's seals account for ten of the twelve that can be dated between 659 and 668. These cover warehouses of Abydus and Galatia in the Opsician Theme, Helenopontus in the Armeniac Theme, Cappadocia in the Anatolic Theme, and at least one other

73. Hendy, *Studies*, 631–34.
74. Oikonomidès, "Silk Trade," 51–53. Though Hendy based his argument on the supposed unreliability of the chronology of Theophanes for this time, that chronology seems generally sound; see Treadgold, "Seven Byzantine Revolutions," 203–27.
75. Oikonomidès, "Silk Trade," esp. 39–40.

place that cannot be read because the seal is damaged. One of these seals identifies Stephen as the Military Logothete, the imperial minister in charge of paying the army.[76] Holding both these offices at once seems nonsensical, unless the commerciarius and his warehouses had something to do with the army at the time. Nor is it easy to conceive of the same man's serving simultaneously as an imperial official on a salary and a private businessman with a government contract.

At this date, the very beginning of the period of abundant seals of commerciarii, Stephen may well have been distributing imperial estates as military lands. His jurisdictions covered so much territory that he seems unlikely to have been working on a contract; and the process of setting up the whole system of military lands and warehouses seems too sensitive to entrust to a private contractor. In most cases, however, commerciarii do appear to have contracted to sell all state goods within certain jurisdictions during certain years. After 659 much the largest category of state goods on sale seems to have been not silk or gold or (most of the time) slaves, but the soldiers' arms and uniforms. In order to refute this theory, one would need to identify some other sort of commodity that could account for this burst of commercial activity at such an improbable time. None is to be found.

Against Hendy's theory Haldon has objected that the soldiers would not have had the money to buy their equipment from the state. Instead Haldon proposes that the state returned to the old system, abandoned since the fourth century, of levying supplies in kind from taxpayers and distributing them to the soldiers as free issues. This, he supposes, was the function of the commerciarii and their warehouses.[77] The objection, at least, seems cogent. If the soldiers had still had enough money to buy their equipment, they could simply have done so, as they did in the sixth century, without the state's needing to make any new provisions for them. In fact their pay was evidently insufficient for this, and we have already seen that the government appears to have been buying them their equipment, with bronze coins, since the reign of Heraclius.

Yet levying equipment in kind, the suggestion made by Haldon, would only have aggravated the state's problems. Transporting goods all over the empire by land was immensely wasteful and expensive. The state had resorted to such measures under Diocletian only because its currency had collapsed. As soon as the currency was partly restored, the state began commuting taxes in kind to cash and paying cash allowances to the sol-

---

76. See Zacos et al., *Byzantine Lead Seals*, I.1, 145 with table 1 and nos. 138–44; notice the double seals of the same type, the note on no. 139, and no. 144's mention of Stephen's being Military Logothete. On the office of Military Logothete, see Oikonomidès, *Listes*, 314.

77. Haldon, *Byzantium*, 238–44.

diers. In the seventh century the currency was sound. The problem was that the government no longer had enough of it to pay the troops. If the government had felt able to raise taxes, it would surely have demanded them in cash. That would have put much less burden on taxpayers than exacting enough goods in kind to cover the expense of restoring the postal network for heavy goods that had been abolished by Justinian, never to be heard of again. The reason that the state did not raise taxes, in money or in kind, is plainly that taxpayers could not be made to pay them.

The only remaining possibility is that the warehouses did sell the soldiers arms and uniforms, but accepted payment in whatever form the soldiers could offer, which would mostly have been farm produce. As private businessmen working under contract for the state, the commerciarii first obtained arms and uniforms. These they bought either from the state factories, which still functioned in Constantinople, or, probably more often, from private workshops and weavers—unless the commerciarii happened to own such workshops themselves.[78] The commerciarii then offered these arms and uniforms to the soldiers. Bargaining with their customers, the commerciarii accepted either cash or whatever goods the soldiers had produced that the commerciarii believed they could resell at a profit.

The commerciarii could have sold some of these goods locally, while others, like livestock that could travel on the hoof, could be transported fairly cheaply to other markets. The state may have regulated the process, or it may have stood back on the assumption that if the commerciarii demanded too much, they would be left with unsold goods at the end of the year. Soldiers would have retained some bargaining power, because they could put off their purchases or dip into their savings to buy with cash. Nonetheless, the warehouse system for selling arms and uniforms seems not to have survived long after 840, when most soldiers gained enough money to do without it. The reason was probably that the business was considerably more advantageous for the commerciarii than for the soldiers, as we might expect of any virtual monopoly.

All this is hypothetical, like every explanation of the activities of the commerciarii and their warehouses. Yet how else could the empire have maintained a working economy, with taxes levied in cash, when so little cash was in circulation? Under Constantine V, the chroniclers record that the imperial gold reserve absorbed so much of the money supply that farmers had to sell their goods at scandalously low rates to collect enough money to pay their taxes. Yet even then the farmers, presumably including those in the farthest reaches of Asia Minor, seem somehow to have found

---

78. On the factories in Constantinople, including the arms factory, see Oikonomidès, *Listes*, 316–18.

merchants to buy their produce, which the people of Constantinople enjoyed in abundance at low prices.[79]

No doubt the commerciarii were given their contracts primarily in order to profit the state and to supply the army, and no doubt they bought and sold for their own advantage. But since they had to resell whatever goods they accepted from the soldiers, they would soon have provided not only soldiers but other farmers a means of doing business with a minimum of money. The commerciarii would have had money to spend, and would have been ready to buy almost anything from anyone if it offered the prospect of a profit. Thus the market that soldiers had afforded rural areas in the earlier Byzantine period would have continued to exist even after their pay was reduced, as the warehouses helped the economy adapt to a shortage of cash. After 840, when more money came back into circulation, the old pattern of trade seems to have resumed. The soldiers spent their pay among the people; the people paid the money to the state in taxes; and then the state paid the money to the soldiers again.[80] The warehouses had nevertheless performed a vital function in supplying the army and supporting the economy in the preceding period.

79. Theophanes, 443; Nicephorus the Patriarch, *Short History*, 85.
80. For this pattern in the Roman Empire, see Hopkins, "Taxes and Trade." For the same pattern in Byzantium, see Hendy, *Studies*, 602–7.

CHAPTER SIX

The Army and the State

The Byzantine army and the Byzantine government needed each other, and relied on each other's good will to a great extent. Even after receiving military lands, the army depended on the government for its pay. Even when Byzantium was largely at peace in the middle years of the eleventh century, no one doubted that the empire needed some sort of defense. The emperor had the authority to dismiss all military commanders, as he repeatedly did, and even to dismiss large numbers of soldiers, though that happened less often. The army had the power to overthrow the emperor, as it sometimes did, and then to purge the government, though it did so only at the beginning and end of the catastrophic seventh century. As the head of both the army and the government, the emperor usually tried to make the two of them work together.

Yet though both were well organized and powerful, and either could dominate the other, in a contest between the army and the government the government had at least a marginal advantage. The army lacked any unified leadership apart from the emperor, who even if he had been a general before his accession soon became primarily a civilian ruler. Except by proclaiming a new emperor, the army could not levy its own taxes and pay itself, and it could hardly find or found another state to serve. The closest it came to doing so was in the late eleventh century, when the general Philaretus Brachamius managed to claim a piece of the disintegrating empire in the East, but only precariously and temporarily. On the other hand, the government could in time let the army atrophy and replace it with another sort of army, as it did in the late eleventh century. The army had armed force on its side, but the government had the ultimately greater power of the purse.

MILITARY AND OTHER SPENDING

Although the Byzantine government seems always to have been able to find enough men to serve as its soldiers, it often seems to have had trouble paying them. Various possible reasons for this difficulty may be suggested; more than one cause may have contributed to the problem, and the explanations need not have been the same at different times. The army could have been needlessly large, or much overpaid. The government could have been negligent in collecting its revenues, or have spent too much on things other than the army. Finally, in times of crisis the empire's maximum revenues could simply have been inadequate, or just barely adequate, to pay for the empire's minimum defensive needs. We can only understand how hard the army was to pay by forming some idea of the state budget, including military spending, other spending, and any overall surplus or deficit.

We already have the elements to compute the military payrolls for most periods of Byzantine history, within a relatively modest margin for error. We also know the amounts of the accessional and quinquennial donatives, and over the length of any given reign we can easily compute how much these would have come to on an annual basis. Computing military supplies is more troublesome, because these were sometimes levied in kind, though we cannot always be sure when and where, and when they were commuted to cash the rates are often not recorded. Yet for comparative purposes supplies need to be included in a budgetary estimate whenever they were provided by the state; otherwise an estimate in cash alone will give the illusion that issues in kind cost the state and taxpayers nothing.

Fortunately for comparisons, the value of the nomisma was admirably stable during all of this period except for the very beginning and the very end. Leaving aside the inflated arms and uniform allowances that Anastasius I introduced as a means of raising military pay, which were higher than the real cost of the equipment, the cost of most military supplies seems to have remained much the same. We can therefore seldom go far wrong by following early Byzantine figures and assuming that throughout the period a horse's fodder cost about 4 nomismata a year, the cost of remounts averaged about a nomisma a year, and the cost of arms and uniforms averaged about 5 nomismata a year.[1] The fairly generous rations of the later tagmata and bodyguards might be valued at 5 nomismata a year, the amount of a sixth-century annona, rather than 4 nomismata, the

---

1. See above, pp. 149, 151, and 148–49.

amount of a less ample though still adequate fifth-century annona. The Optimates' mules should have cost about as much as horses, and probably ate about as much.[2]

The last major item in the military budget was campaign pay. Constantine VII's figures for the expeditions against Crete in 911 and 949 show that campaign pay could range from nothing at all for some Thracesian soldiers in 949 to 9 nomismata, or a full year's pay, for some soldiers of the Scholae in 911. The same figures also show that total campaign pay was about 239,128 nomismata in 911 and 209,622 nomismata in 949, for 44,908 and 27,010 men respectively.[3] The earlier figures average out to some 5.3 nomismata per man, about half the average for regular pay since it includes the officers. No rations were included, since thematic soldiers were expected to bring their own, and the rations of the tagmata would have been the same whether they campaigned or stayed at home.[4] Interestingly, in the ninth century the Arabs spent the equivalent of 200,000 to 300,000 nomismata a year on their campaigns against Byzantium, whether by sea or land.[5] The Byzantine figures for the naval campaigns against Crete also fall within these limits, though they are closer to the lower figure.

Apparently a typical Byzantine campaign cost around 200,000 nomismata in the ninth and tenth centuries, since the expeditions to Crete seem to have been relatively expensive. Emperors who sent out an average of one campaign a year—an unusually high level of military activity—would have spent about that much on campaign pay. For the eighth century, Theophanes records that the Bulgar khan Tervel paid 360,000 nomismata for the campaign in which the deposed emperor Anastasius II tried to regain his throne from Leo III in 719.[6] Though this is somewhat higher than the figures given by Jarmī and Constantine VII for the next two centuries, it probably included something more than campaign pay, since Anastasius lacked an emperor's advantages of possessing the central treasury and the main body of the army.

For the early Byzantine period, we have a figure for the enormous joint campaign of Leo I and the western emperor Anthemius, which was meant to drive the Vandals from North Africa in 468. John the Lydian and the contemporary historian Candidus the Isaurian give figures for the eastern

2. See Cheynet et al., "Prix et salaires," 350.
3. Treadgold, "Army," 100–121 and 123–41.
4. On the thematic soldiers' rations, see Ibn Khurdādhbih, 85, a text dependent on al-Jarmī.
5. Qudāmah, 193.
6. Theophanes, 400.

expenditures, itemized by the department that provided them, that add up to nearly identical totals of some 7.3 or 7.4 million nomismata. John says that this sum was an all-time record.[7] Its stupendous size strongly suggests that it included Leo's quinquennial donative and Anthemius's accessional donative, both theoretically due in 467 but often paid a year late during the fourth and fifth centuries.[8] If so, the total was an inflated one, in the sense that it included regular expenditures for salaries and donatives that would have fallen due even without the expedition.

Thus the total probably included the soldiers' regular pay, their campaign pay, their rations on the campaign, fodder for their horses, the cost of building some additional ships, and a subsidy for the forces from the then-impoverished western empire. Procopius, apparently following the contemporary historian Priscus, says that Leo was extraordinarily generous to both soldiers and oarsmen, and that the whole cost of the expedition was about 9.4 million nomismata.[9] Thus the western empire seems only to have managed to contribute some 2 million nomismata on top of the eastern empire's 7.4 million, though the West should still have been able to supply about half the soldiers and oarsmen.

John the Lydian says that the expedition had 400,000 men, while Procopius says that "the army" had 100,000, apparently omitting the oarsmen.[10] Such numbers seem extremely high, but so does the cost of the expedition. Its failure was an utter catastrophe, leaving the West almost helpless and the East weakened for a generation. The implied proportion of some 75 percent oarsmen tallies well with the three other Byzantine naval expeditions for which we have details; those proportions ranged between 67 percent and 86 percent.[11] The obvious difficulty in sending a really overwhelming expedition against North Africa was finding enough oarsmen to row the soldiers. If we assume that most of the oarsmen were enlisted in preparation for the campaign and were lost or discharged afterward, each half of the empire would then have had to contribute some 50,000 regular soldiers, a large but quite possible number.

7. See Hendy, *Studies*, 221; citing John the Lydian, *On Magistrates*, III.43; and Candidus, p. 470, who specifies that the western emperor Anthemius contributed money in addition to this.

8. See Hendy, *Studies*, 188.

9. Procopius, *Wars*, III.6.1–2.

10. John the Lydian, *On Magistrates*, III.43; Procopius, *Wars*, III.6.1.

11. See Procopius, *Wars*, III.11.2–19 (32,000 rowers, including 2,000 marines, 67% of the 48,000-odd men on the expedition against the Vandals of 533); and Treadgold, "Army," 150–51 (36,837 rowers, 86% of the 42,774 men on the expedition against Crete of 911) and 154 (38,640 rowers, 86% of the 44,908 men on the expedition against Crete of 949).

We might nonetheless be tempted to dismiss John's total of 400,000 and to assume that Procopius's total of 100,000 included oarsmen. But any such theory cannot be made to square with the costs. The highest expenses that seem possible for 100,000 men, even making the improbable assumption that the campaign pay was equal to full regular pay, give a total that is little more than a quarter of the 9.4 million nomismata recorded for both East and West.[12] With 400,000 men, the cost of rations, fodder, and campaign pay at half the regular rates would reach only some 3.7 million nomismata, while regular pay and donatives would bring the total to about 8.4 million.[13] Shipbuilding and incidental expenses could then account for the remaining 1 million nomismata. In fact, the real expense of the campaign, excluding donatives and salaries that should have been paid anyway, would probably have been about 4 million nomismata.

The sources agree that this expedition was absolutely unparalleled. The later campaign against the Vandals in 533 consisted of little more than 48,000 men, with 30,000 oarsmen, 2,000 marines who rowed, and 16,000 soldiers, 6,000 of them cavalry. For each of its two years, that expedition might have cost about 550,000 nomismata in campaign pay, rations, and

12. I assume equal contributions of men from East and West and a proportion of soldiers of about a third and of cavalry about a third of those, as in Belisarius's expedition against the Vandals in 532. The calculations would be:

Expenditure	Number	Rate	Multiplier for officers	Total
regular pay for soldiers	33,000	8 nom.	$\frac{1}{3}$	0.352M nom.
regular pay for oarsmen	67,000	4 nom.	$\frac{3}{4}$	0.335
campaign pay equal to regular pay				0.687
quinquennial donative in East	50,000	5 nom.		0.25
accessional donative in West	50,000	9 nom.		0.45
rations	100,000	4 nom.		0.4
fodder	11,000	4 nom.		0.044
TOTAL				2.518M nom.

13. The calculations for 400,000 men, including 100,000 soldiers, and again assuming that a third of the soldiers were cavalry, would be:

Expenditure	Number	Rate	Multiplier for officers	Total
regular pay for soldiers	100,000	8 nom.	$\frac{1}{3}$	1.067M nom.
regular pay for oarsmen	300,000	4 nom.	$\frac{3}{4}$	1.5
campaign pay at half regular pay				1.283
quinquennial donative in East	200,000	5 nom.		1.0
accessional donative in West	200,000	9 nom.		1.8
rations	400,000	4 nom.		1.6
fodder	33,000	4 nom.		0.132
TOTAL				8.382M nom.

fodder.[14] This, which was about twice the cost of campaigns in the ninth and tenth centuries, seems a reasonable average for years in the earlier period when there was one major campaign. In many years there would have been none.

About nonmilitary expenses we know less. Procopius appears to say that the payroll of the central bureaucracy under Justinian was 10,000 pounds of gold, or 720,000 nomismata.[15] Hendy tentatively accepted this, and used it to make estimates totaling around 1.1 million nomismata for the whole civil service.[16] This fits well enough with an estimate I have made for the civil servants of the mid-ninth century, which is about 450,000 nomismata, including the fees of tax collectors.[17] Since these figures imply that when the empire was rather less than half as big it paid its bureaucrats rather less than half as much, they can be used as guidelines to estimate what the bureaucracy's payroll would have been when the empire was larger or smaller. Then there was the grain dole at Constantinople, which existed from the fourth century until Heraclius was forced to discontinue it. Using fairly good evidence, Hendy has estimated its value at 800,000 nomismata a year, a figure that would apply from the late fourth century to the early seventh.[18]

As for public works, we can estimate the cost of the most expensive of them. Justinian spent about 300,000 nomismata on St. Sophia in 532, which was the first of the six years of its construction.[19] If this annual rate of spending was more or less the average for the whole six years, the entire project would have cost around 2 million. Justinian's somewhat less grand churches of the Holy Apostles in Constantinople and St. John at Ephesus probably cost about a million nomismata each. But a far more modest

14. The private retainers of Belisarius mentioned by Procopius, *Wars*, III.19, can be ignored for this purpose, since they would have been paid by Belisarius, not by the treasury. Figuring campaign pay that averaged half of regular pay, the calculations are:

Expenditure	Number	Rate	Multiplier for officers	Total
campaign pay for soldiers	18,000	10 nom.	⅓	0.24 M nom.
campaign pay for oarsmen	30,000	2.5 nom.	¾	0.094
rations	48,000	4 nom.		0.192
fodder	6,000	4 nom.		0.024
TOTAL				0.55 M nom.

15. Procopius, *Secret History*, 24.30–31.

16. Hendy, *Studies*, 164–71, making estimates totaling 944,800 nomismata for the Eastern Prefecture and 53,000 nomismata for the African Prefecture, to which should be added rather more than another 53,000 nomismata for the Italian and Illyrian prefectures.

17. Treadgold, *Byzantine State Finances*, 37–49.

18. Hendy, *Studies*, 170.

19. John the Lydian, *On Magistrates*, III.76, notes that Justinian spent 4,000 pounds of gold (288,000 nomismata) on St. Sophia during the prefecture of Phocas, which lasted for most of 532.

church like San Vitale at Ravenna, paid for by a private benefactor, cost just 26,000 nomismata.[20] Most of Justinian's fortifications would have been built cheaply from local materials by soldiers on regular pay. No other emperor approached Justinian's level of building. Yet Theophilus was a great builder for his time. We know that his gold ornaments were worth well over 1.44 million nomismata, because his son Michael III melted down that much of them without damaging them irreparably.[21]

As for tribute to the barbarians, when it was paid it was often small, and never truly crushing. The tribute to the Huns that the emperor Marcian ended in 450 had been 151,200 nomismata a year. That rate had itself been raised in 443 from 50,400 nomismata, which had in turn been raised around 435 from 25,200 nomismata.[22] In 506 Anastasius I agreed to pay the Persians 39,600 nomismata a year.[23] The highest sum paid to any foreign power was the 792,000 nomismata for Justinian's Perpetual Peace with Persia in 532.[24] But Justinian actually turned this to a profit by suspending the pay of the eastern frontier troops, who would have earned more than that in a year.[25] In 561 Justinian secured a second peace with the Persians by agreeing to pay an annual tribute of just 30,000 nomismata, though the first seven payments were to be made in advance.[26]

Finally, emperors tried to keep a substantial cash reserve, and consequently often ran a budgetary surplus. The emperor Marcian left a reserve of some 7.2 million nomismata in 457, much of which presumably dated from the reign of his predecessor Theodosius II. Most of this reserve was spent on Leo I's disastrous expedition against the Vandals. Anastasius I left a reserve of some 23 million nomismata in 518; since the treasury had still been low at his accession in 491, most of this sum probably represented his own savings at a rate of perhaps 750,000 nomismata a year. Constantine V was also known as a great saver, and left a reserve of well over 3.6 million nomismata at his death in 775.

Since we have already seen that the reserve stood at some 6,984,000 nomismata in 842 and at some 7,848,000 nomismata in 856, we can compute the government's rate of saving at that time, an average of 62,000 nomismata a year. Basil II also accumulated a great treasure of about 14.4 million nomismata by 1025, most of it doubtless saved since 989,

20. Agnellus, *Liber Pontificalis*, 59.
21. See above, p. 128 and n. 28.
22. Cf. Priscus, 304–6, with 236 and 227.
23. See the references in Stein, *Histoire*, II, 99 n. 5.
24. Procopius, *Secret History*, 24.12–13.
25. At the time of the *Notitia* there had been about 149,500 eastern frontier troops. Even if these had lost 10% of their strength, there would still have been about 135,000 of them left in 532. Counting pay of 5 nomismata apiece and an additional third for their officers, their annual payroll would have been about 900,000 nomismata.
26. Menander Protector, 60–62.

when a series of costly civil wars had ended. His rate of saving might thus have been around 350,000 nomismata a year.[27]

I have used all this evidence, along with that for the size and pay of the army, to make the eleven budgetary estimates shown in Table 12. These of course have considerable margins for error, because the nonmilitary expenses are so uncertain. Yet already in 1919 Ernst Stein arrived at a rough estimate for the budget in the late sixth century of 7 million nomismata, not far from my estimate of 8.5 million for 565.[28] This comparison actually exaggerates the difference between the estimates, because Stein chose not to include monetary equivalents for payments in kind, as I do for military supplies and the grain dole. Without them, my estimate would be about 6.1 million nomismata, less than 1 million lower than Stein's.

Even though Hendy believed that sixth-century soldiers were paid only 5 nomismata apiece, probably a quarter of the correct figure, he still arrived at a budgetary estimate for this time of 5 to 6 million nomismata, including the grain dole but not the military supplies.[29] Without military supplies, my estimate would be about 6.9 million. All three estimates fall within a remarkably narrow range. In any case, Byzantine state budgets, like all state budgets, fluctuated from year to year. As long as we know their approximate size at various dates, we know about as much as can be useful to us.

The estimates in Table 13 show rough percentages of military spending that range from about 58 percent to about 81 percent, with an average around 69 percent.[30] The highest percentage seems to be that of Diocletian around 300. This is no surprise, because his army was not only very large but paid in an inefficient manner, largely in kind. The second-highest percentage appears to be that of Heraclius about 641, naturally enough because he was dealing with a desperate military and financial emergency and still paying his large army a living wage. The lowest percentages seem to be those of Constans II about 668 and Constantine V about 775. This is again only to be expected, because under these two emperors military pay was very low, with the military lands providing most of the army's support.

27. All the references for reserves are conveniently provided by Hendy, *Studies*, 224–26.

28. Stein, *Studien*, 141–60, esp. 155.

29. Hendy, *Studies*, 164–73, esp. 171.

30. Cf. the observation of Starr, *Roman Empire*, 88 and n. 11: "Before the Industrial Revolution the cost of armed forces of a state represented almost always at least 60 per cent of the total expenditures (excluding debt service, which could not exist in the Roman Empire)."

TABLE 12
Estimated Budgets, ca. 300 to ca. 1025

Date and budgetary item	Estimate (millions of nomismata)
CA. 300 (Diocletian)[a]	
pay of soldiers (311,000 × 12 nom. × ⅓)	4.976M nom.
pay of oarsmen (32,000 × 12 nom. × ¾)	0.48
uniforms and arms (311,000 × 5 nom.)	1.555
fodder and horses (26,000 × 5 nom.)	0.13
campaigns and other military expenses	0.5
pay of bureaucracy	1.0
other nonmilitary expenses and surplus	0.8
TOTAL	9.441M nom.
CA. 457 (Marcian)	
pay of Scholae (3,500 × 16 nom. × ⅓)	0.075M nom.
pay of field soldiers (104,000 × 8 nom. × ⅓)	1.109
pay of frontier soldiers (195,500 × 4 nom. × ⅓)	1.043
pay of oarsmen (32,000 × 4 nom. × ¾)	0.16
accessional donative (335,000 × 9 nom./7 yrs.)	0.431
quinquennial donative (335,000 × 5 nom./7 yrs.)	0.239
uniforms and arms (303,000 × 5 nom.)	1.515
fodder and horses (122,500[b] × 5 nom.)	0.612
campaigns and other military expenses	0.2
pay of bureaucracy	0.8
grain dole	0.8
other nonmilitary expenses and surplus	0.8
TOTAL	7.784M nom.
CA. 518 (Anastasius I)	
pay of Excubitors (300 × 40 nom. × ⅓)	0.016M nom.
pay of field soldiers (95,000 × 20 nom. × ⅓)	2.533
pay of frontier soldiers (176,000[c] × 5 nom. × ⅓)	1.173
pay of oarsmen (30,000 × 5 nom. × ¾)	0.188
uniforms and arms (176,300 × 5 nom.)	0.882
fodder and horses (107,400[d] × 5 nom.)	0.537
campaigns and other military expenses	0.2
pay of bureaucracy	0.8
grain dole	0.8
tribute and other nonmilitary expenses	0.6
surplus	0.75
TOTAL	8.479M nom.
CA. 540 (Justinian I)	
pay of Excubitors (300 × 40 nom. × ⅓)	0.016M nom.
pay of field soldiers (145,000 × 20 nom. × ⅓)	3.867
pay of frontier soldiers (195,000 × 5 nom. × ⅓)	1.303
pay of oarsmen (30,000 × 5 nom. × ¾)	0.188
uniforms and arms (195,800 × 5 nom.)	0.979
fodder and horses (126,800[e] × 5 nom.)	0.634
campaigns and other military expenses	1.0
pay of bureaucracy	1.1
grain dole	0.8
other nonmilitary expenses	1.4
TOTAL	11.287M nom.

(*continued*)

TABLE 12 (*continued*)

Date and budgetary item	Estimate (millions of nomismata)
CA. 565 (Justinian I)	
pay of Excubitors (300 × 40 nom. × ⅓)	0.016M nom.
pay of field soldiers (150,000 × 20 nom. × ⅓)	4.0
uniforms and arms (195,800 × 5 nom.)	0.979
fodder and horses (127,800ᶠ × 5 nom.)	0.639
campaigns and other military expenses	0.5
pay of bureaucracy	1.1
grain dole	0.8
tribute and other nonmilitary expenses	0.5
TOTAL	8.534M nom.
CA. 641 (Heraclius)	
pay of soldiers (109,000 × 10 nom. × ⅓)	1.453M nom.
uniforms and arms (109,000 × 5 nom.)	0.545
fodder and horses (21,800ᵍ × 5 nom.)	0.109
campaigns and other military expenses	0.8
pay of bureaucracy	0.5
other nonmilitary expenses	0.3
TOTAL	3.707M nom.
CA. 668 (Constans II)	
pay of soldiers (109,000 × 5 nom. × ⅓)	0.727M nom.
campaigns and other military expenses	0.5
pay of bureaucracy	0.5
other nonmilitary expenses and surplus	0.3
TOTAL	2.027M nom.
CA. 775 (Constantine V)	
pay of bodyguards (400 × 72 nom. × ⅓)	0.038M nom.
pay of soldiers (80,000 × 5 nom. × ⅓)	0.533
pay of oarsmen (18,500 × 5 nom. × ¾)	0.116
uniforms, arms, and rations (18,400 × 10 nom.)	0.184
fodder, horses, and mules (14,400 × 5 nom.)	0.072
campaigns and other military expenses	0.2
pay of bureaucracy	0.4
other nonmilitary expenses	0.2
surplus	0.2
TOTAL	1.943M nom.
CA. 842 (Theophilus)	
pay of bodyguards (400 × 72 nom. × ⅓)	0.038M nom.
pay of soldiers (120,000)ʰ	1.294
pay of oarsmen (14,600)ⁱ	0.148
uniforms, arms, and rations (24,400 × 10 nom.)	0.244
fodder, horses, and mules (20,400 × 5 nom.)	0.102
campaigns and other military expenses	0.2
pay of bureaucracy	0.5
other nonmilitary expenses	0.5
surplus	0.06
TOTAL	3.086M nom.

TABLE 12 (*continued*)

Date and budgetary item	Estimate (millions of nomismata)
CA. 959 (Constantine VII)	
pay of bodyguards (1,200 × 72 nom. × 4/3)	0.115M nom.
pay of soldiers (144,000 × 9 nom. × 6/5)	1.555
pay of oarsmen (34,200 × 9 nom. × 9/8)	0.346
uniforms, arms, and rations (29,200 × 10 nom.)	0.292
fodder, horses, and mules (21,200 × 5 nom.)	0.106
campaigns and other military expenses	0.3
pay of bureaucracy	0.6
other nonmilitary expenses and surplus	0.6
TOTAL	3.914M nom.
CA. 1025 (Basil II)	
pay of bodyguards (1,200 × 72 nom. × 4/3)	0.115M nom.
pay of soldiers (247,800 × 9 nom. × 6/5)	2.676
pay of oarsmen (34,200 × 9 nom. × 9/8)	0.346
uniforms, arms, and rations (43,200 × 10 nom.)	0.432
fodder, horses, and mules (35,200 × 5 nom.)	0.176
campaigns and other military expenses	0.4
pay of bureaucracy	0.8
other nonmilitary expenses	0.6
surplus	0.35
TOTAL	5.895M nom.

[a] Estimated budget includes domains of both Diocletian and Galerius. For purposes of comparison, figures are converted from denarii into later nomismata struck at 72 to the pound of gold.

[b] The number includes 3,500 Scholae, 21,500 field cavalry, and 97,500 frontier cavalry.

[c] This is 90% of the comparable figure under Marcian, to allow for losses.

[d] This is 90% of the comparable figure under Marcian, to allow for losses.

[e] The number includes 300 Excubitors, 29,000 field cavalry (20% of 145,000 at the apparent cavalry ratio), and 97,500 frontier cavalry (see Table 1).

[f] The number includes 300 Excubitors, 30,000 field cavalry (20% of 150,000 at the apparent cavalry ratio), and 97,500 frontier cavalry (see Table 1).

[g] This number is 20% of 109,000 at the apparent cavalry ratio.

[h] The figure for pay is computed from tables 9 and 10, excluding the oarsmen, centarchs of ships, and protocarabi of the Cibyrrhaeot Theme and the Theme of Hellas.

[i] The figure for pay is computed from Table 9, including only the oarsmen, centarchs of ships, and protocarabi of the Cibyrrhaeot Theme and the Theme of Hellas.

Though the other percentages all seem to fall within 4 percent of the average of 69 percent, this relative uniformity conceals some important differences. About 565 Justinian appears to have had about the same revenues as Anastasius in 518. But at the earlier date military expenses can be estimated at 65 percent of the revenues with a surplus of about 9 percent, while at the later date military expenses seem to have absorbed 72 percent of the budget and left no surplus worth mentioning. From 450 to 540, and again from 842 to 1025, the proportion of military expenses seems to have fluctuated between 65 percent and 71 percent. But in the earlier period

TABLE 13

Summary of Budgetary Estimates, ca. 300 to ca. 1025

(*Millions of nomismata*)

Date	Military expenses	Other and surplus	Total
Ca. 300	7.6 M nom. (81%)	1.8 M nom. (19%)	9.4 M nom.
Ca. 457	5.4 (69%)	2.4 (31%)	7.8
Ca. 518	5.5 (65%)	3.0 (35%)	8.5
Ca. 540	8.0 (71%)	3.3 (29%)	11.3
Ca. 565	6.1 (72%)	2.4 (28%)	8.5
Ca. 641	2.9 (78%)	0.8 (22%)	3.7
Ca. 668	1.2 (60%)	0.8 (40%)	2.0
Ca. 775	1.1 (58%)	0.8 (42%)	1.9
Ca. 842	2.0 (65%)	1.1 (35%)	3.1
Ca. 959	2.7 (69%)	1.2 (31%)	3.9
Ca. 1025	4.2 (71%)	1.7 (29%)	5.9

the army included large numbers of ill-paid and second-rate frontier troops, while during most of the later period the pay and quality of the soldiers was much more uniform. In 300 and 540, and especially in 565 and 641, the government met its expenses with difficulty; in 450, 518, and from the eighth century onward, it met them rather easily.

These statistics, like all statistics, can only be understood in context. Yet they can also do much to clarify their historical context. With this in mind, we can return for the last time to these eight hundred years of the Byzantine army's history, and consider events from the government's point of view. Too often modern historians have judged the empire's military and financial measures with only the vaguest ideas of the money and manpower available. At various times the Byzantine government has been blamed for not committing enough troops in a crisis, levying too much in taxes, paying troops too little or too late, and letting the army deteriorate. Such criticisms assume that the empire had the money or men required, but failed to use them as it should have. But did the state really have what it needed, and could it have done much better with what it had?

FENDING OFF BARBARIANS

Diocletian expanded the army in the first place in order to repel the barbarian incursions of the third century. He was also trying to stop the military revolts that had become endemic during the third-century wars with the Germans and Persians. In the short term, until his abdication in 305, he succeeded in both aims. Yet he was a man of real vision, and his elaborate political and military arrangements show that he was planning for the long term. The part of the empire that was under his personal administration was the East, though his colleagues in the West followed the general guidelines of his policies. Perhaps by coincidence—but probably not—his system worked better in the East, where he was familiar with local conditions and supervised his measures himself. The East managed to hold nearly all of its territory until 602. The West lost the last of its territory in 480, though much of it was later reconquered by the East under Justinian.

Diocletian set the size of the army more or less as it was to remain in the East for the next three centuries. His case for increasing the army is easy to conjecture, because a not vastly smaller army had proved unable to keep out the barbarians before his time. The improvement in the empire's security after Diocletian increased the army's size was almost immediate, and there can be little doubt that the improved security was a direct result of the growth of the army. As long as all the troops were paid a living wage, as they were until some time in the later fourth century, they defended the eastern empire adequately. A smaller and better-paid army would probably have been a more satisfactory solution in the long run, but Diocletian's army did its job.

Diocletian was more successful in ending military revolts than may appear from the civil warfare that began in 306. He surely knew that all of his three colleagues had the power to start civil wars, and that their successors would have the same power. But he attempted to avoid this danger by choosing them carefully, allowing all of them a share of imperial power, and giving the junior emperors the prospect of becoming senior emperors later. Since the army was too large for Diocletian to command by himself, appointing general commanders for each sector of the frontier was unavoidable. Diocletian wisely limited those commanders to four and gave them the title of emperor, so that rebellions below the imperial level had little chance of success. The civil wars after 306 were fought only by emperors among themselves. Diocletian's main miscalculation was probably to choose emperors with sons and then to forbid them to name their sons their successors, since the ambitions of the theoretically disinherited sons Constantine and Maxentius set off the civil warfare.

Under the emperors' commands came the frontier ducates. These were smaller than the provincial commands, which had ranged in size up to the whole of Egypt and had been big enough to serve as bases for rebellions in the third century. The legions commanded by the dukes were also broken up, so that the dukes would have needed to have the support of a dozen or more subordinate commanders before they could even mount a general rebellion within their ducates. If they had done so, the rebel dukes would still have had resources that were far inferior to those of emperors. Very few dukes attempted revolt, and none had any success with it.

Paying for the enlarged army was the weakest point in Diocletian's system. Doing it properly required an abundant and stable currency, which Diocletian's determined but blundering efforts, including his edict of 301 setting maximum prices, never managed to establish. Even with a sound currency, paying an army of this size a satisfactory wage was bound to put some strain on the empire's always primitive economy. Paying the smaller army of the third century had already been a problem, and had led the emperors of the time to inflate the currency in the first place. Diocletian resorted to paying soldiers a less than satisfactory wage and enforcing conscription.

Constantine I made some adjustments. Unlike Diocletian, who had no sons, Constantine believed that emperors were less likely to fight each other if they were related by blood. He therefore made his sons his co-emperors and successors. Though after his death even the brothers fought each other, they still fought somewhat less often than Diocletian's emperors by adoption, and at least Constantine left no sons outside the system to mount rebellions against it. Constantine established a gold currency of substantial size and probably used it for donatives to the army, stabilizing their income somewhat even though bronze inflation continued. Finally, because he relied less on colleagues, he found that he needed a personal guard and a field army, though he kept the field army and Scholae that he created to a moderate size.

Constantius II, who eventually ruled alone over most of the East, found that he needed more than one field army, since the Persians were becoming more threatening and his brothers were quarreling in the West. Certainly Constantius ran some danger of rebellion when he formed armies of the East and of Illyricum in addition to his praesental army. But he kept their commanders under control by appointing separate masters of cavalry and infantry and maintaining the separate commands of the dukes on the frontier. With the partial exception of Julian's failed Persian expedition of 363, in which the army was never truly defeated, the soldiers continued to perform rather well. The value of the army's pay seems to have declined somewhat because of the inflation of the base-metal coinage, but both field and frontier soldiers were still paid a living wage, and probably the same wage.

In 364, when Valentinian I divided the empire with his brother Valens, Valens again formed three field armies in the East. The frontier troops were definitely relegated to second-class status only under Valentinian and Valens. By the time their law of 372 assigned the frontier forces the less fit recruits, they had probably already allowed the frontier soldiers' pay to fall behind that of the field soldiers. In 367 Valens won praise for assessing taxes at half the previous rate after forty years of steady tax increases.[31] In 370 or 371 Valens seems to have restored a third of the revenues that the government had confiscated from the cities near the beginning of his reign.[32] Such reductions in revenue imply reductions in expenditure, and spending on the frontier forces was a large and likely item to cut.

Yet at this time taxes undoubtedly remained high. The large mobile armies seemed able to meet the empire's defensive needs, and the upgrading of more of the frontier troops to cavalry would have tended to increase the cost of maintaining them. Spending on the frontier forces appears to have been reduced without attracting too much notice through gradual reductions in their allowances, or simply by letting the inflation of the bronze coinage do its work without compensating for it. The decline in both the pay and the effectiveness of the frontier forces seems to have started near the beginning of the joint reigns of Valentinian and Valens. From then on, the frontier forces continued to decline, though gradually.

At least in the short term, however, deficiencies in the frontier troops were of secondary importance, since the main task of fighting foreign enemies had passed to the mobile forces. The mobile armies were those that lost in 378 at the battle of Adrianople, in which Valens died. Valens' worst mistake was probably to fight any large, set-piece battle with the Goths at all. No doubt he was concerned with his prestige; but he had little to gain by defeating them, while the consequences of his defeat were dire. Though no exact figure is available, some 20,000 to 25,000 troops were evidently lost, enough to cripple the field armies for several years.[33]

Theodosius I worked hard to restore the army, mostly by recruiting barbarians. He had learned the lesson of avoiding large battles with barbarian enemies; for many years to come the lesson stayed learned, perhaps too well. Recruiting barbarians was almost unavoidable, and not the obvious mistake it might seem. The barbarians had little national feeling, and as long as they had Byzantine officers they fought well and

31. Themistius, *Orations*, 8.112a–113c.
32. See Liebeschuetz, "Finances of Antioch."
33. For the Roman losses at Adrianople, see Hoffmann, *Spätrömische Bewegungsheer*, I, 443–49.

loyally. Even barbarian officers seldom went over to the enemy. But they did sometimes try to dictate to the government, especially when it was led by feeble emperors like Theodosius's son Arcadius and grandson Theodosius II.

The real rulers of the eastern empire between 395 and 450 were not those two emperors but their principal advisers, many of whom were capable. Early on some of them, preoccupied with infighting in Constantinople, took the shortsighted attitude that the best way to get rid of barbarians was to send them to the West. The Visigoths did go west, where they caused terrible damage to the western empire and sacked Rome in 410. Meanwhile the leading officials at Constantinople played their barbarian generals off against each other, frustrated the attempted takeover of the government by its Visigoth general Gaïnas in 400, and shortly afterward excluded barbarians from the highest commands.

Then the Huns began to threaten the Balkans. The eastern government defended the frontier just well enough to avoid utterly demoralizing the army and excessively encouraging the Huns. But its main policies were to fortify Constantinople, which it did splendidly in 413, to bribe the Huns with a tribute that seemed large to them but was small in terms of the empire's wealth, and to tolerate their ravaging of the Balkans, a not very valuable region already ravaged by the Visigoths. Thus the army and the empire survived, without glory but without too much damage, until the Huns went west in 450.

As long as the Huns seemed to be the real enemy, other barbarian generals were allowed to take over the chief military commands from which they had been temporarily excluded. Theodosius II's successor Marcian was a lieutenant of the Alan general Aspar, and so was Marcian's successor Leo I. The danger of having barbarians in charge of the army was not so much that they collaborated with other barbarians, as that they wanted to keep the emperors they dominated from becoming strong enough to reclaim full imperial authority.

This was probably the reason that Aspar and his western counterpart, the German general Ricimer, subverted the great expedition against the Vandals of 468. Though that expedition had obviously been risky, it was probably the only hope of saving the western empire. The West's recovery of Africa would greatly have strengthened both its calamitous strategic position and tottering economic base. Yet the only chance of expelling the well-entrenched Vandals was a vigorous and direct attack. The gigantic size of the expeditionary force shows how determined both East and West were that it should not fail.

Although its failure probably spurred Leo to get rid of Aspar, it also meant that the eastern empire was at a disadvantage against Aspar's outraged allies, the Ostrogoths. After losing many soldiers and oarsmen in Africa, the empire lost still more Ostrogoth mercenaries, who deserted to the independent Ostrogoths in the Balkans. Leo and Zeno seem to have replaced some of the mobile armies' losses with Isaurians, but even so the field armies seem to have been almost a tenth smaller at the end of the century than they had been at the beginning. Zeno finally won the struggle with the Ostrogoths not by defeating them in the field but by persuading them to go west, where by this time no western empire remained to be harmed.

Anastasius I was an exceptional emperor in being a better economist than a general. He was also a good politician. As soon as he established a sound currency, he spent it liberally on the army. Yet his liberality was selective. He raised the remuneration of field soldiers from about 14 nomismata to 20 a year, but left that of frontier troops unchanged at about 5 nomismata. As a result, given the losses the armies had sustained in the meantime, his military budget was not much bigger than Marcian's. He was nonetheless able to turn his field armies into an overwhelmingly native force of eager volunteers. In 502 Anastasius mustered 52,000 soldiers on the border, a number contemporaries thought was unprecedented.[34] It may have been slightly more than the number of eastern soldiers sent against the Vandals in 468, which I have guessed at 50,000.

Since Anastasius's budgetary surplus was bigger than Marcian's, despite his reductions in taxes, the empire was plainly better off than before. Some of the credit should doubtless go to Anastasius's good management; but more of it should probably go to a demographic recovery. A richer field army was not necessarily more docile, as Anastasius discovered when his general Vitalian rebelled in 513, winning support because he opposed the Monophysite heresy favored by the emperor. Yet a better-paid army did seem to fight better, and it was certainly much easier to find recruits for.

Thus Justinian was able to increase the field armies by almost 60 percent, and apparently had no trouble attracting the volunteers he needed. He did, however, have some trouble paying them after he had recruited them. The main exception to the army's generally good record under Justinian was its tendency to mutiny, a form of military protest that had been almost unknown in earlier times.[35] Most of the mutineers under Jus-

34. For the number, see the detailed contemporary account of Joshua the Stylite, 54, p. 44, mentioning separate forces of 12,000 and 40,000. Cf. Procopius, *Wars*, I.8.1 – 4; and the comments of Jones, *Later Roman Empire*, 231 – 32.

35. As Jones, ibid., 678, observes, "The recurrent and serious mutinies of the sixth century are something quite new in the history of the empire," but for the reasons indicated here Jones is probably wrong that the mutinies "indicate that the conditions of the troops had seriously deteriorated."

tinian were not backing some rebel who wanted to be emperor, and generally they were not even seeking some privilege or complaining about some government action.[36] They simply wanted their pay, which Justinian had allowed to fall into arrear.

Since Justinian spent heavily on both military and civilian projects, his financial problems must have begun even before the plague started to diminish his revenue in 541. Nearly all the reserve left by Anastasius is said to have been gone by 527.[37] In 536 the soldiers who mutinied in recently reconquered North Africa already complained of late pay; the mutiny was put down only after Justinian sent the arrears.[38] At the same time the army in Sicily threatened mutiny, probably for the same reason.[39]

Yet up to 540 Justinian's conquests in Africa and Italy probably paid for themselves just by capturing the treasuries of the Vandal and Ostrogoth kingdoms. Justinian appears to have failed to send pay for his soldiers because he expected African and Italian revenues to be enough to meet their armies' payrolls at once; in practice, unsettled conditions made this overoptimistic. Once peace was fully established, however, Justinian's expectation should have been justified, at least until the plague broke out. Justinian's military expenses in 540 seem actually to have been less than those of Diocletian and Galerius in 300, when they surely ruled a much smaller population, including neither Africa nor Italy. No doubt Justinian ran a risk when he tried to retake Africa and Italy, but with the aid of Belisarius he succeeded with surprising ease at first, and in the end he completed both conquests despite everything that went wrong.

The plague, which Justinian could not possibly have foreseen, severely upset his plans. He and his finance ministers met the emergency, though with the greatest difficulty, by canceling the pay of the frontier troops, delaying the pay of the mobile troops, and retrenching in the West to the point where the Moors and Ostrogoths could overrun much of Africa and Italy. The emperor went on to confiscate private fortunes and to sell public offices, and we may be sure that nonmilitary spending was curbed as well. All of these measures together proved to be just enough.

Justinian was harshly criticized by his contemporaries, above all by Procopius in his unpublished *Secret History*. The criticism continues today. Yet if Justinian's government had other choices, they are far from obvious. The frontier troops had been second-rate for almost two hundred years,

36. The African mutiny of 536 was a partial exception, since according to Procopius, *Wars*, IV.14.7–21, it was largely fomented by Vandals; but a speech he attributes to the leader of the mutiny (*Wars*, IV.15.55) gives most prominence to the lateness of the army's pay.

37. Cf. Procopius, *Secret History*, 19.7–8.

38. Id., *Wars*, IV.15.55 and 16.5.

39. Ibid., IV.15.48.

and they continued to exist and to be of some use even without regular wages. Though the field army sometimes mutinied or even deserted when its pay was late, it would surely have done the same if its pay had been cut, and then it might even have tried to overthrow Justinian. Justinian might have written off Italy or Africa altogether, but by holding on to their most important strongholds he made it easier for his generals to reconquer both of them after the plague passed. Since Justinian must have expected that the plague would indeed pass after a few years, his task in the meantime was to avoid bankruptcy, revolution, or permanent losses of territory. This he did, and could hardly have done in any very different ways. He would probably have been much more successful, and perhaps conquered all of Spain, if the plague had not returned in 558.

During the rest of the sixth century, the emperors found themselves with fewer taxpayers, longer frontiers, and an enlarged field army that was paid at a high rate. Their margin for making errors was accordingly reduced. Justin II made the serious mistakes of failing to reinforce Italy against the Lombards and provoking an unnecessary war with Persia. Tiberius II, finding that Justin had at least left a large reserve in the treasury, by 577 not unreasonably recruited new troops, the 15,000 Federates, to deal with the Persian war. The field soldiers' pay was high enough that he could still attract this large number of volunteers in the impoverished Balkans, even after several bouts of plague had reduced the population. The arrival of the Federates enabled Tiberius's general Maurice to inflict a severe defeat on the Persians the next year. But the Persians stubbornly refused to make peace. By 579 the 50,000 Byzantine soldiers in the East were becoming hard to pay, and threatened mutiny when their pay was overdue.[40] Then the Avars and Slavs, seeing how much of the empire's army was occupied with the Persians, invaded the Balkans in force.

This was the dangerous but not desperate situation inherited by Maurice as emperor in 582. Maurice tolerated Avar and Slav raids in the Balkans and the Lombard occupation of much of Italy, and tried to reduce military expenses. Like Tiberius before him, Maurice hoped for a quick peace with the Persians, but failed to get it because of Persian obstinacy. Finally, in 590, the Persian king paid for his stupidity with his life. Maurice won the war by prudently choosing to restore the legitimate heir to the Persian throne. The emperor then transferred many troops to the Balkans, and by 599 won that war as well by driving out the invaders.

Maurice must have had a very small financial surplus, and he became obsessed with cutting costs. Since he never actually ran out of money, his aim seems to have been not so much to avoid bankruptcy as to put aside a comfortable reserve in the treasury. His unsuccessful attempts to econo-

40. John of Ephesus, VI.28.

mize provoked not one but four mutinies, the last of which brought him down with truly horrendous consequences. Justinian had managed a far worse financial crisis much more skillfully. Rather than court such a disaster after such clear warnings, Maurice should have made economies elsewhere, perhaps at the expense of the residual frontier troops, or simply decided that having no reserve for an emergency was better than having an emergency.

Over the whole period from 284 to 602, however, the eastern empire defended itself remarkably well. It avoided very real dangers of insolvency and subversion from within, put down every military revolt by those outside the imperial college, lost scarcely any of its original territory, and took and held North Africa and much of Italy. Its field forces became the best army in the western world. Its frontier troops, for all their weaknesses, maintained a fair level of domestic order. Even in the sixth century the only frontier regions that were permanently lost to the enemy, those of Italy and Spain, were the only ones that seem to have lacked frontier soldiers. Although the army suffered two terrible defeats, at Adrianople in 378 and against the Vandals in 468, it survived both of them, and under Justinian it destroyed the Vandals and Ostrogoths by brilliant victories.

SURVIVING CATASTROPHE

The mutiny of 602 almost undid everything. By 610, when Heraclius ended the reign of the mutineers' leader Phocas, even a complete conquest of the empire by the Persians and Avars seemed possible. Heraclius was assisted in managing the empire's financial troubles by the clearness of the danger, which led the army and bureaucracy to tolerate his cuts in pay and the Church to grant him extraordinary loans of gold and silver. The loss of the frontiers at least ended the need to pay for the supplies of the frontier troops. Many field soldiers must have been lost as well, further reducing military expenses.

Yet Heraclius's nerve and strategic sense deserve much, and probably most, of the credit. He wisely concentrated on saving soldiers rather than territory. Though he tried to stop the Persians in Syria, he never risked losing a whole field army there, and he avoided imperiling the Army of the East by a last-ditch attempt to hold Egypt. Though the Avars do seem to have trapped and destroyed most of the Army of Illyricum, the circumstances are extremely obscure. Heraclius is unlikely to have had much control over what happened on the faraway Danube frontier, but he does seem to have evacuated a little of the Army of Illyricum and much of the Army of Thrace to Anatolia. He then left the Avars and Slavs a free hand in the Balkans, realizing that they lacked the knowledge of naval or siege warfare that they needed to cross the straits or to take Constantinople. He refused to become bogged down fighting the Persians in Asia Minor.

After 620, Heraclius tried above all to increase pressure on the Persian government, which had after all succumbed to a military rebellion during another costly war thirty years earlier. The Persians responded as best they could by joining the Avars to besiege Constantinople; but the two allies' forces were too different from each other, and their naval power too weak, to make the siege effective. In the end, Heraclius broke into Persian Mesopotamia and provoked the internal revolt he sought. Then he used his victory carefully and moderately, making an equitable peace, as Maurice had done.

Heraclius's reaction to the Arab invasion, which is as much criticized today as his reaction to the Persian invasion is praised, was in fact rather similar to it. Although he put up a respectable resistance, he took more care to save his soldiers than his land. He managed to withdraw most of the Army of the East to Anatolia, which with its mountainous terrain was always much more defensible than Syria. The only real alternative would have been to mass his remaining forces in Syria for a desperate showdown with the enemy.

What would have happened if he had tried this and failed can be seen in the experience of the Persians, who after failing in a determined defense of Mesopotamia lost their whole empire, including their more defensible heartland in Persia proper. By being more cautious, through all the invasions of the Persians, Avars, Slavs, and Arabs, Heraclius saved something like two-thirds of the eastern field armies that he had taken over in 610. This was not only a remarkable achievement but one vital to the empire's future survival.

Constans II kept those troops by creating the themes and distributing military lands, a necessary financial measure that turned out to be of impressive military value as well. The empire's defensive position had also improved in what remained of its territory after the loss of the Balkans and Syria. The Danube had always been too long to patrol against invaders, who needed only rafts or canoes to cross it; but the walls of Constantinople were strong, the straits were short and wide, and the Aegean was impassable without a fleet. Syria had no natural defenses but the desert, which was no barrier for the Arabs; but the Taurus and Antitaurus mountains formed a barrier broken by only a few passes, and even those were made hazardous by winter snows.

The Arabs were not at their best in mountain fighting, or in snow and cold. Though they raided Anatolia repeatedly through the passes, they almost always returned to Syria before winter set in, and when they failed to do so they usually came to regret it. The only parts of Anatolia that the

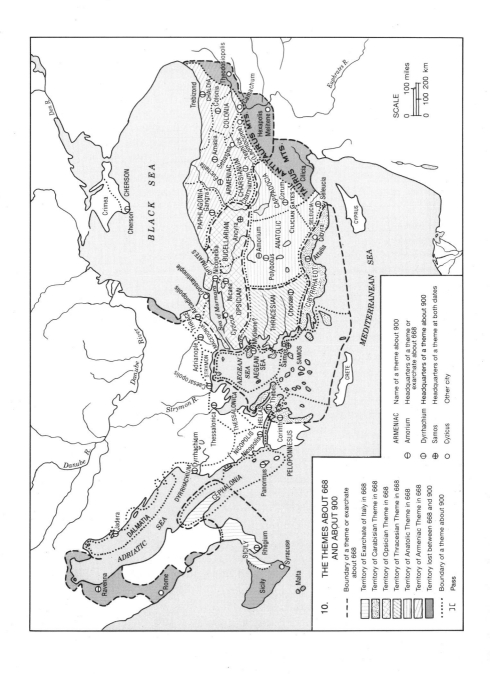

SCALE

0   100 miles

0   100   200 km

10.   THE THEMES ABOUT 668
AND ABOUT 900

- - -   Boundary of a theme or exarchate
about 668

Territory of Exarchate of Italy in 668

Territory of Carabisian Theme in 668

Territory of Opsician Theme in 668

Territory of Thracesian Theme in 668

Territory of Anatolic Theme in 668

Territory of Armeniac Theme in 668

Territory lost between 668 and 900

········   Boundary of a theme about 900

)(Pass

ARMENIAC   Name of a theme about 900

   Amorium   Headquarters of a theme or
exarchate about 668

   Dyrrhachium   Headquarters of a theme about 900

   Samos   Headquarters of a theme at both dates

   Cyzicus   Other city

Arabs conquered after the foundation of the themes were some border areas on their side of the Taurus and Antitaurus. The limit of their advance can be seen in Map 10.

Since the Arabs had already managed to conquer mountainous and snowy Armenia, Byzantine resistance in Anatolia had to be stiff to prevent a conquest. Yet no serious attempt was made to stop the Arabs' summer raids until the ninth century. The deployment of Byzantine soldiers in Anatolia, which had presumably been made under Constans more for financial than for strategic reasons, was thinnest near the frontier in 775. It may well have been thinner still in the parts of the themes beyond the Taurus that by then had been lost. The Arab raiders only began to encounter large groups of soldiers when the raids reached the central Anatolian plateau. Troops were sparsest in Cappadocia, just opposite the main pass through the Taurus, the Cilician Gates, on the route the Arabs took most often.

No region was raided more by the Arabs than the Turma of Cappadocia in the Anatolic Theme. They sacked its forts again and again, and sometimes even wintered there. The region must have become depopulated; the remaining inhabitants resorted to building great underground shelters for themselves and their livestock. Just to the north, the Turma of Charsianum in the Armeniac Theme also had few troops and suffered greatly from Arab raids. In this frontier zone only the tough could survive, and not surprisingly it came to have the largest concentration of great landowners of military background.[41] The Arabs could easily have conquered both Cappadocia and Charsianum, if neighboring Byzantine troops had not been ready to drive them out as soon as winter came.

After the failure of the Arab siege of Constantinople in 717–18, the Byzantines' survival seemed assured, and they lost no more land in Anatolia to the Arabs. After 743, Constantine V made the army somewhat more flexible by creating the tagmata. The main motive for this reform, as with Constans' creation of the themes, seems not to have been to improve the empire's defenses; Constantine rather wanted to reduce the power of the Opsician Theme and even to punish parts of it, certainly including the Optimates. Yet the tagmata turned out to fight well against the enemy, allowing Constantine to make a few tentative raids on Arab territory and to begin advancing the Byzantine frontier in Thrace.

Irene continued what Constantine had begun in Thrace, while Nicephorus I reoccupied most of Slav-held Greece and created new themes there. Since the Slavs were generally unwarlike, this could probably have been done earlier; but emperors had grown accustomed to being on the defensive, and retaking Greece brought little loot or glory. Yet Greece,

---

41. Cf. Hendy, *Studies*, 100–103.

apart from its substantial economic value, was a possible base for future advances against the Bulgars. Significant gains at the expense of the Arabs still seemed beyond the empire's reach at the time.

The Arabs had a far larger army than the empire's. Even their raiding parties were of several thousand men, and when they chose they could put enormous armies into the field. For the siege of Constantinople in 717 they are said to have mustered 120,000 men, well above the strength of the whole Byzantine army.[42] In 782 the Arabs invaded the empire with 95,793 men, again more than the whole Byzantine army. In 806 the Arabs invaded with 135,000 men, perhaps their highest number and certainly an overwhelming force. In 838 they invaded with 80,000 men, which still was more than the Byzantines could put into the field.[43]

The Arabs' military superiority was a result of their economic superiority. Excluding deserts, the Arab Caliphate held about ten times as much territory as the empire in the eighth century. Around 800 the caliph's revenues were the equivalent of some 35 million nomismata, while Byzantine revenues were about 2 million.[44] Though the Byzantines' reliance on military lands made their army much stronger than their cash revenues could have supported alone, their financial inferiority to the Arabs shows how necessary the military lands were. Under the circumstances, the themes did well simply by preventing the Arab conquest of Asia Minor and Constantinople itself.

The themes did, however, pose some threat to the empire's political stability. The danger first appeared in 668, when the Count of the Opsician Theme assassinated Constans II and the Strategus of the Armeniac Theme revolted. The problem became far worse between 695 and 717, when the Carabisian, Opsician, and Anatolic themes made and unmade emperors and allowed the Arabs to extend their conquests to the east of the Taurus and Antitaurus. Constantine V's division of the Opsician Theme reduced the danger of rebellions, and his division and dispersion of the tagmata helped insure that they would never overthrow an emperor.

Troops from the themes nonetheless overthrew Michael I in 813. Thematic troops almost overthrew Michael II in 821–23, and the long civil war in which they tried to depose him contributed to his loss of Crete in 828. As late as 838, the Khurramite rebellion against Theophilus undermined his resistance to the Arab invaders, who were able to defeat the Byzantine army and sack Ancyra and Amorium, probably the largest cities in Anatolia at the time. The Arab campaign of 838 showed Theophilus

42. See Mas'ūdī, 226.
43. See Treadgold, *Byzantine Revival*, 67, 144, and 297.
44. For Arab revenues, see Treadgold, *Byzantine State Finances*, 2–3.

that though the Byzantine army might defeat Slavs and Bulgars and Arab raiding parties, it was still unable to withstand a regular Arab army in the field.[45]

REGAINING SUPERIORITY

When Theophilus recovered from the shock of his defeat, he put down the Khurramite revolt and reformed the army. Probably he had realized that pay of 5 nomismata a year was too little to deter soldiers with self-sufficient farms from rebelling against the emperor. Full pay of 12 nomismata a year was much better, especially because it provided enough cash to free the soldiers from dependence on the imperial warehouses, a system that seems not to have been much to their advantage. Doubtless the soldiers' loyalty and morale improved, and they probably spent some of their additional money on improving their equipment. When Theophilus resettled the Khurramites, he also reinforced the border region by creating the cleisurae. These reinforcements, together with the smaller territorial commands called banda, for the first time permitted a rapid and vigorous defense against Arab raiders in the border region itself.

The only major weakness in Theophilus's reform was his failure to create a cleisura in the region of Colonia in the Armeniac Theme. Apparently he relied on the fact that earlier Arab raids had mostly attacked the regions of Cappadocia, Charsianum, and Seleucia, all of which he did turn into cleisurae. But the Arabs soon learned that they could avoid these cleisurae and reach the Anatolian plateau by advancing up the Euphrates valley and around the end of the Antitaurus into Colonia. There the low mountains and the narrow Upper Euphrates provided little defense against invaders; past the Euphrates, the way was clear to the middle of the Anatolian plateau. The Paulician heretics set up their rebel principality in just this region at the end of the Antitaurus, and joined the Arabs of nearby Melitene in raiding the Armeniac Theme, whose soldiers had received relatively few reinforcements. Yet these raids were not much more than nuisances. The Byzantine army defeated Arab and Paulician raiders whenever it had a chance to muster troops against them. Before long, it crushed them.

Though the Byzantines twice mishandled the difficult amphibious operations needed to retake Crete from the Arabs, Basil I largely restored Byzantine control of the seas by his reform of the Imperial Fleet. Basil also finished off the Paulicians. At last, in 900, Leo VI began to retake some territory from the Arabs. Significantly, his new themes screened the weak point in the frontier around Colonia. They also occupied the barren re-

45. On this campaign, see Treadgold, *Byzantine Revival*, 297–305.

gion between the Taurus and Antitaurus, most of which had long been a no-man's-land. Even so, the empire was not ready to attempt significant conquests across the mountains for another sixty years. The conquests of Melitene and Theodosiopolis simply brought Byzantine control up to the Taurus.

Nicephorus II began the empire's breakthrough by retaking Crete in 961. His conquests of Cyprus, Cilicia, most of Armenia, and some of Syria followed rapidly. John I then conquered most of Bulgaria and an additional part of Syria before his death in 976. These had been an extraordinary fifteen years. The empire turned large new territories into dozens of themes, and seemed quite capable of advancing farther in any direction it chose. Though Nicephorus and John were certainly military geniuses of a high order, they could hardly have done all they did so quickly if their armies had been less than satisfactory.

Naturally these ambitious campaigns cost money, for campaign pay if nothing else. Nicephorus made requisitions of various kinds, but his main economy seems to have been the introduction of the tetarteron. Since the tetarteron was a lightweight nomisma rather than a debased one, the usual Byzantine practice of weighing coins to allow for wear prevented the tetartera from causing any loss of revenue in taxation, or even much confusion in commerce. Though Nicephorus would have saved money on any payments he made in tetartera, military or civilian, he would primarily have reduced military spending if, as suggested above, he used the lighter coins to pay thematic troops in the interior who had become less active, and whom he did not really need. Other such troops may have been called upon to contribute toward the expenses of his new heavy cavalry.

Nicephorus and John won their victories with armies that seem to have ranged between 25,000 and 70,000 men, with between 16,000 and 40,000 infantry.[46] The highest number, the about 70,000 men led by Nicephorus against Aleppo in 962, was quite exceptional, and created supply problems. Before the major conquests began in 959, the whole army had had some 144,000 men, including 88,000 infantry. These were already more than twice the maximum needed for offensive campaigns, and with the collapse of Arab military power most of Byzantine Anatolia needed no local defense against the Arabs. Nicephorus and John added themes that probably brought the army up to more than 200,000 men, almost three times the maximum they needed for offensive campaigns.

Many of the new recruits were cavalry. Most of them were probably Armenians with recent fighting experience, who were far better soldiers than the largely inactive Byzantines of the central and western Anatolian

46. See above, pp. 113–14.

themes. Perhaps 120,000 of those Byzantines, the size of the whole ninth-century army, were unlikely to be needed in any foreseeable contingency. But they still drew pay. If Nicephorus reduced their real wages by just a twelfth, while saving their pride by keeping it at the same nominal figure, he acted generously. Yet the soldiers involved cannot be expected to have seen things in quite this way. Even if they had become accustomed to draw pay without fighting, they had never done anything to deserve discharge. Though they had no desperate need for the money they were paid, it made a very handy supplement to their income. They would have reacted to any suggestion that they were useless with indignation, and would have fought if necessary to keep their ranks and pay as soldiers.

Such considerations seem to lurk in the background during the two great civil wars that lasted from 976 to 980 and from 987 to 989. In these wars the old themes of Anatolia found opportunities to fight, and for the most part they fought the central government of the legitimate emperor Basil II. The tagmata and western themes generally remained loyal to Basil. Ostensibly the rebels were fighting either for Bardas Phocas, the heir of Nicephorus II, or for Bardas Sclerus, the heir of John I—or at one point for both, when the two Bardases made a temporary alliance. At least at first, each of the rebel leaders would probably have been content to be co-emperor along with the young and apparently weak Basil II. But the supporters of each Bardas naturally expected that their leaders would protect their interests if they won; and many of the thematic soldiers of Anatolia must have felt that their interests were endangered at the time.[47]

Basil II finally emerged the victor, and despite his vengeful disposition he took no measures against the soldiers of Anatolia. If they were indeed the ones who had been paid in tetartera, he must have begun paying them in full nomismata again, since he minted no tetartera during much of his reign. He had evidently had too much trouble from them to want any more of it. But he cannot have made much use of them in his wars. The armies he led seem to have been of fairly modest size, composed of troops from the border themes, the tagmata, and his faithful Varangian Guard. Basil was essentially a cautious and conservative ruler, though he recognized that too much caution could be dangerous. Much of his military effort simply restored the conquests of Nicephorus II and John I. He annexed western Bulgaria and eastern Armenia almost against his will, as results of wars he had neither started nor wanted.

By 1025 the empire had plenty of land, which produced revenues that were more than sufficient to pay even the inflated military payroll. The last three emperors, Nicephorus, John, and Basil, had used the empire's

47. For a recent discussion of these civil wars, see Cheynet, *Pouvoir et contestations*, esp. 321–36.

new revenues as any prudent Byzantine aristocrat would have used his money. They invested it in land—not directly, but by paying for campaigns of conquest. The army was strong enough to go on conquering, and Basil himself had been planning to conquer Sicily when death forestalled him. Though no particularly valuable land remained to the north or east of the empire's borders, John I had already shown the Byzantine standard in southern Syria, which was relatively prosperous, and beyond it lay the even richer land of Egypt. Yet the rest of Syria and Egypt would have been difficult to assimilate, because Christians were already in the minority there. The Byzantines disliked ruling Muslims, and had expelled most of them from their conquests in Cilicia and northern Syria. So seemingly the easiest course was to sit back and enjoy a secure and prosperous peace.

LOSING THE PEACE

Even peace, however, presented certain problems. The tagmata and border themes had become used to fighting and winning booty, and many of their soldiers had no desire to settle down for good. Not only the army but most other Byzantines had come to expect military glory from their emperors. While up to the early tenth century many provincials would have been glad enough just to be spared enemy raids, the victories that followed had created some enthusiasm for successful wars. The songs that were to become the epic of the heroic warrior Digenes Acrites appear to belong to this time.[48] With such superiority over its enemies as the empire had attained, keeping the peace was no great credit to the emperor or his army.

The army of the old Anatolian themes was absurdly large and well paid, and in peacetime the absurdity of paying so many men so much for nothing became more evident. However, especially after the long reign of the austere Basil II, emperors had got out of the habit of nonmilitary spending. Most ways of spending immense sums of money risked creating powerful rivals to the emperor among the recipients. Basil had already left some taxes uncollected; but cutting them permanently meant reducing the government's power and renouncing money that might be needed someday. Similarly, since occasional military troubles were bound to recur, the empire clearly needed a strong army, if not as large a one as it had. Some fighting, and probably some conquests, still seemed to be necessary.

Basil's elderly brother Constantine VIII was able to ignore such prob-

48. For this still problematic poem, which exists in several versions that probably go back to an original of the tenth century, see the combined edition with introduction by Trapp, *Digenes Akrites*. The English translation with edition by Mavrogordato could well be improved upon.

lems during his brief reign of three years. But Constantine's successor Romanus III was dimly aware of them, even though he had been chosen for his dimness by Constantine's ministers to enhance their own power. Romanus sought to expand in the most obvious way, by annexing the neighboring Emirate of Aleppo, which for many years had been a Byzantine client. Realizing that he lacked military experience but had money to spare, he offered to buy Aleppo from its rulers and to give them another city; but they refused. In 1030, Romanus mustered a large and disorderly army, invaded the emirate in the worst heat of summer, lost 10,000 men in two ambushes, and fled. Eager to avoid further tests of strength with the empire, the Aleppines offered to become clients again, and were accepted.[49]

The Aleppines were wise, because the Byzantine army still fought well when it was capably led. In 1031 the Strategus of the little Theme of the Euphrates Cities, George Maniaces, took the large city of Edessa in Mesopotamia and held it. As for Romanus III, he decided that the safest way to win glory for himself was to build an expensive church. His successor Michael IV was also a builder of churches, and relied on his generals to repel Arab pirates from Sicily and Pecheneg raiders from across the Danube. Michael merely bid for vicarious glory by sending George Maniaces to conquer Sicily.

Though George took Syracuse and was well on his way to success, Michael became worried that the victorious general might rebel, and had him arrested. Maniaces' Norman mercenaries did revolt, and attacked Byzantine Italy. Then the Bulgarians also rebelled, but luckily for Michael they fell to quarreling among themselves and surrendered by the time that the emperor marched out against them in person. Yet the expedition Michael sent to claim the Armenian Kingdom of Ani, which under a treaty of 1022 was due to be inherited by the empire, met with defeat. Some fighting clearly could not be avoided. But for the emperor to do it himself took some skill; using skillful generals ran the risk that they would want to be emperor themselves; and unskillful generals failed.

So matters stood when Constantine IX became emperor in 1042, then was almost deposed by George Maniaces the next year. Constantine survived, and had a long enough reign that he needed to take some major steps to deal with the army. The army did not much care for Constantine, and tried to overthrow him twice more in 1047. He in turn spent so freely on buildings and largess that by about 1050 he had exhausted the vast reserves left by Basil II. Constantine resumed minting tetartera, which if my conjecture is correct meant reducing the pay of the older themes by a twelfth again. He also debased both his tetartera and his regular nomis-

---

49. On this whole episode, see Felix, *Byzanz und die islamische Welt*, 82–94.

mata, and released the soldiers of the Armenian themes from their duties in return for a tax.

The latter two measures were explicable but indefensible. Behind them, and probably behind the reintroduction of the tetarteron, was the reasonable feeling that the army was unnecessarily big and costly. Since the soldiers might rebel if the government reduced their pay openly and substantially, debasing the coinage by a fifth was the easiest way of cutting their pay by a fifth—or for those paid in tetartera by over a quarter. As for the second measure, Constantine doubtless thought it reasonable that soldiers who were not going to fight should pay for the privilege. Already in the early tenth century the government had asked for money in return for excusing troops from individual campaigns.[50] Constantine seemed simply to be regularizing that practice.

The main error in all of this from the strategic point of view was that Constantine failed to distinguish between the soldiers the empire needed and those it did not need. Those it needed were in the tagmata, the naval themes, and the border themes. The latter were more or less those grouped under the various dukes and the Catepan of Italy, and certainly included the Armenian themes. Apart from the fact that in the long run debasing the coinage would save no money, because the debased coins would just reduce the value of tax revenues, the debasement affected all the soldiers, even those who were needed most.

Although by all accounts Constantine more than compensated the civil service for the debasement by giving them donatives and promotions, he seems not to have been so liberal even with the tagmata, let alone with the naval or border themes. No doubt Constantine remembered that troops that included the tagmata had tried to overthrow him three times. Perhaps he considered campaign pay, which could be adjusted as needed, to be sufficient compensation for the soldiers who really fought.

The demobilization of the Armenian themes was an even worse mistake, and attracted the sharp condemnation of Constantine's contemporaries Scylitzes, Attaliates, and Cecaumenus.[51] The 50,000 men affected should have been among the empire's very best thematic troops, since they were Armenian and Iberian veterans defending their ancestral lands. They had defeated the Seljuk Turks as recently as 1048.[52] The Seljuk Turks were the empire's most dangerous enemies, and had begun attacking precisely this sector at just this time. Furthermore, the Armenian themes were what protected the old weak spot in Byzantine defenses on the Upper Euphrates, the back door to Asia Minor that Theophilus had strangely failed to bar by his military reforms of 840.

50. See above, pp. 138 and 139.
51. See above, p. 80.
52. Felix, *Byzanz und die islamische Welt*, 164.

Officials like Scylitzes, Attaliates, and Cecaumenus saw that Constantine had made a fatal error. But the emperor wanted more money, and he had reasons for not demanding it from the soldiers of the nearly useless themes of central and western Anatolia. Most of those men would never have done military service in their lives, except possibly in a rebellion, and probably they had never been asked even for money in place of military service. To ask this late for regular tax payments from as many as 50,000 of them, in return for their not having to do something that they had never done anyway, would have looked like extortion and invited a revolt.

Since the soldiers of the Armenian themes had fought recently, the taxes that they paid replaced real duties and real danger. Even if the Armenians might have preferred to go on being soldiers, they were far from Constantinople and unlikely to rebel. The revenues of their poor and rocky themes may well have been less than the cost of their pay before Constantine began his tax, which even so does not seem to have involved canceling their pay. Probably Constantine was willing to tolerate some Turkish raiding of the Armenian themes themselves, though he could never have imagined that some backward Turks might threaten the Anatolian heartland of the empire. The Byzantines' traditional enemies were the Arabs, who faced the themes under the dukes of Antioch and Edessa that Constantine did nothing to dismantle. Besides, he had already stationed tagmatic troops and mercenaries in Armenia, and he could always use some of the money from his new taxes to hire more mercenaries.

The absence of the troops of the Armenian themes was felt as early as 1054, when the Turks raided Armenia with impunity. But then they interrupted their attacks on the empire while they conquered the Buwayhid Sultanate of Baghdad. By the time that an uprising backed by troops from the tagmata, mercenaries, and Syrian themes put Isaac I on the throne in 1057, he was appalled to find the financial disarray that Constantine IX had left behind. The full seriousness of the Turkish threat was still not clear; after sacking Melitene in 1057, a Turkish raiding party was destroyed by the empire's Armenian client prince of Sasun. The treasury needed the new taxes from the Armenian themes. During his short reign Isaac spent his energies on finance and never got around to reforming the army; neither did his successor Constantine X.

Then the Turks began attacking the empire in earnest. In 1059 they passed through the Armenian themes, crossed the Upper Euphrates, and sacked Sebastea. In 1064 they conquered Ani outright. In 1067 they penetrated through the Armenian themes to sack Caesarea in Cappadocia, then went back through the Cilician Gates to raid Cilicia and the region of Antioch from the rear.[53] Byzantine Armenia was on the point of falling,

53. See Cahen, "Première pénétration," 22–25.

and Anatolia itself was in danger. Military disaster was plainly impending when Romanus IV became emperor in 1068.

Romanus needed to do something drastic, and he chose to try to revive the old themes in Asia Minor. Like the tagmata, the ducates of Antioch and Edessa seem still to have been ready to fight; reviving the Armenian themes probably needed to wait until some semblance of order was restored there. Ani and most of Vaspurakan were already lost. Yet Romanus was surely right not to abandon all the Armenian themes. Ravaged though they were, they formed a buffer, and fighting in them was better than fighting in Anatolia. In such an emergency, Romanus's accepting the Norman conquest of the empire's small foothold in Italy in 1071 was only sensible. Even Romanus's further debasement of the nomisma may have been justifiable as a temporary expedient.

In an amazingly short time, Romanus turned men with scarcely any fighting experience into usable soldiers. But while Romanus used his new army to campaign, Turks continued to raid across the Upper Euphrates into Anatolia, sacking not only Neocaesarea but Amorium and Iconium in the very center of the plateau. Romanus concentrated on trying to reestablish a barrier against them as far east as Manzikert. Even if he failed to stop them from raiding, he could hope to stop them from making permanent conquests. A victory at Manzikert would probably have given him the respite he needed to finish training the themes.

His defeat, even through treachery, was a devastating blow to his prestige. Nevertheless, weakened though he was, Romanus could still have ruled better than the Ducas family, who first betrayed and then killed him. They never secured control of the forces under Romanus's lieutenant Philaretus Brachamius, which evidently included the eastern tagmata and soon the ducates of Edessa and Antioch. Unable to conceive that the Turks might go beyond raiding actually to conquer Anatolia, the government allowed them to advance unhindered across the Upper Euphrates. The Turks spread over the themes of Colonia, Sebastea, Cappadocia, Charsianum, Chaldia, the Bucellarians, the Anatolics, the Armeniacs, Paphlagonia, and the Optimates.

After Byzantine civil wars in which the Turks participated, Alexius I took over in 1081 with only the rump of an army and the broken shell of Asia Minor. To repel the Norman invasion of the Balkans, he withdrew the last effective troops from Anatolia, giving up most of the empire's remaining outposts there. Then he lost most of what remained of the army fighting the Normans at Dyrrhachium. Although Antioch, Edessa, and Cilicia still held out under Philaretus and his soldiers, they were independent of Constantinople.

The preposterous result was that Nicaea and Smyrna in western Anatolia fell in 1081, while in faraway Syria and Mesopotamia Antioch fell only in 1084 and Edessa in 1086. Though Armenia proper succumbed almost at once, Armenian troops held Cilicia for generations. Such an outcome makes no sense in terms of military geography, economics, or demographics. The difference was simply the presence or absence of soldiers competent to conduct a defense. Anatolia was defensible, rich, and populous, but it fell because the Byzantines scarcely defended it. Though sufficient troops screened the southeastern approaches of Anatolia, Constantine IX had dismissed the army that guarded the northeast.

Byzantine historians have long wondered why the empire, after successfully weathering so many reverses, collapsed so abjectly before the Turkish invasion and the Fourth Crusade of 1204. The evidence now seems clear that the empire was quite prosperous in the eleventh century, and that it retained most of its prosperity even in the twelfth century.[54] Although in time Alexius I put together a new army, he did not and could not replace the large professional force of native troops that Byzantium had inherited from Rome, maintained for so long, and thrown away in the course of the eleventh century. Without it, Byzantine power would never be the same again.

54. See esp. Hendy, "Byzantium, 1081–1204: An Economic Reappraisal"; and "Byzantium, 1081–1204: The Economy Revisited."

Reference Matter

Appendix: List of Eastern Roman (Byzantine) Emperors (284–1118)

The principal Eastern Roman Emperor is listed in capitals, with other rulers (if any) listed under him.

DIOCLETIAN 284–305
  Galerius, Caesar in Egypt and Syria 293–99
    Caesar in Balkans 299–305

GALERIUS 305–11
  Maximin, Caesar in Egypt and Syria 305–10
    Augustus in Egypt and Syria 310–11
  Licinius, Augustus with Galerius in Balkans 308–11

LICINIUS 311–24
  Maximin, Augustus in Egypt, Syria, and Anatolia 311–13
  Constantine I, Augustus in Balkans except Thrace 317–24

CONSTANTINE I 324–37
  Constantius II, Caesar in Egypt and Syria 335–37
  Dalmatius, Caesar in Balkans 335–37

CONSTANTIUS II 337–61
  Constans I, Augustus in Balkans except Thrace 337–50
  Gallus, Caesar in Egypt and Syria 351–54

JULIAN 361–63

JOVIAN 363–64

VALENS 364–78
  Valentinian I, Augustus in Balkans except Thrace 364–75
  Gratian, Augustus in Balkans except Thrace 375–79

THEODOSIUS I   379–95
  Valentinian II, Augustus in Balkans except Thrace 382–92

ARCADIUS   395-408

THEODOSIUS II   408-50

MARCIAN   450-57

LEO I   457-74

LEO II   474
  Zeno Tarasius, Augustus and regent

ZENO Tarasius   474-91
  Basiliscus, rival Augustus in most of East except Isauria 475-76

ANASTASIUS I   491-518

JUSTIN I   518-27

JUSTINIAN I   527-65

JUSTIN II   565-78
  Tiberius, Caesar and regent 574-78

TIBERIUS II Constantine   578-82

MAURICE Tiberius   582-602

PHOCAS the Tyrant   602-10

HERACLIUS   610-41

CONSTANTINE III Heraclius   641

HERACLONAS (Heraclius) Constantine   641
  Martina, regent

CONSTANS II (Constantine) Heraclius the Bearded   641-68

CONSTANTINE IV   668-85

JUSTINIAN II the Slit-Nosed   685-95

LEONTIUS (Leo)   695-98

TIBERIUS III Apsimar   698-705

JUSTINIAN II the Slit-Nosed (again)   705-11

PHILIPPICUS Bardanes   711-13

ANASTASIUS II Artemius   713-15

THEODOSIUS III   715-17

LEO III the Syrian ("Isaurian")   717-41

CONSTANTINE V Name of Dung   741 - 75
  Artavasdus, rival emperor at Constantinople 741 - 43

LEO IV the Khazar   775 - 80

CONSTANTINE VI the Blinded   780 - 97
  Irene, regent

IRENE the Athenian   797 - 802

NICEPHORUS I the General Logothete   802 - 11

STAURACIUS   811

MICHAEL I Rhangabe   811 - 13

LEO V the Armenian   813 - 20

MICHAEL II the Amorian   820 - 29

THEOPHILUS   829 - 42

MICHAEL III the Drunkard   842 - 67
  Theodora, regent 842 - 56

BASIL I the Macedonian   867 - 86

LEO VI the Wise   886 - 912

ALEXANDER   912 - 13

CONSTANTINE VII Porphyrogenitus   913 - 59
  Nicholas Mysticus, regent 913 - 14
  Zoë Carbonopsina, regent 914 - 20
  Romanus I Lecapenus, co-emperor 920 - 44

ROMANUS II Porphyrogenitus   959 - 63

BASIL II the Bulgar-Slayer   963 - 1025
  Theophano, regent 963
  Nicephorus II Phocas, co-emperor 963 - 69
  John I Tzimisces, co-emperor 969 - 76

CONSTANTINE VIII Porphyrogenitus   1025 - 28

ROMANUS III Argyrus   1028 - 34

MICHAEL IV the Paphlagonian   1034 - 41

MICHAEL V the Caulker   1041 - 42

ZOË Porphyrogenita   1042

CONSTANTINE IX Monomachus   1042 - 55

THEODORA Porphyrogenita   1055 - 56

MICHAEL VI Bringas   1056-57

ISAAC I Comnenus   1057-59

CONSTANTINE X Ducas   1059-67

MICHAEL VII Ducas   1067-78
  Eudocia Macrembolitissa, regent 1067-68
  Romanus IV Diogenes, co-emperor 1068-71

NICEPHORUS III Botaniates   1078-81

ALEXIUS I Comnenus   1081-1118

Bibliography

This bibliography includes only works cited in the notes, and uses the following abbreviations:

BAR	British Archaeological Reports
BZ	Byzantinische Zeitschrift
CFHB	Corpus Fontium Historiae Byzantinae
CSHB	Corpus Scriptorum Historiae Byzantinae
DOP	Dumbarton Oaks Papers
GRBS	Greek, Roman and Byzantine Studies
JÖB	Jahrbuch der Österreichischen Byzantinistik
JRS	Journal of Roman Studies
MGH	Monumenta Germaniae Historica
PG	Patrologia Graeca, ed. J.-P. Migne
TIB	Tabula Imperii Byzantini
TM	Travaux et Mémoires

The Abinnaeus Archive: Papers of a Roman Officer in the Reign of Constantius II. Ed. H. I. Bell et al. Oxford, 1962.

Agathias of Myrina. *Histories.* Ed. Rudolf Keydell. *CFHB* 2: Berlin, 1967.

Agnellus. *Liber Pontificalis Ecclesiae Ravennatis.* Ed. O. Holder-Egger. In *MGH, Scriptores Rerum Langobardicarum et Italicarum,* 265–391. Hannover, 1878.

Ahrweiler, Hélène. *Byzance et la mer: La marine de guerre, la politique et les institutions maritimes de Byzance aux VIIe–XVe siècles.* Paris, 1966.

Allen, P. "The 'Justinianic' Plague." *Byzantion* 49 (1979) 5–20.

Anonymous of Valois [*Excerpta Valesiana*]. *Origo Constantini Imperatoris.* Ed. Jacques Moreau and Velizar Velkov. Leipzig, 1968.

Antoniadis-Bibicou, Hélène. *Études d'histoire maritime de Byzance à propos du "thème des Caravisiens."* Paris, 1966.

Attaliates, Michael. *History.* Ed. Immanuel Bekker. *CSHB:* Bonn, 1853.

Bar Hebraeus, Gregorius. *Chronography.* Trans. E. A. W. Budge. Oxford, 1932.

Biraben, J.-N. *Les hommes et la peste en France et dans les pays européens et méditerranéens,* I. Paris, 1975.

Bivar, A. D. H. "Cavalry Equipment and Tactics on the Euphrates Frontier." *DOP* 26 (1972) 271–91.

Blockley, R. C., ed. and trans. *The Fragmentary Classicizing Historians of the Later Roman Empire: Eunapius, Olympiodorus, Priscus and Malchus.* 2 vols. Liverpool, 1981–83.

Brooks, E. W. "Arabic Lists of the Byzantine Themes." *Journal of Hellenic Studies* 21 (1901) 67–77.

Brown, Thomas S. *Gentlemen and Officers: Imperial Administration and Aristocratic Power in Byzantine Italy, A.D. 554–800.* Rome, 1984.

Bryennius, Nicephorus. *History.* Ed. and French trans. Paul Gautier. *CFHB* 9: Brussels, 1975.

Bryer, A. "Rural Society in Matzouka." In A. Bryer and H. Lowry, eds., *Continuity and Change in Late Byzantine and Early Ottoman Society,* 53–95. Birmingham, 1986.

Bryer, A., and D. Winfield. *The Byzantine Monuments and Topography of the Pontos.* 2 vols. Washington, D.C. 1985.

Bury, J. B. *The Imperial Administrative System in the Ninth Century.* London, 1911.

Cahen, Claude. "La première pénétration turque en Asie-Mineure." *Byzantion* 18 (1948) 5–67.

Canard, Marius. *Histoire de la dynastie des H'amdanides de Jazîra et de Syrie,* I. Paris, 1951.

Candidus. In Blockley, ed., *Fragmentary Classicizing Historians* [q.v.], II, 463–73.

Cecaumenus. *Strategicon.* Ed. and Russian trans. G. G. Litavrin. Moscow, 1972.

Charanis, Peter. "Observations on the History of Greece during the Early Middle Ages." *Balkan Studies* 11 (1970) 1–34.

Cheesman, G. L. *The Auxilia of the Roman Imperial Army.* Oxford, 1914.

Cheynet, Jean-Claude. "Du stratège de thème au duc: Chronologie de l'évolution au cours du XIe siècle." *TM* 9 (1985) 181–94.

———. "Mantzikert: Un désastre militaire?" *Byzantion* 50 (1980) 410–38.

———. *Pouvoir et contestations à Byzance (963–1210).* Paris, 1990.

Cheynet, Jean-Claude, and J.-F. Vannier. *Études prosopographiques.* Paris, 1986.

Cheynet, Jean-Claude, et al. "Prix et salaires à Byzance (X^e–XVe siècle)." In *Hommes et richesses* [q.v.], II, 339–74.

Comnena, Anna. *Alexiad.* Ed. and French trans. Bernard Leib. 4 vols. Paris, 1937–76.

Constantine VII. *De Administrando Imperio.* Ed. G. Moravcsik and trans. R. J. H. Jenkins. Washington, D.C., 1967.

———. *De Ceremoniis.* Ed. Johann Reiske. *CSHB*: Bonn, 1829.

———. *De Thematibus.* Ed. A. Pertusi. Studi e Testi 160. Vatican City, 1952.

———. *Three Treatises on Imperial Military Expeditions.* Ed. John Haldon. *CFHB* 28: Vienna, 1990.

Corpus Iuris Civilis. 3 vols. Berlin, 1912–20.

Dagron, G., and H. Mihăescu. *Le traité sur la guérilla (De velitatione) de l'empereur Nicéphore Phocas.* Paris, 1986.

Dennis, George, trans. *Maurice's Strategikon.* Philadelphia, 1984.

———, ed. and trans. *Three Byzantine Military Treaties.* *CFHB* 25: Washington, D.C., 1985.

De Rebus Bellicis. Ed. and trans. Robert Ireland. BAR International Series 63.2. Oxford, 1979.

Digenes Akrites. Ed. E. Trapp. Vienna, 1971.

————. Ed. and trans. J. Mavrogordato. Oxford, 1956.

Diocletian. *Edict.* Vol. I. Ed. and Italian trans. Marta Giacchero. Pubblicazioni dell'Istituto di Storia Antica e Scienze Ausiliare dell'Università di Genova, VIII. Genoa, 1974.

Duncan-Jones, R. P. "Pay and Numbers in Diocletian's Army." *Chiron* 8 (1978) 541–60.

Escorial Tacticon. In Oikonomidès, *Listes* [q.v.], 255–77.

Evagrius Scholasticus. *Ecclesiastical History.* Ed. J. Bidez and L. Parmentier. London, 1898.

Felix, Wolfgang. *Byzanz und die islamische Welt im früheren 11. Jahrhundert: Geschichte der politischen Beziehungen von 1001 bis 1055.* Vienna, 1981.

Ferrill, A. *The Fall of the Roman Empire: The Military Explanation.* London, 1986.

Forsyth, John. *The Byzantine-Arab Chronicle (938–1034) of Yaḥyā b. Saʿīd al-Antākī.* Ann Arbor, 1977.

Fourmy, M.-H., and M. Leroy. "La vie de S. Philarète." *Byzantion* 9 (1934) 85–170.

Frank, R. I. *Scholae Palatinae: The Palace Guards of the Later Roman Empire.* Papers and Monographs of the American Academy in Rome, XXIII. Rome, 1969.

Genesius. *Emperors.* Ed. A. Lesmüller-Werner and J. Thurn. *CFHB* 14: Berlin, 1978.

Goodburn, Roger, and Philip Bartholomew. *Aspects of the Notitia Dignitatum.* BAR Supplementary Series 15. Oxford, 1976.

Gouillard, Jean. "Aux origines de l'iconoclasme: Le témoignage de Grégoire II?" *TM* 3 (1968) 243–307.

Grierson, Philip. *Catalogue of the Byzantine Coins in the Dumbarton Oaks Collection and the Whittemore Collection,* II–III. Washington, D.C., 1968–73.

Grosse, Robert. *Römische Militärgeschichte von Gallienus bis zum Beginn der byzantinischen Themenverfassung.* Berlin, 1920.

Güriz, A. "Land Ownership in Rural Settlements." In Peter Benedict et al., *Turkey: Geographic and Social Perspectives,* 71–91. Leiden, 1974.

Haldon, John. *Byzantine Praetorians: An Administrative, Institutional and Social Survey of the Opsikion and Tagmata, c. 580–900.* Bonn, 1984.

————. *Byzantium in the Seventh Century: The Transformation of a Culture.* Cambridge, 1990.

Hendy, Michael. "Byzantium, 1081–1204: An Economic Reappraisal." *Transactions of the Royal Historical Society,* ser. 5, 20 (1970), 31–52.

————. "Byzantium, 1081–1204: The Economy Revisited, Twenty Years On." In M. Hendy, *The Economy, Fiscal Administration and Coinage in Byzantium,* chap. 2. Northhampton, 1989.

————. *Studies in the Byzantine Monetary Economy, c. 300–1450.* Cambridge, 1985.

Hild, Friedrich, and Marcel Restle. *Kappadokien. TIB* 2. Vienna, 1981.

Hoffmann, Dietrich. *Das spätrömische Bewegungsheer und die Notitia Dignitatum.* 2 vols. Epigraphische Studien 7. Düsseldorf, 1969–70.

Hommes et richesses dans l'empire byzantin. 2 vols. Paris, 1989–91.

Honigmann, Ernst. *Die Ostgrenze des byzantinischen Reiches.* Brussels, 1935. [A. A. Vasiliev et al., *Byzance et les Arabes,* III.]

Hopkins, Keith. "Taxes and Trade in the Roman Empire (200 B.C.–A.D. 400). *JRS* 70 (1980) 101–25.

Ibn Khurdādhbih. *Kitāb al-Masālik.* Ed. and French trans. M. J. de Goeje, in *Bib-*

liotheca Geographorum Arabicorum, VI, 1 – 143. Leiden, 1889. [Page numbers refer to translation.]

Irmscher, J. "Einiges über Preise und Löhne in frühen Byzanz." In H. Köpstein and F. Winkelmann, eds., Studien zum 8. und 9. Jahrhundert in Byzanz, 23 – 33. Berlin, 1983.

Isaac, Benjamin. The Limits of Empire. Oxford, 1990.

John Malalas. Chronographia. Ed. L. Dindorf. CSHB: Bonn, 1831.

John of Ephesus. Ecclesiastical History. Latin trans. E. W. Brooks. Corpus Scriptorum Christianorum Orientalium 106, Scriptores Syri 55. Louvain, 1936.

John of Nikiu. Chronicle. Trans. Robert Charles. London, 1916.

John the Lydian. On Magistrates. Ed. and trans. Anastasius Bandy. Philadelphia, 1983.

————. On Months. Ed. Richard Wuensch. Leipzig, 1898.

Jones, A. H. M. The Later Roman Empire, 284 – 602: A Social, Economic, and Administrative Survey. 2 vols. Oxford, 1964.

Joshua the Stylite. Chronicle. Ed. and trans. W. Wright. Cambridge, 1882.

Justinian. Novels. Ed. R. Schoell and W. Kroll. Corpus Iuris Civilis [q.v.], III.

Justinian Code. Ed. Paul Krueger. Corpus Iuris Civilis [q.v.], II.

Kaegi, Walter. Byzantine Military Unrest, 471 – 843: An Interpretation. Amsterdam, 1981.

————. Byzantium and the Early Islamic Conquests. Cambridge, 1992.

————. "Some Reconsiderations on the Themes (Seventh – Ninth Centuries)." JÖB 16 (1967) 39 – 53.

Karlin-Hayter, Patricia. "The Revolt of Andronicus Ducas." Byzantinoslavica 27 (1966) 23 – 25.

King, C. E. "The Sacrae Largitiones: Revenues, Expenditure and the Production of Coin." In C. E. King, ed., Imperial Revenue, Expenditure and Monetary Policy in the Fourth Century A.D., 141 – 73. BAR International Series 76. Oxford, 1980.

Kolias, Taxiarchis. Byzantinische Waffen. Vienna, 1988.

Kühn, Hans-Joachim. Die byzantinische Armee im 10. und 11. Jahrhundert. Vienna, 1991.

Lactantius. De Mortibus Persecutorum. Ed. and trans. J. L. Creed. Oxford, 1984.

Lefort, Jacques. "Radolibos: Population et paysage." TM 9 (1985) 195 – 234.

Lemerle, Paul. The Agrarian History of Byzantium from the Origins to the Twelfth Century. Galway, 1979.

————. Les plus anciens recueils des miracles de S. Démétrius et la pénétration des Slaves dans les Balkans. 2 vols. Paris, 1979 – 81.

————. Prolégomènes à une édition critique et commentée des "Conseils et Récits" de Kékauménos. Brussels, 1960.

————. "La vie ancienne de S. Athanase l'Athonite." In Le millénaire du mont Athos, 963 – 1963: Études et mélanges, I, 59 – 100. Chevetogne, 1963.

Leo III. Ecloga. Ed. and German trans. L. Burgmann. Frankfurt, 1983.

Leo VI. Naumachica. Ed. A. Dain. Paris, 1943.

————. Tactica. In PG 107, cols. 669 – 1120. Paris, 1863.

Leo the Deacon. Historia. Ed. B. G. Niebuhr. CSHB: Bonn, 1828.

Libanius. Orations. Ed. R. Foerster. 4 vols. Leipzig, 1903 – 8.

Liber Pontificalis. Vol. 1. Ed. L. Duchesne. Paris, 1886.

Liebeschuetz, W. "The Finances of Antioch in the Fourth Century A.D." BZ 52 (1959) 344 – 56.

Life of Philaretus. In Fourmy and Leroy, "Vie" [q.v.], 111–70.

Lilie, Ralph-Johannes. *Die byzantinische Reaktion auf die Ausbreitung der Araber: Studien zur Strukturwandlung des byzantinischen Staates im 7. und 8. Jhd.* Munich, 1976.

———. "Die byzantinische Staatsfinanzen im 8./9. Jahrhundert und die *stratiotika ktemata*." *Byzantinoslavica* 48 (1987) 49–55.

———. "Stellungnahme zu der Entgegnung W. T. Treadgolds." *Byzantinoslavica* 50 (1989) 62–63.

———. "'Thrakien' und 'Thrakesion': Zur byzantinischen Provinzorganisation am Ende des 7. Jahrhunderts." *JÖB* 26 (1977) 7–47.

———. "Die zweihundertjährige Reform: Zu den Anfängen der Themenorganisation im 7. und 8. Jahrhundert." *Byzantinoslavica* 45 (1984) 27–39, 190–201.

Liudprand of Cremona. *Antapodosis*. Ed. Joseph Becker. *MGH*, Scriptores Rerum Germanicarum, XLI, 1–158. Hannover and Leipzig, 1915.

McEvedy, Colin, and R. Jones. *Atlas of World Population History*. Harmondsworth, 1978.

MacMullen, Ramsay. "How Big Was the Roman Imperial Army?" *Klio* 62 (1980) 451–60.

———. "The Roman Emperors' Army Costs." *Latomus* 43 (1984) 571–80.

McNeill, William H. *Plagues and Peoples*. New York, 1976.

Mann, J. C. "What Was the *Notitia Dignitatum* for?" In Goodburn and Bartholomew, *Aspects of the Notitia Dignitatum* [q.v.], 1–9.

Marcellinus Comes. *Chronicle*. Ed. Theodor Mommsen. In *MGH,* Auctores Antiquissimi 11, 37–109. Berlin, 1894.

Masʿūdī. *Tanbīh*. French trans. B. Carra de Vaux [as *Le livre de l'avertissement et de la revision*]. Paris, 1896.

Maurice. *Strategicon*. Ed. George Dennis. German trans. Ernst Gamillscheg. *CFHB* 17: Vienna, 1981.

Menander Protector. *History*. Ed. and trans. R. C. Blockley. Liverpool, 1985.

Morrisson, Cécile. "La dévaluation de la monnaie byzantine au XIᵉ siècle: Essai d'interpretation." *TM* 6 (1976) 3–47.

———. "Monnaie et prix à Byzance du Vᵉ au VIIᵉ siècle." In *Hommes et richesses* [q.v.], I, 239–60.

Morrisson, Cécile, and Werner Seibt. "Sceaux de commerciaires byzantins du VIIᵉ siècle trouvés à Carthage." *Revue Numismatique,* 6th ser., 24 (1982) 222–40.

Nesbitt, John, and N. Oikonomidès. *Catalogue of Byzantine Seals,* I. Washington, D.C., 1991.

Nicephorus II. *Military Precepts*. Ed. J. A. Kulakovskij. Zapiski Imperatorskoj Akademii Nauk po Istoriko-filologičeskomu Otdeleniju, VIII. 9. St. Petersburg, 1908.

———. *On Skirmishing*. Ed. and trans. Dennis, *Three Byzantine Military Treatises* [q.v.], 137–239.

———. ———. Ed. and French trans. Dagron and Mihǎescu, *Traité* [q.v.].

Nicephorus the Patriarch. *Short History*. Ed. and trans. Cyril Mango. *CFHB* 13: Washington, D.C., 1990.

Notitia Dignitatum. Ed. Otto Seeck. Berlin, 1876.

Oikonomidès, Nicolas. "Une liste arabe des stratèges byzantins du VIIᵉ siècle et les origines du Thème de Sicile." *Rivista di Studi Bizantini e Neoellenici* 11 (1964) 121–30.

———. *Les listes de préséance byzantines des IXe et Xe siècles.* Paris, 1972.
———. "Silk Trade and Production in Byzantium from the Sixth to the Ninth Century: The Seals of Kommerkiarioi." *DOP* 40 (1986) 33–53.
———. "Terres du fisc et revenu de la terre aux Xe–XIe siècles." In *Hommes et richesses* [q.v.], II, 321–37.
On Campaign Organization and Tactics. Ed. and trans. Dennis, *Three Byzantine Military Treatises* [q.v.], 241–335.
Ostrogorsky, George. *History of the Byzantine State.* 2d ed. Trans. Joan Hussey. Oxford, 1968.
Oxford Dictionary of Byzantium. Ed. Alexander Kazhdan et al. 3 vols. New York, 1991.
Paschal Chronicle. Vol. 1. Ed. L. Dindorf. *CSHB*: Bonn, 1832.
Paulys Realencyclopädie der classischen Altertumswissenschaft. Ed. A. von Pauly, G. Wissowa, and W. Kroll. Stuttgart, 1894–.
Philotheus. *Treatise.* In Oikonomidès, *Listes* [q.v.], 65–234.
Pliny the Elder. *Natural History.* Ed. and French trans. J. Beaujeu et al. 37 vols. Paris, 1950–72.
Priscus of Panium. Ed. and trans. Blockley, *Fragmentary Classicizing Historians* [q.v.], II, 221–400.
Procopius of Caesarea. *Opera Omnia.* Ed. Jakob Haury and Gerhard Wirth. Rev. ed. 4 vols. Leipzig, 1962–64.
———. *Secret History.* Vol. 3 of *Opera Omnia* [q.v.].
———. *Wars.* Vols. 1 and 2 of *Opera Omnia* [q.v.].
Psellus, Michael. *Chronographia.* Ed. and French trans. Émile Renauld. 2 vols. Paris, 1926–28.
Pseudo-Codinus. *Origines.* Ed. T. Preger. *Scriptores Originum Constantinopolitarum*, II. Leipzig, 1907.
Pseudo-Symeon. *Chronicle.* Ed. [as "Symeon Magister"] Immanuel Bekker. In *Theophanes Continuatus* [q.v.], 601–760.
Qudāmah ibn Ja'far. *Kitāb al-Kharaj.* Ed. and French trans. M. J. de Goeje. In *Bibliotheca Geographorum Arabicorum*, VI, 144–208. Leiden, 1889. [Page numbers refer to translation.]
Scylitzes, John. *History.* Ed. J. Thurn. *CFHB* 5: Berlin, 1973.
Scylitzes Continuatus. Ed. E. Tsolakes. Thessalonica, 1968.
Shahid, Irfan. "Heraclius and the Theme System: Further Observations." *Byzantion* 59 (1989) 208–43.
———. "Heraclius and the Theme System: New Light from the Arabic." *Byzantion* 57 (1987) 391–406.
de Slane, W. M. *Ibn Khaldun: Histoire des Berbères et des dynasties musulmanes de l'Afrique septentrionale*, I. Paris, 1925.
Speidel, M. Alexander. "Roman Army Pay Scales." *JRS* 82 (1992) 87–106.
Starr, Chester. *The Roman Empire, 27 B.C.–A.D. 476: A Study in Survival.* New York, 1982.
———. *The Roman Imperial Navy, 31 B.C.–A.D. 324.* Cambridge, 1960.
Stein, Ernest. *Histoire du Bas-Empire.* 2 vols. Paris, 1949–59.
———. *Studien zur Geschichte des byzantinischen Reiches, vornehmlich unter den Kaisern Justinus II und Tiberius.* Stuttgart, 1919.
Stephen of Taron. French trans. Frédéric Macler. Paris, 1917.
Symeon the Logothete. Ed. [as "Georgius Monachus"] Immanuel Bekker. In *Theophanes Continuatus* [q.v.], 761–924.

Tacticon Uspensky. In Oikonomidès, *Listes* [q.v.], 41–63.

Themistius. *Orations.* Ed. G. Downey and A. Norman. 3 vols. Leipzig, 1965–74.

Theodosian Code. Ed. Theodor Mommsen and Paul Meyer. 2d ed. 2 vols. Berlin, 1952.

Theophanes Confessor. *Chronicle.* Vol. 1. Ed. C. de Boor. Leipzig, 1883.

Theophanes Continuatus. Ed. Immanuel Bekker. *CSHB:* Bonn, 1838.

Theophylact Simocatta. *Histories.* Ed. C. de Boor and P. Wirth. Rev. ed. Stuttgart, 1972.

Toynbee, Arnold. *Constantine Porphyrogenitus and His World.* London, 1973.

Treadgold, W. "The Army in the Works of Constantine Porphyrogenitus." *Rivista di Studi Bizantini e Neoellenici,* n.s., 29 (1992) 77–162.

———. "The Break in Byzantium and the Gap in Byzantine Studies." *Byzantinische Forschungen* 14 (1990) 289–316.

———. *The Byzantine Revival 780–842.* Stanford, 1988.

———. *The Byzantine State Finances in the Eighth and Ninth Centuries.* New York, 1982.

———. "The Military Lands and the Imperial Estates in the Middle Byzantine Empire." *Harvard Ukrainian Studies* 7 (1983) 619–31.

———. "The Missing Year in the Revolt of Artavasdus." *JÖB* 42 (1992) 87–93.

———. "A Note on Byzantium's Year of the Four Emperors (641)." *BZ* 83 (1990) 431–33.

———. "Notes on the Numbers and Organization of the Ninth-Century Byzantine Army." *GRBS* 21 (1980) 269–88.

———. "On the Value of Inexact Numbers." *Byzantinoslavica* 50 (1989) 57–61.

———. "The Problem of the Marriage of the Emperor Theophilus." *GRBS* 16 (1975) 325–41.

———. "Remarks on the Work of al-Jarmī on Byzantium." *Byzantinoslavica* 44 (1983) 205–12.

———. "Seven Byzantine Revolutions and the Chronology of Theophanes." *GRBS* 31 (1990) 203–27.

———. "Three Byzantine Provinces and the First Byzantine Contacts with the Rus'." *Harvard Ukrainian Studies* 12–13 (1988–89) 132–44.

Vasiliev, A. A., et al. *Byzance et les Arabes.* 3 vols. Brussels, 1935–68.

Vegetius. *Epitoma Rei Militaris.* Ed. and trans. Leo Stelton. New York, 1990.

Vryonis, Speros. "An Attic Hoard of Byzantine Coins (668–741) from the Thomas Whittemore Collection and the Numismatic Evidence for the Urban History of Byzantium." *Zbornik Radova Vizantinološkog Instituta* 8 (1963) 291–300.

———. *The Decline of Medieval Hellenism in Asia Minor and the Process of Islamization from the Eleventh through the Fifteenth Century.* Berkeley and Los Angeles, 1971.

Watson, G. R. *The Roman Soldier.* London, 1969.

Webster, Graham. *The Roman Imperial Army of the First and Second Centuries A.D.* London, 1969.

Winkelmann, F. *Byzantinische Rang- und Ämterstruktur im 8. und 9. Jahrhundert.* Berlin, 1985.

———. "Probleme der Informationen des al-Ġarmī über die byzantinischen Provinzen." *Byzantinoslavica* 43 (1982) 18–29.

Yaḥyā of Antioch. *Chronicle.* Ed. and French trans. I. Kratchkovsky and A. Vasiliev. Patrologia Orientalis 18.5 and 23.3. Paris, 1924–32.

Zacos, G., A. Veglery, and John Nesbitt. *Byzantine Lead Seals.* 2 vols. Basel and Bern, 1972–84.

Zepos, I., and P. Zepos. *Jus Graecoromanum.* 8 vols. Athens, 1931.

Zosimus. *New History.* Ed. and French trans. François Paschoud. 3 vols. Paris, p3–89.

Index

In this index an "f" after a number indicates a separate reference on the next page, and an "ff" indicates separate references on the next two pages. A continuous discussion over two or more pages is indicated by a span of page numbers, e.g., "pp. 57–58." *Passim* is used for a cluster of references in close but not necessarily consecutive sequence.

Library of Congress Cataloging-in-Publication Data

Treadgold, Warren T.
     Byzantium and its army, 284–1081 / Warren Treadgold.
          p.   cm.
     Includes bibliographical references and index.
     ISBN 0-8047-2420-2 (cl.) : ISBN 0-8047-3163-2 (pbk.)
     1. Byzantine Empire — Army — History.   2. Byzantine
Empire—History. Military—To 527.   Byzantine Empire—
History, Military—527–1081.   I. Title
U43.B9T74   1995
355'.009495—dc20

                                        94-42463
                                            CIP

This book is printed on acid-free paper.

Original printing 1995
Last figure below indicates year of this printing:
06   05   04   03   02   01   00   99   98